Penguin Books
Lloyds Bank Tax Guide
1987/8

CW00815821

SARA WILLIAMS is a financial jo
analyst and lecturer in finance. For a number of years she wrote for
Which?, including the *Which? Tax-Saving Guide* and *The Which? Book
of Tax*. She has also contributed many articles on personal finance and
tax to newspapers and magazines. She is the author of *Lloyds Bank
Small Business Guide* and forthcoming books are *Go for Growth: The
Hidden Entrepreneur* (Viking) and *Unit Trusts*. She runs her own business, Tudor Myles & Co., which has interests in consumer affairs and
communication material for the financial sector. Sara Williams is a
public interest member for LAUTRO (Life Assurance and Unit Trust
Regulatory Organization).

JOHN WILLMAN is a financial journalist who has written for *Which?*
and Peat, Marwick, McLintock (the City accountants). A contributor
to the *Which? Tax-Saving Guide* and *The Which? Book of Tax*, he has
also contributed articles on tax and personal finance to many magazines. He was editor of *Assessment* and *Taxes*, published by the Inland
Revenue Staff Federation. He currently works as General Secretary of
the Fabian Society.

**SARA WILLIAMS
and JOHN WILLMAN**

LLOYDS
BANK
TAX GUIDE
1987/8

PENGUIN BOOKS

Penguin Books Ltd, 27 Wrights Lane, London w8 5tz (Publishing and Editorial)
and Harmondsworth, Middlesex, England (Distribution and Warehouse)
Viking Penguin Inc., 40 West 23rd Street, New York, New York 10010, U.S.A.
Penguin Books Australia Ltd, Ringwood, Victoria, Australia
Penguin Books Canada Ltd, 2801 John Street, Markham, Ontario, Canada l3r 1b4
Penguin Books (N.Z.) Ltd, 182–190 Wairau Road, Auckland 10, New Zealand

First published by Penguin Books 1987

Filmset in 9 on 11½pt Monophoto Times
Made and printed in Great Britain by
Richard Clay Ltd, Bungay, Suffolk

CONTENTS

6

SECTION V SPENDING YOUR MONEY

SECTION VI OTHER TAXES

ACKNOWLEDGEMENTS

We should like to convey our gratitude to a number of people without whom this book could not have appeared. At Lloyds Bank, Peter Shears, Jim Hepburn, Brian Clutterbuck, Mike Harkess, Brian Miles, Philip Laidlow, and Steve Onions have been as enthusiastic and as helpful as with last year's Guide. And at Penguin, Andrew Franklin has managed to retain his usual optimism and cheerfulness against all the odds. Thanks also to Mary Omond for her astute copyediting, and to Andrew Welham, Patrick Hutchinson and everyone in the sales and marketing department for all their efforts.

Our thanks go also to the Controller of Her Majesty's Stationery Office for permission to reproduce Inland Revenue Forms P1, 11P, P2, P70 and R185. These forms are Crown copyright.

Writing the Guide has caused inevitable dislocation in our households; Margaret and Peter became single parents (temporarily) and Charles, Michael and Kate must have become more than irritated with 'Go away, I'm writing.' We couldn't have done it without them all.

But we dedicate this year's Guide to two very small heroes, Freddie and Claire, who bounded into the world somewhere between fringe benefits and capital gains tax. We hope it doesn't affect their thinking in future life.

INTRODUCTION

Tax changes do not often make world news. The US tax reform now being carried out is an exception. It is normally impossible for the President and both Houses of Congress to agree on anything to do with public finance – except fudged compromises. This time the US amazed itself and the rest of the world by agreeing on the abolition of higher rates of tax and a wide range of tax shelters. The US tax reform has been the talk of tax experts everywhere. In the UK, tax reform has remained at the stage of talk. All the bold plans orbiting in the capacious mind of Mr Nigel Lawson, the Chancellor of the Exchequer, were grounded when it came to the March 1987 Budget. The need to avoid giving offence to any group of voters overrode the desire to emulate the radicalism of the US tax reform. The pill of tax reform usually has to be sweetened by making a net giveaway, so that some taxpayers gain and none lose. The Chancellor could have done this, because he had money to give away – rather to his surprise. He blew it on an old-fashioned 2p cut in income tax to 27p in the pound, with the hint of another cut to 25p if the voters showed their gratitude by re-electing the Conservatives.

The higher rates of tax were left untouched, and were not even fully indexed in line with inflation. Mortgage interest relief, the biggest and most controversial of the many tax shelters, emerged unscathed. There was no attempt to carry out the proposal for allowances transferable between husband and wife. The cut in income tax rates is a difference in degree but not a difference in kind, so it hardly qualifies as even a step towards a reform. Any serious reform of income tax would have to either merge or bring about a more rational relationship between income tax and employee National Insurance contributions. For example, if the higher rates of income tax were done away with, or reduced to one higher rate, then the upper earnings limit on National Insurance contributions might have to be raised or abolished for employees, as it already has been for employers.

Some of these reforms may see the light of day in the 1988 Budget, so the next Budget may be more interesting than the last one. There is still a regrettable uncertainty about the economic results to be expected from tax reform. The Conservatives have not excluded a further switch from income tax to VAT, such as they carried out in 1979. This could be seen as a move towards an expenditure-based tax system, as advocated by the Meade Committee a decade ago and more recently favoured by the CBI. The effect of higher VAT on the inflation rate is undoubted, if once for all. The effect of income tax changes on work incentives is ambiguous. In response to an income tax cut, some people will work more, others less. The supply-side metaphysics on which the US tax reform was based is still unproven. Income tax cuts may or may not be a vote-winner, but that is another matter.

The main reforms of personal taxation for the Conservative government are PEP and the proposed PRP – which surely deserve to become cartoon characters just as much as that great beneficiary of tax-free capital gains, Sid. PEP (Personal Equity Plans) are described in this Guide since they are now in operation, following their introduction in the 1986 Budget. Lloyds and the other clearing banks are among the intermediaries offering their customers these schemes for tax relief on dividends and capital gains – but not, alas, on the original sum invested. PRP (Profit-Related Pay) is a clever dodge to keep down fixed labour costs by increasing, with a tax sweetener, the variable part of the pay package. It is easy to confuse it with other, already existing, profit-sharing schemes, based on the issue of company shares to employees. It remains to be seen whether employers will find PRPs worth the extra auditing costs.

The authors of this year's Tax Guide describe the changes, in the 1987 Budget as 'more a question of tinkering than fundamental reform'. That is a widely shared view. However, there is no point in tax reform for its own sake. Better muddle through with the existing system than take a sharp turn in the wrong direction. Spare a thought for your poor harassed underpaid Tax Inspectors. They are having quite enough problems operating the existing system. A tax reform could cause the whole rickety machine to grind to a halt. The reform of the tax-collecting machinery is as important as the reform of the tax system itself. It is unnecessary to go to the lengths of actually privatizing the tax-collection business, in view of some of the obvious objections which arise. It would be sufficient to give the Inland Revenue the status of a public corporation, and assess it by means of performance criteria similar to those

which apply in the efficient and booming private financial services
sector.

Christopher Johnson
Chief Economic Adviser
Lloyds Bank

Chairman of the Executive Committee
Institute for Fiscal Studies

June 1987

1 · THE BASIC TAX SYSTEM

The man who first thought of income tax probably had little idea of its future importance. In 1799 William Pitt introduced income tax to Britain to finance the Napoleonic Wars. Then, it was a relatively simple affair (10p in the pound). Today, it is a complicated, confusing and, by comparison with what it was like when it was introduced, all-embracing structure.

One reason why the system is complicated is that it hasn't grown in a planned and orderly fashion; its development has been higgledy-piggledy. First, as public spending has increased, successive governments have wanted to raise more money from taxes. So, at regular intervals, Chancellors of the Exchequer have looked for ways to increase the rates and to spread the net wider. For example, before the Second World War there were fewer than four million income taxpayers. In recent years, the number has been around twenty million.

Second, taxpayers are an ingenious bunch who want to pay as little tax as legally possible. Every so often, the government has to step in to block a loophole which taxpayers use to reduce their tax bills. Hence, tax laws can sometimes be rather piecemeal.

It is not just the haphazard nature of its development which makes the tax system difficult to understand; it is also made more complex by the historical throwbacks of the system, the desire to be fair to all and the attempt to encourage particular types of activities.

There are two main features of the tax system today which were there from the very early days. One is the Victorian notion that a wife's income belongs to her husband. In today's society, with the increase in families where the parents are divorced, separated or not married in the first place, this has led to anomalies. The second absurdity is the way the taxman divides income up into a system of Schedules (p. 33). This system was introduced in 1803. It's hardly surprising that a way of grouping income suitable nearly two hundred years ago does not come up to scratch today.

Governments also try to be equitable to taxpayers. This means that rates of tax are progressive and, because of the allowances available, there is a band of income which is tax-free. There are also allowances to help particular needs, for example, an allowance for the blind. All this increases the difficulties of working out how much tax should be paid.

The income tax system is also tinkered with to stimulate certain activities in the economy. For example, there are special allowances to encourage business to invest in capital equipment or to encourage individuals to put up money to help small businesses grow.

As governments have needed to raise more money than they could from incomes, so other taxes have been introduced. There have been three attempts to tax people's wealth, culminating in the latest, inheritance tax. And in 1965 a tax was introduced on gains you might make on certain items as they increase in value; this tax is called capital gains tax.

HOW THE TAX RULES ARE CHANGED

Nowadays, most changes in the tax rules are announced once a year in the Budget. This takes place before the start of each tax year, so that as well as announcing proposed new tax laws the Chancellor sets the rates of tax and personal allowances for the tax year ahead. A month or so after the Budget, the Finance Bill is published and after debate in Parliament, the Finance Act will be passed, usually in July. This pattern has not been followed in 1987 because of the election. The Finance Act was hurried through in May, which meant that it did not include all the proposed Budget changes. The principal casualties were changes in personal pensions (p. 215) and profit-related pay, but the government has reintroduced them.

The Finance Act can run to a large number of pages, one or two hundred or more, which means a lot of changes to what happens in the tax system. Occasionally, there can be an Act which consolidates all the changes which take place year by year; the last time this was done for income tax was in 1970.

HOW THE TAX RULES ARE PUT INTO PRACTICE

The tax system is operated by the Inland Revenue. Tax Inspectors are responsible for assessing how much tax each taxpayer should pay. The taxpayer has the responsibility for providing the information which the Tax Inspector needs to do the assessment. This is done by filling in a

Tax Return. In some other countries, the burden of the work is not shared in the same way. For example, in the United States taxpayers have to work out how much tax they should pay; the American system is known as self-assessment.

Tax Inspectors are not allocated to certain taxpayers. Instead, they are allocated according to the type of income. This can lead to confusion for the taxpayer. If you change your jobs frequently, it's also likely that you will have frequent changes in Tax Inspectors.

If you get income from different places in a tax year, you could be dealing with more than one Tax Inspector at a time. For example, if you have a job and also run a business on the side, only by pure coincidence would both these sources of income be dealt with by the same person. It is far more likely that for the earnings from your job, you are corresponding with one Tax Inspector located at one end of the country, while the earnings from your business are dealt with by a local Tax Inspector.

TYPES OF TAXES

There is a variety of different taxes. The taxes included in this Guide are:

● *income tax*

● *capital gains tax:* this is a tax on the increase in the value of certain assets you own

● *inheritance tax:* this attempts to tax money being passed from one person to another on death and sometimes in gifts before death

● *National Insurance:* this is a tax on people who work.

There are other taxes which are beyond the scope of this Guide. These include:

● *corporation tax:* the government raises money from companies through this tax

● *value added tax:* it is charged on most goods and services which you buy as a consumer and it is passed on through the sellers of the goods, rather than straight to the government

● *excise duties:* this will be paid by everyone who smokes, drinks or drives a car. It is also an indirect tax, like VAT, which is paid by the consumer.

2 · HOW TO USE THIS GUIDE

The Guide is written in simple, everyday language to help you sort out your tax affairs. You will not find the normal complicated tax jargon that is in other books or used by the professionals. Instead, the intricacies of the tax system are laid bare so that you and your family can understand what's going on. However, the Guide also helps you to understand the words used by the tax people; these are explained in the text and there is a Glossary on p. 309.

The Guide covers all the important tax points which the vast majority of taxpayers need to know, but it can't cover the minute details of the more unusual problems. However, even if you hand over your tax affairs to a tax adviser, because you quake at the very thought of the tax system, this Guide will help you keep an eye on what your tax adviser says or does.

There are a number of specific tasks which this Guide will enable you to do.

TASK 1 *Filling in your Tax Return*. In Chapter 9 'The Forms', p. 55, the Guide explains the different sorts of Tax Returns there are and who has to fill one in; it uses an illustration of a Tax Return to show you where to find the particular points that *you* need to know to fill in your Tax Return. Each chapter covers a different tax topic. At the end of each chapter there is a summary of what you should put in your Tax Return.

The Guide uses as an illustration the form which you should fill in at the start of the 1987/8 tax year. But you can also use the Guide to help you fill in the Tax Return you will be receiving at the start of the 1988/9 tax year. The forms are similar from one year to the next, and all the important tax changes for the 1987/8 tax year which you would need to know are detailed in each chapter.

TASK 2 *Checking your PAYE code*. For taxpayers who do not have to fill in a Tax Return every year, it is vital to keep track of what is going on. The Guide shows you how to check your Notice of Coding and your PAYE code, so you can ensure that you are not paying too much tax. It is a common fallacy to believe that if your tax affairs are very simple you will not be able to save tax. Do not fall into this trap. Use this Guide to check that you are getting all the reliefs and allowances that you can.

TASK 3 *Checking your tax bill.* Whether you get a Tax Return to fill in or not, it is important to check at the end of the tax year that you have not paid too much tax. If you use this Guide, you should be able to make sure that the taxman has not included income he should not have or left out allowances or reliefs you should have had. Do not forget to check the arithmetic, too. Chapter 10, 'Checking Your Income Tax Bill', p. 67, will help you work out what your tax should be for the tax year 1986/7. If your affairs are a bit more complicated, you may be sent a Notice of Assessment; Chapter 9, 'The Forms', p. 55, shows you how to understand this.

TASK 4 *Saving tax.* There may be simple steps you can take to rearrange your affairs to help you cut the amount of tax you pay. The Guide is packed with lots of useful tips to help you do that. And on p. 314, there is a list of the more common tax-saving tips.

TASK 5 *Dealing with the taxman.* Finding your way around the Inland Revenue can be difficult. It can be very confusing if, for example, you find yourself corresponding with more than one Inspector at a time. Chapter 8, 'Your Tax Inspector', p. 48, explains why this might happen to you; it tells you who is the right person to go to for queries, problems, claiming relief, or appealing against decisions. Throughout the book are practical hints on the best method of presenting information to your Tax Inspector to achieve what you want.

TASK 6 *Checking specific tax points.* If you are puzzled about a particular tax treatment, you will find the answer to virtually all of your queries here in this book. Use the Index as your starting point.

HOW THIS GUIDE IS ORGANIZED

There are six sections to this Guide. In each section is a number of chapters; the individual chapter headings are on pp. 5 and 6. Here is a brief description of what you can find in each section.

SECTION I · AN OUTLINE OF INCOME TAX
This section starts off by explaining why the income tax system is so

complicated (Chapter 1, p. 13) and gives a summary of how it works (Chapter 3, p. 20). Next it outlines in simple detail what makes up income (Chapter 4, p. 25) and what can be deducted from it to reduce your tax bill (Chapters 5 and 6, pp. 36 and 40). Finally, it describes the changes which occurred in the 1987 Budget (Chapter 7, p. 43).

SECTION II · YOU AND YOUR TAX INSPECTOR

This gives an explanation of how the Inland Revenue works and how you should communicate with your Tax Inspector (Chapter 8, p. 48). The next chapter, Chapter 9, p. 55, describes the process of filling in Tax Returns and checking other forms. You can use this to find out where each specific entry in your Tax Return is covered in detail in the Guide. Chapter 10, p. 67, shows you a simple way of checking that you are paying the right tax. Finally, Chapter 11, p. 77, explains how you can appeal against a tax bill and what happens if you are investigated.

SECTION III · HOW THE FAMILY IS TAXED

You can find here clear details of what happens if you are single (Chapter 12, p. 86), marry (Chapter 13, p. 90) and subsequently separate or divorce (Chapter 15, p. 106). The anomalies of the tax treatment of couples who live together without marrying are shown in Chapter 14, p. 101. The tax affairs of the widowed (Chapter 16, p. 113), children, students and dependants (Chapter 17, p. 117) and the elderly (Chapter 18, p. 124) are also explained.

SECTION IV · IN WORK OR OUT OF WORK

The income which you earn from your work is the main source of income taxed by the UK system. This section looks at how your income from work is treated. Employees can be paid earnings (Chapter 19, p. 131) and fringe benefits (Chapter 20, p. 151). What happens when you start or leave a job is explained in Chapter 21, p. 164. When unemployment strikes, Chapter 22, p. 168 should help you organize your financial affairs (details of other benefits are also given here). How you will be taxed if you work abroad is explained in Chapter 23, p. 174.

Earning money on the side as a freelance can be useful (Chapter 25, p. 199). And if you set up in business it can be on your own (Chapter 24, p. 178) or in partnership (Chapter 26, p. 202).

SECTION V · SPENDING YOUR MONEY

This section explains how your money is taxed if you invest it (Chapter 30, p. 241) or give it to charity (Chapter 32, p. 269). Some investments are dual purpose, such as your home (Chapter 28, p. 218) or life insurance (Chapter 31, p. 260). The best way of saving for your retirement is through a pension scheme (Chapter 27, p. 206) and there are other ways of investing in property, as well as buying your home (Chapter 29, p. 230).

SECTION VI · OTHER TAXES

Income tax may not be the only tax you have to pay. You may find yourself having to pay capital gains tax (Chapter 33, p. 275) or inheritance tax (Chapter 34, p. 291).

3 · HOW INCOME TAX WORKS

The government gets much of *its* income by taxing *your* income. Income tax is likely to make the biggest hole in your pay packet: bigger than your mortgage payments, bigger than National Insurance contributions, bigger than your food bill. So why pay more than you have to? Spend some of your time keeping your tax affairs organized, checking that you are not paying too much income tax and claiming it back if you are. There may be ways you can alter your tax bill by following the tax-saving tips on p. 314. But as a first step, try to understand how the income tax system works.

Cutting through all the complexities, income tax works like this:

STEP 1   Calculate your income from your job, investments, self-employment or other sources. Chapter 4, 'Income', p. 25, tells you what is, and what is not, income and which income is, or is not, taxed.

STEP 2   From your income for tax purposes, deduct the items on which you get tax relief. These are known as 'outgoings' and are listed in Chapter 5, 'Outgoings', p. 36. After you have done this, you will be left with a figure which in most cases will be what the taxman calls 'total income' – quite a misnomer. But if you are retired, or nearing retirement, knowing what your 'total income' is can be important.

STEP 3   Deduct the personal allowances you can claim; these also give you tax relief and reduce the amount of income on which you must pay tax. This leaves you with taxable income.

STEP 4   Work out how much tax you are going to pay on your taxable income. If your taxable income is below a certain amount, you will pay tax at the basic rate only. Above the limit, tax is charged at higher rates on succeeding slices of income. On the next page are the rates of tax charged for the tax years 1986/7 and 1987/8.

TAX RATES FOR 1986/7

INCOME BAND £	SIZE OF BAND £	TAX RATE %	TAX ON BAND £
1–17,200	17,200	29	4,988
17,201–20,200	3,000	40	1,200
20,201–25,400	5,200	45	2,340
25,401–33,300	7,900	50	3,950
33,301–41,200	7,900	55	4,345
Over 41,200		60	

TAX RATES FOR 1987/8

INCOME BAND £	SIZE OF BAND £	TAX RATE %	TAX ON BAND £
1–17,900	17,900	27	4,833
17,901–20,400	2,500	40	1,000
20,401–25,400	5,000	45	2,250
25,401–33,300	7,900	50	3,950
33,301–41,200	7,900	55	4,345
Over 41,200		60	

EXAMPLE

In the tax year 1987/8, Freddie Noble's earnings from his job are £25,000. Before he is paid, his employer deducts pension contributions of £1,200. He can claim the married man's allowance for the year. How much tax will he pay?

	£
Income	25,000
less *Outgoings*	
Pension contributions	1,200
Total income	23,800
less *Allowances*	
Married man's allowance	3,795
Taxable income	20,005

Tax:	17,900 at 27%	£4,833
	2,105 at 40%	842
	TOTAL TAX	£5,675

WHEN DO YOU PAY INCOME TAX?

Taxpayers pay their tax bills on different days during the tax year. For 1987/8:

TAXABLE INCOME	WHEN IS TAX DUE
Earnings from a job, pensions from employer	Tax deducted as you are paid, for example, weekly, monthly
Profits from self-employment, a partnership, normally furnished holiday accommodation, and Enterprise Allowance	First instalment 1 January 1988; second equal instalment 1 July 1988
Taxable investment income paid without deduction of tax, for example, small maintenance payments, interest on National Savings investments	1 January 1988
Rents which are unearned income	1 January 1988
Higher-rate tax due on income from investments paid after deduction of tax; other payments made with basic-rate tax deducted, for example, maintenance payments, annuities	1 December 1988
Taxable social security benefits	Normally after you return to work, weekly or monthly

If you are an employee and the bulk of your income comes from your job, you may find that your Tax Inspector includes your other bits of income in your PAYE code and collects tax weekly or monthly rather than on the dates shown. If this means that you would be paying tax earlier than you would otherwise do, you can ask to pay on the dates above instead. Sometimes, however, your Tax Inspector may include it in next year's calculation of your P A Y E code which means that this is the best way for you to pay.

On occasion the amount of income tax you are supposed to pay may not have been settled by the dates above. In this case, you should pay within thirty days after you receive what's called a Notice of Assessment from your Tax Inspector. This shows your Tax Inspector's calculation of the income tax you owe or are owed, if you have paid too much.

THE IMPORTANCE OF TIME

As you read through the Guide, you will find that there are some deadlines to meet if you want a bit of income to be taxed in one way rather than another or if you want to tell your Tax Inspector that your tax bill is wrong. Here are some of the important income tax deadlines:

WITHIN THIRTY DAYS
- appealing against a Notice of Assessment   p. 52
- applying for a postponement of tax due   p. 52

WITHIN SIXTY DAYS
- telling your tax office you disagree with the statement of taxable social security benefits you receive from the benefit office   p. 169

BEFORE 6 JULY IN THE TAX YEAR
- choosing to be separately assessed   p. 98
- changing your mind about being separately assessed   p. 98

WITHIN A YEAR OF THE END OF THE TAX YEAR
- having the wife's earnings taxed separately   p. 98
- changing your mind about having the wife's earnings taxed separately   p. 98

WITHIN TWO YEARS OF THE END OF THE TAX YEAR
- setting losses made in a new business against other income   p. 189
- setting business losses against other income   p. 189

WITHIN SIX YEARS OF THE END OF THE TAX YEAR
- claiming allowances   p. 41
- changing which allowances claimed   p. 41
- claiming tax relief on outgoings   p. 38
- setting business losses against future profits of the same business   p. 189

GETTING HELP AND ADVICE

This Guide cannot cover every single point of income tax. For a few specialized areas, for example, if you are a director or a partner or if you are not resident or domiciled in the UK, you will need further advice. The obvious people to turn to are an accountant or your bank. If you want help on some fairly easy problem, you could try your Citizens' Advice Bureau to see if it can handle it.

4 · INCOME

The first step in working out how much income tax you are going to have to pay is to sort out what your income is for the tax year. This is not as obvious as it may seem; income is not necessarily the same as money. For example, what you get from selling some unit trusts is not income, but the value the taxman puts on your company car does count as income for tax purposes.

Once you have worked out what does count as income (see below), you may find that not all of it is taxed. Some income is specifically excluded from the calculation because it is said to be tax-free (p. 27). You do not have to include it when working out your tax bill.

Even more confusing for the ordinary taxpayer can be the question of which income is being taxed. In most cases, the income the taxman is interested in is what you get during the current tax year between 6 April in one year and 5 April in the next. So, for the tax year 1987/8, this is what you earn or receive between 6 April 1987 and 5 April 1988.

But sometimes the taxman may be talking about the income which you got in the preceding tax year. So, for example, if you are an employee with a part-time self-employed business you will find your tax bill based on two different years. For 1987/8, the tax bill for your earnings from your job will be based on what you receive during that year. But the tax bill for your earnings from self-employment, if it has been going a number of years, will be based on earnings made in 1986/7 (strictly, the accounting year ending during the preceding tax year, (see p. 191).

A further complication to be faced up to is that sometimes you receive the income without any tax deducted and on other occasions tax has been paid, at basic rate or even higher rates, if due. So you need to sort out which is which; p. 31 gives you guidance.

WHAT IS INCOME?

Some of the commonest ways you get income are from:

● your job, including salary, bonuses, the value the taxman puts on fringe benefits, holiday pay (pp. 131, 151)

● your business, if you are self-employed (p. 178) or in partnership (p. 202)

● letting out property, such as rent (p. 230)

● investments, such as interest or dividends (p. 241)

● the state, such as the state retirement pension (p. 126) or unemployment benefit (p. 168)

● past employer, such as a pension from your employer's pension scheme (p. 126)

● casual earnings, such as occasional freelance work (p. 199)

● someone else, such as maintenance payments from your ex-spouse (p. 108) or covenant payments (p. 119).

What counts as income can change from time to time. This may occur when the Chancellor announces that some particular money or proceeds will now be treated as income. Sometimes, the money has formerly been treated as something quite different – a capital gain, say. This happened in recent years with two rather specialized investments, roll-up funds (p. 255) and accrued interest on British Government stocks (p. 247). In both these examples, the change occurred because these investments were being used by higher-rate taxpayers to pay less income tax than they might otherwise have done.

The taxman has the power to classify proceeds from the same action as two different types of money, for example, sometimes income and sometimes gain. This might occur with buying and selling houses. Any gain you make is not normally treated as income. But if you do it too often, the taxman may decide that you are doing this as a business and treat it as income instead.

IS IT EARNED OR UNEARNED?

The tax laws distinguish between income which is earned and income which is unearned also called investment income. Broadly, from the list above, income from investments, rent from property (but see p. 235) and maintenance and covenant payments are treated as unearned income. In some circumstances, for example, a wife with unearned income (p. 104), you need to know the distinction between earned and unearned as the tax treatment for the two can be different.

The distinction is not as important now as in previous years. Before 1984/5, if you had unearned income, apart from maintenance, above a certain amount in a tax year, there was an extra tax (called the investment income surcharge) to pay.

You may receive money or proceeds during the year, which the taxman does not count as income. This does not mean that this money will not be taxed; it may well be, but by some other tax, not income tax.

The commonest examples are likely to be:

● gifts or presents (but there may be inheritance tax to pay, p. 291)

● gain from selling an asset, for example, shares, antiques (but there may be capital gains tax to pay, p. 275)

● money you inherit (but there may be inheritance tax to pay, p. 291)

● premium bond prizes (no tax to pay)

● winnings from a lottery or from gambling (no tax to pay, unless it is your business)

● money you borrow (no tax to pay).

WHICH INCOME IS TAX-FREE?

There is no logical pattern to help you distinguish income which is tax-free from income which is not. Instead the government at different times has specified that taxpayers will not have to pay tax on some bits of income:

From investments
● interest on National Savings Certificates and the Yearly Plan (and Ulster Savings Certificates for Northern Ireland inhabitants)

● what you get back at the end of SAYE contracts

● the first £70 interest each year on National Savings Ordinary account (if you are married, you can get £70 each free of tax; £140 in a joint account)

● part of the income from an annuity (that is, the bit which is treated as a return of your money, p. 248)

● normally what you get from a regular-premium life insurance policy, such as a with-profits endowment policy or unit-linked one (p. 262)

- loan interest paid to members of a credit union

- income from a personal equity plan, as long as it is reinvested in the plan (p. 251)

Pensions and benefits
- war widows' pensions and equivalent overseas pensions

- tax-free lump sum instead of part of a pension (pp. 207, 210)

- some social security benefits (p. 171)

- the increase paid on 28 July 1986 to the state retirement pension, widow's allowance, widowed mother's allowance, widow's pension, invalid care allowance, and industrial death benefit. This applies to the 1986/7 tax year only

- certain compensation payments made to victims of Nazi persecution

- certain pensions paid to victims of Nazi persecution (before 6 April 1986, only half was tax-free)

- wound and disability pensions

- pension paid to a former employee who retires because of a disability due to injury at work or a work-related illness

- allowances and gratuities paid for additional service in the armed forces

- additional pensions paid to holders of some awards for bravery, for example, Victoria Cross

- rate and rent rebates

- improvement and insulation grants for your home

From jobs
- genuine personal gifts from your employer, for example, a wedding present

- some fringe benefits (p. 153)

- in special circumstances, earnings from working abroad (p. 175)

- some payments on leaving a job (£25,000 or less) (p. 164)

- half the pay received under a registered profit-related pay scheme as proposed in the 1987 Budget, subject to certain limits (p. 132)

● awards from suggestion schemes within limits

● travelling and subsistence allowances paid to employees if public transport is disrupted

● income paid to an employee attending a full-time course (for example, sandwich course) at college, within certain limits (p. 119)

● expenses (for example, books, fees) paid by employer for attending a job-related course (or course of general education if under a certain age) (p. 154)

● some allowances under the Job Release scheme (those open only to men aged sixty-four and women aged fifty-nine)

● the first 15p of luncheon vouchers

● statutory redundancy payments

● miners' free coal or cash allowances instead of the coal

● foreign service allowances paid to servants of the Crown, for example, diplomats

● certain payments from your employer, for passing an exam, for example

Other payments
● gambling profits (if not your business), premium bond prizes, lottery prizes and winnings on the football pools

● income from life insurance policies, such as family income benefit policies and mortage protection policies

● income from a permanent health insurance policy paid for the first complete tax year, if you paid the premiums for the policy yourself

● interest on a tax rebate

● interest on a settlement for damages for personal injury

● scholarships or grants for full-time students (p. 119), but probably not if from the parents' employer (p. 154).

WHOSE INCOME IS TAXED?

Not many escape the income tax system. Even if your child has some income, tax could be payable (although unlikely because your child can claim personal allowances, too). Broadly speaking, the system tries to tax all the income of UK residents no matter where in the world it comes from, but also the income of non-residents if the income comes from the UK. The tax treatment of non-residents is beyond the scope of this Guide and you should take professional advice.

You may also be responsible for paying tax for someone else, for example one partner for another partner who has not paid up, an executor of a will or an agent acting for someone living abroad.

EXAMPLE

During 1987/8, Peter Wong and his wife Elizabeth receive the following bits of money:

PETER:

1 Salary from his job, including a London weighting allowance and use of a company car

2 Proceeds from selling some shares in Trustee Savings Bank

3 Proceeds from selling part of a collection of antique silver

4 A £100 win on the premium bonds

5 An award of £25 for putting up a good suggestion in his firm's suggestion scheme (even though his idea was not adopted)

6 Interest of £21.46 on British Government stocks bought on the National Savings Stock Register.

ELIZABETH:

1 Salary from her job, including luncheon vouchers

2 During the year, the firm closes down the department Elizabeth works for and pays her a lump sum, part of it pay, including holiday pay, and part of it money in lieu of notice

3 She borrows £1,000 from her bank and her granny gives her £1,000 and she starts her own business

4 During the year a ten-year unit-linked life insurance policy comes to an end and she receives a lump sum

5 Interest on a building society account.

What is income?

Out of the money Peter and Elizabeth receive, the following is income:

Salary, London weighting allowance, company car, award from suggestion scheme, interest on British Government stocks, luncheon vouchers, holiday pay, money in lieu of notice, income from self-employment, the proceeds of the unit-linked life insurance policy, interest from a building society account.

None of the other proceeds are income (including the prize from the premium bond, which is in any case tax-free).

Which income is tax-free?

The following income received by Peter and Elizabeth is tax-free:

Award from the suggestion scheme, first 15p of luncheon vouchers, money in lieu of notice (if £25,000 or less) but not the other income received when Elizabeth left, proceeds from the unit-linked life insurance policy.

HOW IS THE INCOME PAID TO YOU?

To work out what your income is for tax purposes, you need to tot up all the amounts you have received from various different sources. A complication arises here because some income you receive has already had tax deducted (p. 32); it is called 'net' income. Other income you receive without any tax deducted is called 'gross' income (p. 32). You may have to put both lots of income on the same footing and you do this by turning the 'net' income figure into the 'gross' figure.

You do this as follows for the 1987/8 tax year when the basic rate of tax is 27 per cent:

$$\text{net income} \times \frac{100}{73} = \text{gross income.}$$

The exact calculation alters with the basic rate of tax. So, for the 1986/7 tax year, when the basic rate of tax was 29 per cent, the sum is:

$$\text{net income} \times \frac{100}{71} = \text{gross income.}$$

EXAMPLE

Wayne Peters has received a 'net' distribution of £10.55 from a unit trust in the 1987/8 tax year. This is paid with the equivalent of basic-rate tax already deducted. To check his tax bill, Wayne needs to know the 'gross' amount. This is:

$$£10.55 \times \frac{100}{73} = £14.45.$$

In fact, Wayne could have got this information another way, as the distribution is paid with a tax credit of £3.90. Adding the two together gives the 'gross' income figure.

INCOME PAID WITH TAX DEDUCTED: 'NET' INCOME

The following types of income will have had tax deducted before you receive it. With all these types of income there will be no more basic-rate tax to pay, but if you pay tax at higher rates, you will have to pay more tax on it. In a couple of cases, higher-rate tax has also been deducted from the income before you receive it. With one major exception, non-taxpayers can claim back the tax deducted:

● what you earn in your job (any higher-rate tax due also deducted before you receive it). If you receive taxable fringe benefits, tax on those will be deducted from your earnings

● pension from an employer's pension scheme (any higher-rate tax due also deducted before you receive it)

● interest from an account with a bank, building society, licensed deposit-taker, local authority loan (p. 244). Note that you cannot claim back any tax deducted if you are a non-taxpayer

● interest from British Government stocks, except for those bought through the post office, or War Loan

● usually income from an annuity (basic-rate tax deducted from the income part, not the part which is regarded as returning what you invested) (p. 248). The insurance company should give you a tax deduction certificate

● dividends from shares and distributions from unit trusts (p. 244). You should receive tax credits with these

● maintenance payments, except for small ones (p. 107)

● income paid out by an executor before the will is sorted out

● income from a trust

● covenant payments.

INCOME PAID WITHOUT TAX DEDUCTED: 'GROSS' INCOME

The following types of income will be paid to you without any tax deducted from it, although the income is taxable:

● what you earn as a self-employed person, with some exceptions in the building industry

● what you earn as a partner

● social security benefits like unemployment benefit or supplementary benefit paid while unemployed or on strike. If you return to work before the end of the tax year, any tax you should have paid will be deducted from your earnings

● the state retirement pension (but if you have other earnings taxed under P A Y E, tax on the pension will be deducted from them)

● small maintenance payments (p. 108)

● interest on British Government stock, if bought at the post office on the National Savings Stock Register, and interest on War Loan, however you buy it

● rent from property you let

● interest on some National Savings investments, such as the Investment Account, Income Bonds, Deposit Bonds.

EXAMPLE

Elizabeth and Peter Wong check which income they receive net and which income gross (see Example on p. 30 for what income they receive).

The following they receive after tax has been deducted:

Salary, London weighting allowance, holiday pay, interest from a building society account. Although tax has obviously not been deducted from the company car and the luncheon vouchers, tax has been collected on these from Peter and Elizabeth's salary (p. 139 for how P A Y E codes are worked out).

The following income they receive without tax deducted:

Interest on British Government stocks bought through National Savings Stock Register, income from self-employment. None of the tax-free income has had tax deducted.

SCHEDULES: HOW THE TAXMAN GROUPS INCOME

One of the more confusing parts of the tax system is the way the taxman divides most types of income up into what is called Schedules. In some cases, the Schedules are divided up further into Cases. These divisions can seem illogical and bizarre. To understand your tax bill, you do not need to know which income goes into which Schedule, except in the case of losses. So this section of the Guide is mainly for 'keenies'. Nevertheless, it may be helpful to have some idea of what is going on, as the names are sometimes used to describe taxpayers; for instance, a

Schedule E taxpayer is an employee. And if you get a Notice of Assessment (p. 63), knowing what the Schedules are is useful.

In practice, there are two main differences which still exist in the treatment of income under one Schedule rather than another. First, the tax is due on different dates (p. 22). Second, you may be allowed to charge up more in expenses against the income from one Schedule rather than another.

Note that interest paid under the composite rate scheme (p. 244), for example from banks or building societies, does not come under a Schedule.

SCHEDULES: WHICH INCOME GOES WHERE?

SCHEDULE A — Income from land or property, for example, letting a house. But income from furnished lettings is normally taxed under Schedule D Case I or Case VI. Tax is normally worked out on a current-year basis and is based on the rent due during the tax year, whether you receive it or not. Schedule A income is unearned income. Further details, including the expenses you can claim, are on pp. 231, 235.

SCHEDULE B — Commercially managed woodlands are taxed either under this schedule or Schedule D Case I.

SCHEDULE C — Interest on British Government stocks (also stock issued by some foreign governments). Schedule C income is unearned income. There are no expenses you can claim.

SCHEDULE D Case I, Case II — Income from your business, trade, profession or vocation. Tax is normally worked out on a preceding-year basis. This income is earned income. For details of the expenses you can claim, see p. 180.

SCHEDULE D Case III — Interest, for example, from loans, income from annuities and other regular yearly payments, such as maintenance or covenant payments received. Tax is normally worked out on a preceding-year basis if it is interest; current-year basis normally applies to covenant and maintenance payments. Schedule D Case III income is unearned income. There are no expenses you can claim.

SCHEDULE D Case IV, Case V — Income from abroad, such as interest on foreign securities, rent, trading profits. The income is normally taxed on a preceding-year basis. Trading profits are earned income; the rest unearned income. There are no expenses you can claim on the unearned income; for further details of what expenses you can claim against the earned income, see p. 180.

SCHEDULE D Case VI — Odds and ends of income, such as income from occasional freelance work, Enterprise Allowance, income received after you close down a business and income from furnished lettings and furnished holiday lettings (unless it amounts to a business, in which case it comes under Schedule D Case I). Tax is normally worked out on a current-year basis. The income is unearned income, apart from Enterprise Allowance and income received after you close down a business. However, you can set personal pension payments and the wife's earned income allowance against income from furnished holiday letting, even though it is unearned. For details of the expenses you can claim, see p. 235.

SCHEDULE E — Earnings from your job. The income is taxed on a current-year basis. For details of the expenses you can claim, see p. 135. There are three Cases, but the vast majority of you come under Case I.

SCHEDULE F — Share dividends and unit trust distributions. The income is taxed on a current-year basis. There are no expenses you can claim. For further details, see p. 244.

EXAMPLE

The income received by Peter and Elizabeth Wong (pp. 30, 31) is all taxed under Schedule E, except the interest on British Government stocks (Schedule D Case III) and income from self-employment (Schedule D Case I). The interest from their building society account does not come under a Schedule.

5 · OUTGOINGS

You do not have to pay income tax on all the income you have. You can get tax relief for a number of payments you make, called outgoings. What outgoings do is reduce the amount of income you pay tax on. And they may also reduce the rate of tax you pay on the top slice of your income. This chapter gives a checklist of the main outgoings you can claim; the details are elsewhere in the Guide.

Tax relief is not given in the same way for all outgoings. This chapter tells you briefly how to claim the tax relief you are entitled to. The main ways you can get your tax relief are:

● making lower payments (for example the MIRAS system for mortgages)

● when your Tax Inspector works out your tax bill after the tax year in a Notice of Assessment (the form which is filled in showing the calculations)

● your Tax Inspector gives you a higher PAYE code so that less tax is deducted from your earnings

CHECKLIST OF OUTGOINGS

OUTGOING	HOW YOU GET TAX RELIEF	DETAILS ON
pension contributions	given by employer through PAYE system. The amount is deducted from your earnings before income tax is worked out	p. 208
personal pension payments	tell your Tax Inspector who will give you a higher PAYE code for regular payments; relief for single payments will be given in a lower tax bill after the tax year	p. 214

mortgage interest	you make lower payments to the lender, that is, the MIRAS system. Any higher-rate tax relief may be given through a higher PAYE code or a lower tax bill after the tax year	p. 223
job expenses	either through a higher PAYE code the following year or in a lower tax bill after the tax year	p. 139
payments under a home income scheme	either by making lower payments to the lender (that is, the MIRAS system) or by telling your Tax Inspector who will give you a higher PAYE code or give the tax relief in a lower tax bill after the tax year	p. 128
covenant payments	making lower payments, that is, you deduct and keep basic-rate tax, giving yourself tax relief. If the payment is to a charity, any higher-rate tax relief is given either through a higher PAYE code or by a lower tax bill after the tax year	pp. 120, 269
maintenance payments	making lower payments, that is, you deduct and keep basic-rate tax from payment, giving yourself tax relief. If small, or if any higher-rate relief is due, you get it through a higher PAYE code or by a lower tax bill after the tax year	p. 107

mortgage interest on a home you let	tell your Tax Inspector; you get tax relief either through a higher PAYE code or by a lower tax bill after the tax year	p. 232
interest on some business loans	tell your Tax Inspector; you get tax relief either through a higher PAYE code or by a lower tax bill after the tax year	see below, pp. 182, 204
interest on loan to pay inheritance tax	tell your Tax Inspector; you get tax relief either through a higher PAYE code or by a lower tax bill after the tax year	p. 305
investments in Business Expansion Scheme	get tax certificate from the company to send to your Tax Inspector, who gives you tax relief either through a higher PAYE code or by a lower tax bill after the tax year.	p. 254

You can get tax relief on various loans, of any size, taken out for business purposes, for example, to buy shares in a close company, buying a share of or putting capital into a partnership (but not if you are a limited partner), and buying plant or machinery for use in your business (or your job if an employee).

WHAT HAPPENS IF YOU HAVE FORGOTTEN TO CLAIM AN OUT-GOING?

You can go back six years to check your tax bills and have them put right. So, if you have forgotten to claim some outgoing for the last six years, do so now and get a tax rebate. If you have paid too much tax in any year, your Tax Inspector will work out the bill for that year again, but using the tax rates and rules which applied for that year, not the current ones.

Going back six years means that, for example, before 6 April 1988 you can ask for an outgoing which would apply as long ago as the 1981/2 tax year.

EXAMPLE

Charlie Barnard decides to make a lump sum payment of £1,000 into a personal pension scheme. On the last slice of his income, Charlie pays tax at a rate of 40 per cent so he saves £40 of tax for each £100 of pension payment. His £1,000 payment actually costs Charlie £600.

WHAT TO PUT IN YOUR TAX RETURN

Turn to the appropriate pages for most outgoings to find out what to do. With interest on business loans which qualify for tax relief, you will find you can claim it under the OUTGOINGS section of the Tax Return. With Forms 11 and 11P, the heading is *Interests on other loans*; with Form P1, enter the details under *Other loan interest paid.* Put the lender's name and the amount of interest you paid in the tax year. You should be able to obtain a certificate of loan interest paid from your lender. Enclose it with the Tax Return.

Form 11P

Interest on other loans *enclose certificates*	Self	Wife
Name of lender	£	£

If you pay property rents or interest to someone who normally lives outside the UK, you have to tell the taxman about it under *UK property rents or yearly interest paid to persons abroad* (Forms 11 and 11P) or *Rents and yearly interest* paid to persons abroad (Form P1). Before you pay rent or interest of this type, you have to deduct basic-rate tax which you pay to the taxman. Put the amount before you deduct tax.

Form 11P

UK property rents or yearly interest paid to persons abroad	Details	£	£

6 · ALLOWANCES

You may not all have outgoings to deduct from your income and thus reduce your tax bill that way. But nearly everybody with an income is entitled to at least one allowance, ensuring some tax-free pay.

CHECKLIST OF ALLOWANCES FOR 1986/7 AND 1987/8 TAX YEARS

ALLOWANCE	1986/7	1987/8	DETAILS ON
	£	£	
single person's	2,335	2,425	p. 86
married man's	3,655	3,795	p. 91
wife's earned income	2,335	2,425	p. 91
additional personal	1,320	1,370	p. 87
single age allowance	2,850	2,960	p. 124
married age allowance	4,505	4,675	p. 124
single age allowance for eighty-plus	2,850	3,070	p. 124
married age allowance for eighty-plus	4,505	4,845	p. 124
income limit for age allowance	9,400	9,800	p. 125
widow's bereavement	1,320	1,370	p. 113
blind person's	360	540	see next page
dependent relative	100 (or 145)	100 (or 145)	p. 122
housekeeper	100	100	p. 113
son's or daughter's service	55	55	p. 125

Anyone registered as blind with a local authority can claim blind person's allowance. If you are married and both husband and wife are blind, you can claim two allowances.

EXAMPLE

Alexander Groom has an income of £5,000; he automatically gets the single person's allowance. The income tax he pays for 1987/8 is:

Income	£5,000
less single person's allowance	2,425
Taxable income	£2,575
Tax at basic rate (27%)	£695.25

But Alexander realizes that as a registered blind person he can also claim the blind person's allowance of £540. This reduces his taxable income to £2,035. Tax at the basic rate (27 per cent) is £549.45, a reduction of £145.80. So Alexander has saved tax of that amount.

WHAT HAPPENS IF YOU HAVE FORGOTTEN TO CLAIM AN ALLOWANCE?

You can go back six years to claim allowances, just as you can with outgoings. The details are on p. 38. You will be able to claim the allowances which applied for the year you missed them, not the current one.

WHICH ALLOWANCE SHOULD YOU CLAIM?

In most cases, it is clear cut which allowance you should claim, for example, if you are single, divorced or widowed you claim the single person's allowance. But there are five choices you can make about which allowance you can claim:

1 If you are married, it may save you tax if you choose to have the wife's earnings taxed separately and to claim the single person's rather than married man's allowance. Chapter 13, 'Married', p. 90, explains and tells you how to work out which is best for you.

2 You cannot claim both additional personal allowance and housekeeper allowance. If you qualify for both, choose additional personal allowance as it will save you more tax.

3 A man can choose to keep additional personal allowance (if he is entitled to it) and single person's allowance rather than married man's allowance in the tax year of marriage. Unless he marries before 6 May, he would be better off foregoing the married man's allowance.

4 A blind person cannot claim both the blind person's allowance and the son's or daughter's services allowance. As the blind person's is larger choose that.

5 You cannot claim both the housekeeper allowance and the son's or daughter's services allowance. Widows and widowers should turn their son or daughter into a housekeeper and claim the larger allowance.

EXAMPLE

Alexander Groom (p. 41) is a widower and his daughter lives with him to look after him, but Alexander pays for her food and keep. This would qualify for the son's or daughter's services allowance, except that Alexander cannot claim it as well as the blind person's allowance. Alexander sticks with the blind person's as it is larger.

However, as Alexander is a widower, he can claim the housekeeper allowance for his daughter. The amount of the allowance is £100 in 1987/8. Alexander's taxable income is reduced to £1,935 and tax is £522.45, a further saving of £27.

WHAT TO PUT IN YOUR TAX RETURN

For how to claim most allowances, turn to the pages listed in the Checklist on p. 40; the information is at the end of each chapter.

If you want to claim blind person's allowance, tick the box in Form P1 in the ALLOWANCES section to indicate whether husband, wife or both of you are claiming the allowance. And put the name of the local authority you are registered with and the date it was done. Give the same information for the other forms, and say whether it is being claimed for 'self', that is, husband or wife.

Form 11P

> **Blind person's allowance**
> Local Authority with which registered and the
> date of registration – *say if self or wife*

7 · TAX CHANGES FOR 1987/8

What has altered since last year's Guide? There haven't been the dramatic changes to the tax system seen in recent years, more a question of tinkering than fundamental reform.

The 1987 election meant that not all the changes proposed in the Budget became law before this Guide went to the printers. Where this has happened we have noted that these are proposals only.

TAX RATES

Basic-rate tax has come down from 29 per cent in 1986/7 to 27 per cent for this tax year. And the amount of income taxed at basic rates has increased from £17,200 to £17,900. The higher rates of 40 and 45 per cent now don't start biting until your income is a little higher than last year, but rates above that start at the same level of income as previously.

PERSONAL ALLOWANCES

The size of the main allowances, such as single person's and married man's allowance have been increased by the rate of inflation (which is what has to be done by law). There has also been an increase in blind person's allowance from £360 to £540.

The increase in age allowance has been pushed up higher for the most elderly section of the population, those aged eighty or over during the tax year. For 1987/8, it is £3,070 for a single person and £4,845 for a married man.

SEPARATE TAXATION OF THE WIFE'S EARNINGS

For 1987/8, this will normally be worthwhile only if your joint income (before any allowances or outgoings you can deduct) is at least £26,870, including a wife's earned income of at least £6,545.

From the 1987/8 tax year, unemployment benefit will now be treated as earned income for separate taxation of the wife's earnings.

COMPANY CARS

Figures were announced in the Budget for the taxable values of cars for

1988/9. These have been increased by 10 per cent over the 1987/8 level. These figures apply only to the higher-paid, broadly those earning £8,500 or more a year and directors (p. 152).

	UNDER 4 YEARS OLD	4 YEARS OLD PLUS
1,400 cc or less	£580	£380
1,401 cc –2,000 cc	770	520
More than 2,000 cc	1,210	800

The taxable value of petrol provided for a company car stays the same as in 1987/8: up to 1,400 cc, £480; 1,401 cc–2,000 cc, £600; more than 2,000 cc, £900.

BUSINESS EXPANSION SCHEME

In previous years, there has been a madcap rush to invest the money you want to in a Business Expansion Scheme before the end of the tax year. But you can now invest up to £5,000 before 6 October 1987 and claim the relief for the tax year 1986/7. But the amount you want to take back to the previous year can't be more than half your total claimed for that year. For example, if you want to invest the full £5,000 between 6 April and 5 October, you must have invested at least £10,000 before 6 April 1987.

The Budget also made it easier for film production companies to qualify for investment under the scheme.

PROFIT-RELATED PAY

The government has proposed this new scheme which will give some tax relief on the part of employee's pay linked to the profits of the employer, that is a part of pay which automatically rises and falls with the profits of the business.

With a registered scheme, you will get half of your profit-related pay free of tax up to a maximum of £3,000 (or 20 per cent of pay if this is less).

PENSIONS

It is proposed that a new era of pensions will begin in April 1988; the much-heralded personal pension will compete with the state earnings-related scheme. And there are changes in the rules for employer's pension schemes and the pension plans currently in existence for the self-employed and those employees who do not save in an employer's pension scheme. Chapter 27, 'Pensions', p. 206, explains what the changes will be and helps you prepare for them.

WOMEN: INVALID CARE ALLOWANCE

If you are a married woman receiving invalid care allowance, you can now claim the wife's earned income allowance to set against it. This change has been backdated to include amounts paid in earlier years, starting with the 1984/5 tax year. This should mean less tax to pay in future and a rebate if you have received the allowance in the past.

FRIENDLY SOCIETIES

From 1 September 1987, friendly societies can issue tax-free policies with yearly premiums of £100 or less. Before that date, the limit for tax-free policies has been based on the amount of life insurance you get with the policy rather than the amount of the premium. In practice, the change will make little difference to someone taking out a policy.

TRADE UNION PROVIDENT BENEFITS

Members of trade unions can receive tax-free payments. For example, if they are sick or injured or if they die, money can be paid out to their children. The amount which can be tax-free has been increased to a lump sum of £3,000 or yearly income of £625.

INHERITANCE TAX

There has been an increase in the amount of money you can leave on your death, or gifts you can pay out in the seven years before your death, before any inheritance tax is due. The tax-free band has been raised from £71,000 to £90,000. On amounts above that, tax is paid at rates of 30 per cent and over. There are now only four possible rates of tax, whereas previously there were seven. However, the maximum rate remains the same at 60 per cent.

If you are passing on a substantial minority shareholding (at least 25 per cent over the previous two years) you can now get IHT business relief of 50 per cent (was 30 per cent). This applies only to unquoted companies. And companies dealt on the Unlisted Securities Market no longer count as unquoted for inheritance tax purposes.

CAPITAL GAINS TAX

The tax-free amount of net capital gains has increased from £6,300 to £6,600 for a single person or a married couple.

The retirement relief if you sell or dispose of your business when you retire at sixty (or earlier if you are ill) has increased from £100,000 to £125,000.

UNPAID AND OVERPAID TAX

From 6 November 1986, the rate of interest charged on unpaid income and capital gains tax (and paid to you if you overpaid tax) went up from 8.5 per cent to 9.5 per cent. From 6 April 1987, it was reduced to 9 per cent and on 6 June 1987 to 8.25 per cent.

There is now only one rate of interest which applies to late or overpaid inheritance tax. From 16 December 1986, the rate became 8 per cent, and from 6 June 1987, 6 per cent. Previously, there had been two rates, one which was used for transfers made in life (11 per cent) and a different one (9 per cent) for those on death.

GETTING THE BENEFIT OF HIGHER PERSONAL ALLOWANCES AND REDUCTION IN BASIC-RATE TAX

Employees should have felt the effect of the drop in basic-rate tax in their first pay packet after the start of the new tax year (but the effect of higher personal allowances would have taken longer to come through).

With income paid after deduction of basic-rate tax, the new rate would have been introduced at different times:

● annuities and maintenance payments could have been paid with deduction at the old rate until 5 May 1987, but payments later in the year should have adjusted for this

● in the case of British Government securities and foreign dividends paid in the UK, you should ask your Inspector of Taxes for a refund (or your tax bill for the year may be adjusted)

● if you are paying a gross covenant (p. 120) you should deduct tax at the new basic rate of 27 per cent and increase what you pay to the person receiving it. If you receive a gross covenant, and can claim back the tax deducted, you will be claiming back a lower amount. If you pay a net covenant, there is no alteration in what you pay; the person receiving it will claim back a lower amount, see p. 270

● dividends should be paid on or after 6 April 1987 with the correct tax credit. If you have received a dividend voucher showing a tax credit at the old rate, this will not apply. If you are a non-taxpayer claiming back tax, you will receive it calculated at the new rate

● income from trusts will be taxed at an overall rate of 45 per cent (that is, basic rate of 27 per cent plus an additional rate of 18 per cent). If you receive income from a trust in 1987/8, you will receive a credit for 45 per cent tax, just the same as in 1986/7.

IF YOU ARE EXPECTING A BABY

The way in which you receive pay while on maternity leave is changing during this tax year. Taxable maternity pay and tax-free maternity allowance are being replaced for employees by statutory maternity pay. The details are on p. 134.

8 · YOUR TAX INSPECTOR

The person with responsibility for assessing how much tax you should pay is your Tax Inspector. He or she is the local representative of the Inland Revenue, the government organization with responsibility for collecting direct taxes in the UK. With well over twenty million customers on its books, the Inland Revenue is the largest financial services organization in the UK, employing nearly seventy thousand civil servants to collect more than £56,000m in tax each year.

But what sort of organization is the Inland Revenue and how will it relate to you as a taxpayer? When should *you* get in touch with your Tax Inspector and how do you find out whom to contact?

THE INLAND REVENUE

The Inland Revenue at Somerset House in London is responsible for assessing and collecting income tax, capital gains tax, inheritance tax, stamp duty, corporation tax and various petroleum royalties and taxes. But the point of contact for most individual taxpayers will be one or more of some six hundred tax offices which cover most of the country.

Each of these tax offices (or districts) is run by a District Inspector: your Inspector of Taxes. Under the District Inspector is a team of Inspectors, most of whom will specialize in either PAYE taxpayers or the self-employed. Next in order of seniority are Tax Officers (Higher Grade), who manage the day-to-day work of the district and deal with routine cases. They are assisted by Tax Officers, and there will be a number of Clerical Assistants to send out Tax Returns, write out assessments, file papers and so on.

Most tax districts in England, Wales and Northern Ireland deal with the tax affairs of both employees (that is PAYE taxpayers) and the self-employed, though different groups of staff deal with each type of work. But the tax affairs of London PAYE taxpayers are dealt with mostly by special London Provincial Offices located in areas like Scotland and the North where it is easier to recruit staff. PAYE in Scotland is dealt with at the giant Centre 1 office in East Kilbride. Civil servants and members of the armed forces are dealt with by the Public Departments (PD) office at Llanishen, near Cardiff. And work on trusts is concentrated in just fifty-five districts.

The assessment of PAYE income tax is currently being put on to computers in what is the largest computerization exercise in Western Europe. Eleven giant regional computer centres will store the tax records of PAYE taxpayers under conditions of strict security to keep the information confidential. Taxpayers will still deal with their tax district, where the staff will have terminals to call up the information stored in the regional computers. When computerization is finished, it should mean a much better service for taxpayers. But while the computers are being installed, the work of tax offices is subject to disruption and you can expect longer than normal delays in getting answers to letters.

COLLECTORS OF TAXES

Tax districts assess your tax bill, that is, work out exactly how much you should pay. The collection of tax is handled by a separate section of the Inland Revenue known as Collectors of Taxes.

There are over 130 collectors' offices across the UK, but most tax has to be sent to the two large computerized Accounts Offices at Shipley in West Yorkshire and Cumbernauld in Scotland. If you fail to pay tax which is owed to the accounts office, you will be approached by your local Collector of Taxes, who will, if necessary, take you to court to get the money.

OTHER SPECIALIST OFFICES

Other specialist Inland Revenue offices deal with particular taxes or aspects of taxes. Among these you might come into contact with are:

● the Inspector of Foreign Dividends in Surrey which specializes in investment income from abroad

● the Claims Branch at Bootle which deals with rebates for non-residents, queries over covenants and repayments of tax to charities, among other matters

● the three Capital Taxes Offices for inheritance tax

● the ten Stamp Offices for the collection of stamp duty.

CONTACTING YOUR TAX INSPECTOR

You must tell your Tax Inspector if any of the following applies:

● you have a new source of income (for example, you start up as self-employed or start letting out your weekend cottage) or you make a taxable capital gain

● you are getting a tax allowance and are no longer entitled to it (for example, for looking after a dependent relative who no longer depends on you)

You should also contact your Tax Inspector promptly if you have overpaid tax or are entitled to a new tax relief or allowance. If you delay, you could lose tax relief: the deadlines for claiming various allowances and reliefs are given on p. 23.

WHICH TAX OFFICE?

Before you can contact your Tax Inspector, you will have to find out which office deals with your tax affairs. This depends on the type of income you get, and you may find that you have to deal with more than one tax office. The following are the general rules:

● *employees*: normally your tax office will be the one which looks after the tax affairs of everyone working for your employer. In most cases, this will be an office near your place of work, but people in London may have to use one of the London Provincial offices well away from the capital, while Scots must communicate with Centre 1 (see p. 49). If you change employer, you may also change tax office

● *civil servants and armed forces*: Public Departments office near Cardiff (see p. 49)

● *self-employed*: your tax office will generally be near where you work (near where you live, if you work from home)

● *property income*: may be dealt with by a tax office near where the property is

● *pensioners*: if you get a pension from your former employer, a tax office near where the pension fund is administered may deal with your tax affairs (ex-civil servants and military pensioners continue to be assessed by Public Departments office in Cardiff)

● *unemployed*: the tax office of your last employer will normally deal with your tax affairs.

If in doubt about your tax office, ask your employer (or your employer's pension administrators if you are retired). Otherwise, approach the tax office nearest home: you can find the address in the phone book under INLAND REVENUE – TAXES, HM INSPECTORS OF.

COMMUNICATING WITH YOUR TAX INSPECTOR

You can write to or telephone your tax office, but it's probably better to write in the first place (if only to save your phone bill). Address your letter to HM Inspector of Taxes, even if you've already spoken to someone else. Always quote your reference number, if possible: you'll find it on any previous correspondence with the tax office; with a new job, your employer will tell you the reference (it's the same for all employees). If you work for an employer, giving your National Insurance number may also be helpful – it's the key to your records in the new computerized PAYE system.

Keep a copy of whatever you write (and of your Tax Return when you send one in). And don't expect an instant reply as delays of a month or more in replying to letters are not uncommon. If you haven't heard after a month, a follow-up telephone call might help and have your reference number ready to quote.

Whatever the reason for getting in touch with your Tax Inspector, the most likely response will be to send you a Tax Return (see p. 55 for the different types). This should be completed and returned within thirty days. If you need longer, write and explain the delay.

Putting in a personal appearance may speed up communications, especially if it is a simple query which can be easily cleared up. If your tax office isn't close to home, you can arrange to discuss your tax affairs at a nearby office (they'll send for your papers, if needed). In London there are three PAYE Enquiry Offices which can liaise with the distant London Provincial offices. Lastly, you may be able to discuss your tax affairs with Inland Revenue staff in your local shopping centre when the mobile Inland Revenue exhibition stand pays a visit.

HOW YOUR TAX BILL IS WORKED OUT

When you return a completed Tax Return, it will be compared with previous returns you have sent in. The Tax Inspector will also match up what you have written with information supplied by people and organizations about payments made to you.

For example, banks, building societies and other savings organizations must tell the Inland Revenue if they pay you interest of £400 a year or more (and the taxman can ask for details of payments as low as £15 a year). Companies and unit trusts provide lists of dividend payments and distributions. And details of fees, commission, royalties and other payments made to you by businesses are also supplied to the Inland Revenue.

If your Tax Inspector thinks that you haven't come clean (or wants further information), you will get further letters to reply to. For details of how an investigation is carried out if the Inspector thinks you haven't told the whole truth, see Chapter 11, 'Appeals and Investigations', p. 82.

Once your Tax Inspector is satisfied that he or she has all the information necessary, your tax bill is worked out. Many taxpayers with simple tax affairs will have paid more or less the right amount of tax through PAYE (Chapter 19, 'Employees: Earnings and Expenses', p. 138) and tax is deducted from a lot of investment income before it is paid to you, with no further tax to pay unless you are a higher-rate taxpayer. But if there is still tax to pay, or you have paid too much tax and are entitled to a rebate, this should emerge from the assessment process.

If you have not paid the right amount of tax, your Tax Inspector is likely to issue you with a Notice of Assessment. This sets out your income, outgoings and allowances, and explains how your tax bill is calculated (for how to check Notice of Assessment, see p. 63). A Notice of Assessment will also be issued if you ask for one: do this if there's something you don't understand about your tax bill.

APPEALING AGAINST AN ASSESSMENT

Whether or not you're issued with a Notice of Assessment, you can appeal against your tax bill (or any other decision by your Tax Inspector). An appeal must be made in writing within thirty days of the date of issue of a Notice of Assessment or the decision in question. After the thirty-day deadline, you will be able to appeal only if you can convince your Tax Inspector that there was a good reason for the delay (for example, you were away on holiday or had moved house). But you can appeal against a Notice of Assessment issued after 30 July 1982, even though the thirty-day period is up, if something has happened which makes you think you have paid too much tax (for example, working through your accounts has thrown up an error).

The tax due on a Notice of Assessment must be paid even if you are appealing against the assessment, unless you also ask for a postponement of payment. The Tax Inspector is likely to agree to postpone only the amount of tax which is in dispute: for example, if the bill is £5,000 and you think it should be £3,000, £2,000 can be postponed. If you cannot agree on the amount of tax to be postponed, you can appeal to the General Commissioners (p. 77).

The tax which has not been postponed must be paid within thirty days of the postponement agreement. Once the appeal is settled, a revised assessment will be issued and any further tax which is due must be paid within thirty days of the date on this (or the date the original tax was due, if this is later). And interest will be charged on any tax which has to be paid after the appeal is decided (see below).

If you don't appeal against an incorrect assessment within the thirty-day time limit, you won't be able to correct your tax bill later – unless you can show that something has happened to make you realize that it was wrong. So always check a Notice of Assessment quickly and put in an appeal if you are at all sceptical about its correctness. If you want to postpone payment of the tax, apply for postponement at the same time as you appeal against the assessment, and within the same thirty-day time limit.

ESTIMATED ASSESSMENTS

A Notice of Assessment can be issued with an estimate of your income, marked *E*, if your Tax Inspector does not have the actual figure. This will often happen because you have not replied to letters asking for information: the Inspector can use whatever assumptions he or she finds reasonable (for example, your previous income, typical income figures for people in your line of business). And Schedule A property income is usually assessed on an estimated basis, since tax bills are issued before the end of the tax year (p. 233).

You can appeal against an estimated assessment as for any other Notice of Assessment, but you will have to prove that the estimate is wrong. Issuing an estimated assessment is often a useful way of getting reluctant taxpayers to come up with the figures, and if you get one, be sure to get the appeal in quickly. You won't be able to overturn the assessment otherwise, even if the estimate is wildly exaggerated.

INTEREST ON OVERDUE TAX

If you don't pay a tax bill on time, you can be charged interest on the unpaid amount. The rate is currently 8.25 per cent a year, but the Inland Revenue can waive the interest if it is £30 or less. This limit can quickly be reached, however: owing £3,000 for just over six weeks will result in an interest charge.

If you appeal against a Notice of Assessment, you have to pay the tax which has not been postponed: interest will be charged if you pay this late. And when the appeal is settled, any remaining tax must be paid within a set time (see above). Interest must also be paid on this, usually running from six months after the tax would have been due if there had been no appeal. Note that if the appeal ends up with your having to pay more tax than was originally assessed, you have to pay interest on the whole amount, including the bit that was not assessed in the first place.

You may also have to pay interest on tax if it is paid late because you didn't tell your Tax Inspector something which would have increased your liability (p. 84).

PAYMENT OF TAX IN INSTALMENTS

If you get a large tax bill which you cannot afford to settle, you can ask the Collector of Taxes to let you pay by instalments. You will have to show that hardship would be involved in paying in one go. And interest will probably have to be paid on the tax paid late.

9 · THE FORMS

In most cases your main means of communication with your Tax Inspector will be through pre-printed forms, of which the Tax Return is the most important. Great efforts have been made in recent years to make Inland Revenue forms more 'user-friendly' and the Inland Revenue has won bouquets from the Plain English Campaign for some of the results. But there are few people who greet the arrival of a buff Inland Revenue envelope with pleasure. This chapter looks at two of the more complicated forms you might have to deal with: the Tax Return and a Notice of Assessment.

THE TAX RETURN

In theory your Tax Inspector could ask you to fill in a Tax Return every year (and many taxpayers are asked to do just that). But people with relatively simple tax affairs may find that they have to fill in a Tax Return every three years or so, or even less frequently. And the complexity of your tax position will also determine which of the three commonest types of tax return you are sent:

● *Form P1* is the simplest Return issued to most employees who pay tax at the basic rate only and whose tax affairs are fairly straightforward

● *Form 11P* is sent to employees with more complicated tax affairs (for example, who get substantial fringe benefits, or who pay tax at the higher rates)

● *Form 11* is for the self-employed, including partners in a partnership (a partnership also gets *Form 1* to give details of the partners' income as a whole).

To find out which you've been sent, check the number at the bottom left-hand corner of the first page.

WHAT'S IN THE TAX RETURN?

The Tax Return asks for details of your income, outgoings and capital gains for the last complete tax year and for the allowances you wish to claim for the next tax year. So the 1987/8 Tax Return, which was sent out from April 1987 onwards, asks about:

● income, outgoings and capital gains for the 1986/7 tax year (ending on 5 April 1987)

● allowances for the 1987/8 tax year (beginning on 6 April 1987).

The 1988/9 Tax Return will be going out from April 1988 onwards and covers income, outgoings and allowances for the 1987/8 tax year and allowances for the 1988/9 tax year.

The Tax Return is designed to provide space to enter details of every type of income (though the simpler P1 leaves some types of income to be declared under *Any other income or gains*). This means that you may find that there are large parts of the Return which do not apply to you. If your only sources of income are your job and a building society account, you would need to do little more than enter details of the income from both and sign the Return (remembering to claim any allowances you might be eligible for).

But if you have a number of different types of savings accounts and investments, there could be several entries to make on the Return. You may have to search out other documents to send in with your Return (for example, a certificate of interest paid if you're claiming tax relief on interest payments). And collecting the facts and figures necessary can be a time-consuming exercise.

A Tax Return should be completed and returned within thirty days of issue (though if you're held up for any reason, write and ask for an extension). It is an offence knowingly to give wrong information on a Tax Return, so before you put your signature to the Return be sure to check the details carefully. And keep a copy of what you send in (there's space in the notes which come with the Return to make a duplicate of your entries). This will make it easier to deal with any queries which your Tax Inspector raises with you and is a useful *aide memoire* for filling in the next Tax Return.

MARRIED COUPLES

If you're married, you should get one Tax Return for the two of you, unless you have chosen separate assessment (p. 98) or, in some cases, if you got married during the current tax year.

Unless you get a Tax Return each, the Return you get must be signed by the husband. And the husband is responsible for making sure that the information given is correct: for example, he is expected to give details of his wife's savings accounts. This requirement has been greatly criticized in recent years and the government published proposals in 1986 for changing the income tax system to give wives their own Tax Returns (p. 90). But until the system changes, the husband must continue to sign the Return and get the letters from the Tax Inspector. However, as a concession to more enlightened times, Tax Inspectors are expected to reply directly to wives who write in about tax, even though legally it's their husband who is the taxpayer.

WHAT TO PUT IN YOUR TAX RETURN

At the end of each chapter in this Guide, there are details of what to enter in the Tax Return about your income, outgoings and capital gains and how to claim your allowances. The relevant section of Form 11P is illustrated, since it's the form you're most likely to get if your tax affairs are complicated. What to put if you get Forms 11 and P1 is also explained. Use the illustration of Form P1 overleaf to find the information you need to complete your Return: the relevant page number is given against each heading.

When entering details of income or outgoings, you can round sums of money down to the nearest whole pound (except for share dividends, unit trust distributions and tax credits). You don't need to write anything in spaces for types of income, outgoings and allowances which don't apply to you. If there is insufficient room under any heading to give full details, set them out on a separate sheet of paper with the same headings as the section of the Tax Return and write 'See attached schedule' on the Return. If there are several schedules, number them.

You do not need to enter details of genuine gifts, unless made under deed of covenant (p. 119), and certain other forms of exempt income such as student grants, adoption allowances and many social security benefits. But if in doubt, give details of the income and ask your Tax Inspector for guidance.

If you've got a source of income and can't figure out where it should go on the Tax Return (or are fairly sure that it doesn't fit in under any of the headings), enter details under *All other profits or income* on Forms 11P and 11 and *Any other income and gains* on Form P1.

Form 11P

Any other income not entered elsewhere eg: accrued income charges and taxable gains on life assurance policies

58

Form P1

Earnings

If you had earnings during the year ended 5 April 1987 from any of the sources listed below,
please tick the appropriate boxes, enter the annual amounts and give details in the space provided.

			Self	Wife	Self	Wife	Details including name and address of employer and job
p. 132	Earnings from full-time employment				£	£	
p. 132, p. 202	All other earnings (for example, part-time or casual earnings)						
p. 178, p. 202	Profits from a trade or profession						
p. 132	Tips						
p. 151	Value of benefits in kind from your work						
p. 164	Redundancy, compensation or other leaving payment						

Please tick if you received any of the other benefits listed below. You do not need to give amounts.

		Self	Wife	Details
p. 158	Transport vouchers, other vouchers or credit cards			
p. 161	Taxed sum from trustees of an approved profit-sharing scheme			
p. 168	Unemployment or Supplementary Benefit			

		Self	Wife
p. 174	If any part of your work during the year ended 5 April 1987 took place outside the United Kingdom, please tick here.		

Pensions

If you received any of the pensions listed below during the year ended 5 April 1987,
please tick the appropriate boxes, enter the annual amounts and give details in the space provided.

		Self	Wife	Self	Wife	Details
p. 126	Retirement or Old Person's pension			£	£	
p. 168	Widow's or other state benefits					
p. 126	Pension from former employer					

If you are receiving a pension now or expect to start one after 5 April 1987 but before 6 April 1988,
please give the following information. It will help me to give you the right PAYE code.
Write the amount of any pension you receive now in the appropriate box.

Type of pension you receive now	Weekly	4-weekly	Monthly	Quarterly	Type of pension you are expecting	Date pension starts
Self	£	£	£	£		
Wife						

p. 124, p. 125	If part or all of your wife's pension is paid as a result of her own contributions, please tick this box and give full details to claim wife's earned income allowance.	If either of you were born before 6 April 1928, give your dates of birth. Self ____ Wife ____

Form P1 continued

Investments, savings, etc

If you received income during the year ended 5 April 1987 from any of the sources listed below, please tick the appropriate boxes, enter the annual amounts and give details in the space provided.

		Self	Wife	Self	Wife	Details
p. 242. p. 249	Rents from land or property in the UK			£	£	
p. 249	National Savings Bank interest Ordinary account					
	Investment account					
p. 244	Interest from any other banks and building societies					
p. 249	Interest from banks not already taxed					
p. 249	Interest not already taxed from any other source					
p. 238. p. 255	Income from abroad					
p. 244	Company dividends and unit trusts					
p. 243	Other dividends, interest, etc, including income from trusts					
p. 117. p. 248	Payments from settlements and estates (gross amount)					
p. 107	Maintenance, alimony or aliment received (gross amount)					
p. 57. p. 199 p. 259	Any other income or gains					

Remember to read the notes 'How to fill in your tax return' as you complete each section.

Outgoings

If you wish to claim for a tax deduction or any allowable payment which you made in the year ended 5 April 1987, please tick the appropriate boxes, enter the annual amounts paid in the year and give details in the space provided.

		Self	Wife	Self	Wife	Details
p. 135	Expenses paid in connection with your work			£	£	
p. 135	Subscriptions to professional bodies					
p. 218	Interest on loans for buying or improving your home					
p. 230	Interest payments on UK property for letting					
	Number of weeks let					
p. 39. p. 308	Other loan interest paid					
p. 119. p. 273	Covenants					
p. 107	Maintenance, alimony or aliment paid					
p. 39	Rents and yearly interest paid to persons abroad					

Form P1 continued

Capital gains

If you or your wife disposed of any chargeable assets during the year ended 5 April 1987:

p. 275

Tick if:	If you ticked any of these boxes, please give:	
total combined proceeds exceeded £12,600 chargeable gains (before allowable losses) exceeded £6,300	Description of asset	
you or your wife made an allowable loss	Date of disposal	Amount of gain or loss £

Allowances

If you are entitled to claim any of the following allowances for the year ending 5 April 1988, tick the appropriate boxes and fill in the details asked for:

p. 90	**Married man's allowance** Allowance for a married man living with or wholly maintaining his wife	Wife's first names		If married since 5 April 1986, date of marriage
p. 40	**Blind person's allowance** Self Wife	Local authority with which registered		Date of registration
p. 125	**Son or daughter whose services you depend on**	Details see Notes for details required		
p. 111	**Housekeeper allowance**			
p. 87	**Additional personal allowance**			
p. 122	**Dependent relative allowance**	Name and address of dependent relative		

		Relationship to you or your wife	Date of birth of dependant
Dependant's annual income, excluding voluntary contributions	£		
If the dependant is not living with you please enter the weekly amount you contribute	£	What is the dependent relative's illness or disability?	
If any other relative contributes, please enter the weekly amount	£		

p. 268 **Death and superannuation benefits**   Name of friendly society, union or scheme

If you and your wife between you paid more than £85 in deferred annuity premiums in the year ended 5 April 1987 including any compulsory payments to provide annuities for widows and orphans, enter the total amount paid £	Full contribution for year ending 5 April 1988 £	Portion for life assurance relief and superannuation benefits (friendly society or trade union only) £

Declaration   Remember that you can be prosecuted for making false statements.

To the best of my knowledge and belief, the particulars I have given on this form are correct and complete

Signature   Date

Please give your National Insurance number in the box below, if not already shown on the front of this form.

If there is any other information which you think may affect your tax liability, please give details here or on a separate piece of paper

CHANGES IN YOUR CIRCUMSTANCES

There is space on Forms 11P and 11 to enter details of *Changes in untaxed income or outgoings since 5 April 1986.*

Form 11P

Changes in untaxed income or outgoings since 5 April 1986	Details

The Tax Inspector wants to know about changes in sources of income paid to you without deduction of tax. So you should enter details if, for example, you have closed a National Savings Investment Account or stopped letting out your holiday cottage. You should also tell the Tax Inspector about changes in your outgoings: if you have been claiming tax relief on loan interest, for example, and have repaid the loan.

But note that this isn't the place to give details of changes in a building society mortgage for your only or main home. There's space elsewhere on the Return to give these details (p. 229).

There's no equivalent space on Form P1, but it might avoid further correspondence and delay if you give similar details in a covering letter.

CHECKLIST OF PAPERS NEEDED TO COMPLETE A TAX RETURN

You will need the following documents to complete your Tax Return:

● a copy of the last Tax Return you sent in as a prompt for things to enter on the new one

● Form P60 setting out your earnings from your job or income from an employer's pension scheme

● a copy of the Form P11D filled in by your employer about your fringe benefits and expense allowances if you count as 'higher-paid' (p. 138)

● your business accounts if you have income from self-employment or property

● your passbooks for National Savings investments (these will need to be sent off to have the interest added – do this after 1 January for the previous calendar year)

● bank deposit and high interest account statements

● building society interest statements

- share dividend and unit trust distribution counterfoils

- tax vouchers from stock and loan interest

- Form R185 or Form R185E if you get maintenance payments or alimony, or income from a trust or the estate of someone who has died

- Form R185AP if you get covenant payments

- receipts, etc. for expenses in employment and allowable professional fees and subscriptions

- certificates of interest paid for loans on which you're claiming tax relief for interest paid

- contract notes for shares you've bought and sold, and records for any other assets bought or sold on which tax may be due.

TAX CLAIM FORM

If you receive income after tax has been deducted from it, you may be able to claim back some or all of the deducted tax. This would apply, for example, to:

- non-taxpayers who get share dividends and can reclaim the basic-rate tax on them (p. 245)

- students who receive covenant payments and can reclaim some or all of the basic-rate tax deducted from the payments (p. 119)

- beneficiaries of discretionary trusts who pay tax at less than the 45 per cent rate at which the trust's investment income is taxed (p. 248).

You may be sent the rather simpler form of Return known as Tax Claim Form R40 to claim back the tax. This asks you about the income paid after deduction of tax and for details of any other income. Send it back with the documents you got with the income which set out the tax deducted: for example, with a covenant payment, the Form R185AP; with share dividends and unit trust dividends, the tax vouchers.

You'll normally be sent a new form with the tax repayment to claim the next repayment. You can send in the completed form before the end of the tax year to get repayment as soon as possible, as long as you've had all the income for the tax year which is paid after deduction of tax. In certain circumstances, your Tax Inspector may even agree to refund the tax in instalments through the year (for example, with student covenants, after each of the three payments is made).

THE NOTICE OF ASSESSMENT

Many people will never see a Notice of Assessment throughout their taxpaying careers because more or less the right amount of tax will be deducted from their earnings through PAYE (and interest on their savings is likely to be paid after deduction of tax). But if you have several sources of income, pay tax at the higher rates or are self-employed, you'll probably be issued with a Notice of Assessment setting out your income, outgoings, allowances and tax bill. Anyone with complicated tax affairs could also get one, and you can ask to be issued with one if you want to know more about how your tax bill was worked out.

There are different types of assessment notice – which you get depends on the type of income:

● *Schedule E* Notice of Assessment is sent if most of your income is taxed under PAYE (that is, you work for an employer or live off a pension). There's space on this notice for other types of income such as small amounts of investment income, property income or freelance earnings

● *Schedule A or Schedule D* Notice of Assessment will be issued if you have substantial property income, investment income or earnings from self-employment

● *capital gains tax* Notice of Assessment is issued if you have a capital gains tax bill to pay

● *Form 930* may be issued if you pay tax at the higher rates, explaining how your higher-rate tax bill has been worked out.

You may get more than one Notice if you have both substantial investment income, say, and work for an employer. And you could get more than one Schedule A or Schedule D Notice if you have both property income and earnings from self-employment.

CHECKING A NOTICE OF ASSESSMENT

You should always check a Notice of Assessment as soon as you get it. Any appeal against it must normally be made within thirty days of its issue (p. 52).

An example of a Schedule E Notice of Assessment (P70) is illustrated overleaf, completed for Robert and Philippa Grange for the 1986/7 tax year. You can follow how the Granges checked their notice as follows (it is easier to tackle the sections in this order):

Section 1 lists earned income, which includes pay, bonus, commission,

64

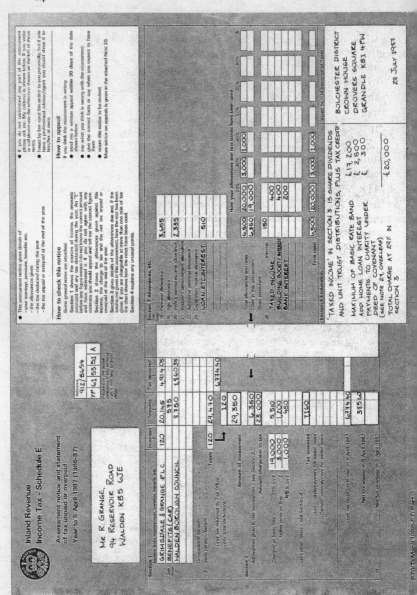

Schedule E Notice of Assessment

the taxable value of fringe benefits and any pension (whether from an ex-employer or the state). Both the Granges work and their earnings after pension contributions are listed, as is the value of Robert's company car. In each case, the tax deducted is also listed, together with any deductions allowed against the income (for example, Robert's £120 subscription to his professional association is set off against his earnings from the job). The Granges check that the figures are correct and that expenses have not been overlooked.

Section 3 sets out the allowances and outgoings the Granges are entitled to: married man's allowance, wife's earned income allowance and loan interest which qualifies for tax relief. Interest paid under MIRAS will not be included here, because the Granges have had the basic-rate tax relief on it. The Granges check that all their allowances and outgoings are included – the total comes to £6,500.

The Granges have a National Savings Investment Account and the £150 interest they got on this was paid without deduction of tax. Their total allowances of £6,500 are reduced by £150 to £6,350 in order to collect the tax due on this interest.

Section 3 also shows how much of the Granges' income is taxed at the basic rate. For 1986/7, up to £17,200 of taxable income is taxed at the basic rate, but this amount can be increased or decreased to give you extra tax relief at the higher rates or to tax income at the higher rates which has already been deducted at the basic rate.

For example, the Granges pay mortgage interest under MIRAS, getting basic-rate tax relief by making reduced payments. The grossed-up amount of this interest was £2,500, and the Granges can be given higher-rate tax relief on this by *increasing* the amount of income taxed at the basic rate by £2,500 to £19,700. The £300 of gross covenant payments the Granges made to charity are also added to their basic-rate band to give them higher-rate tax relief: this gives a total taxable at the basic rate of £20,000.

At the same time, *reducing* this basic-rate band will collect higher-rate tax due on income paid after deduction of basic-rate tax. The Granges got a grossed-up amount of £1,000 in such income for the tax year from bank and building society interest, share dividends and unit trust distributions. After all these adjustments (explained in *Section 4*) the Granges have a basic-rate band given for this assessment of £19,000.

Section 2 works out the Granges' tax bill using the results of the other three sections. It begins by deducting the £6,350 of allowances worked out in *Section 3* from the total income to be taxed on this assessment of £29,350 to produce an amount chargeable to tax of £23,000. £19,000 of this is to be taxed at the basic rate (29 per cent for 1986/7) and the rest at the higher rates. The result is a tax bill of £7,160, which is compared with the tax actually deducted of £6,774.40 to show that an extra £385.60 is due.

If you get more than one Notice of Assessment, it won't always be obvious how the various notices relate to each other, and what allowances you've been given. Ask for Form 930 which explains how the various types of income have been taxed.

10 · CHECKING YOUR INCOME TAX BILL

During the tax year you will have opportunties to check that you are paying the right amount of income tax. These opportunities include receiving:

● your payslip, if you are an employee

● your P60, given to employees at the end of the tax year

● your Notice of Coding, which tells your employer what tax to deduct. If your outgoings and allowances have not changed from last year, you may not receive one

● a Notice of Assessment, if you receive one. If you are self-employed, this is always how your tax bill is worked out; if you are an employee, you may receive a Notice of Assessment, for example, if you are a higher-rate taxpayer.

Just because you are an employee does not mean that you should have great faith that you will have paid the correct tax at the end of the year. When the Inland Revenue have checked in the past to see if employees were paying the right amount of tax under the PAYE system, it estimated that over a quarter of employees had not. So get out your pens and paper. Gather together all the bits and pieces of information that you need to add up your income, outgoings and allowances – much the same list as you need to fill in your Tax Return, see p. 61.

This chapter explains how to satisfy yourself that the income tax deducted for the 1986/7 tax year is correct. But you can also work through your Notice of Assessment to see if you have paid the right amount of tax. How to do this is explained on p. 63.

There may be some special circumstances in which you will not be able to use this chapter to check your income tax bill and will have to check your tax using the Notice of Assessment and by doing some extra work. This applies, for example, if you have received leaving payments of over £25,000, or if you are cashing in part of a single-premium bond and claiming top-slicing relief (p. 263). You will also find that you cannot use this method if your net outgoings (which are paid after you have deducted basic-rate tax, for example mortgage interest under the MIRAS system) come to more than your taxable income. In this case, you will have to pay some of the tax deducted to the Inland Revenue but you will not be able to work out how much.

CHECKING AN INCOME TAX BILL FOR 1986/7

Fill in the figures below. Note that the page number beside each entry tells you where to look for more information. Ignore pence in your calculations. Do not enter any income which is tax-free.

If you have chosen to have the wife's earnings taxed separately for 1986/7, you can use the following method but will need to follow the additional instructions under *Note 1*. If you are claiming age allowance, see *Note 2* before you do your sums.

INCOME	PAGE NO.	£
SECTION I: FOR THE HUSBAND		
Your before-tax earnings from job (from your P60)	144	...
Amount of expenses and taxable value of fringe benefits	137, 151	...
Amount of tips	148	...
Taxable income from self-employment, partnership	179	...
Before-tax amount of taxable social security benefits, for example, unemployment benefit	169	...
Before-tax pension from state, your employer or your own scheme (include wife's if based on your contributions, not hers; see p. 126 for what happens to pensions from abroad)	126	...
Casual or occasional freelance income; Enterprise Allowance	199, 196	...
Income from furnished holiday lettings and any other earned income	237	...

69

	PAGE NO.	£
ADD UP ALL THESE ITEMS:	**A**	...

DEDUCT

Allowable expenses in your job	137	...
Payments to employer's pension scheme	208	...
Payments for personal pension and Sec. 226A life insurance	214, 266	...
Loss relief claimed against husband's earned income	188	...

TOTAL DEDUCTIONS	**B**	...
DEDUCT **B** from **A**	**C**	...

SECTION 2: FOR THE WIFE

Your before-tax earnings from job (from your P60)	144	...
Amount of expenses and taxable value of fringe benefits	137, 151	...
Amount of tips	148	...
Taxable income from self-employment, partnership	179	...
Before-tax amount of invalid care allowance and unemployment benefit	172	...
Before-tax pension from state, your employer or your own scheme (if based on own contributions)	126	...
Casual or occasional freelance income; Enterprise Allowance	199, 196	...
Income from furnished holiday lettings and any other earned income	237	...

ADD UP ALL THESE ITEMS	**D**	...

DEDUCT

Allowable expenses in your job	137	...
Payments to employer's pension scheme	208	...
Payments for personal pension and Sec. 226A life insurance	214, 266	...
Loss relief claimed against wife's earned income	188	...

TOTAL DEDUCTIONS	**E**	...

	PAGE NO.	£
DEDUCT **E** from **D**	**F**	...
DEDUCT Wife's earned income allowance		2,335
TOTAL (if minus, put zero)	**G**	...

SECTION 3: NOW ADD UP THESE (for both of you if married, even if wife's earnings taxed separately)

Investment income received without deduction of tax	249	...
Grossed-up value of investment income received after deduction of tax (net amount × 100/71)	243	...
Income from property less expenses	230	...
Gross amount of maintenance payments received	107	...
Any other unearned income (including covenants received, but not gains on life insurance policies)	120	...
TOTAL UNEARNED INCOME	**H**	...
TOTAL Add **C** + **G** + **H** (but see *Note 2* on p. 73)	**I**	...

SECTION 4: GROSS OUTGOINGS (that is, you pay in full)

Loan interest which qualifies for tax relief but not paid under MIRAS scheme	223	...
Small maintenance payments you make	108	...
Loss relief claimed against husband's or wife's investment income	188	...
TOTAL GROSS OUTGOINGS	**J**	...

SECTION 5: ALLOWANCES

Single person's (£2,335), married man's (£3,655) or amount of age allowance (see **e** in *Note 2* on p. 47), but not wife's earned income allowance		...
Other allowances	40	...
Investment in a BES scheme	253	...
TOTAL ALLOWANCES	**K**	...
ADD **J** + **K**	**L**	...

SECTION 6: NET OUTGOINGS (that is, your pay with basic-rate tax deducted. Enter actual amount you pay)

PAGE NO. £

	PAGE NO.	£
Loan interest which qualifies for tax relief, paid under MIRAS scheme	223	...
Amount of maintenance payments you actually pay (excluding small ones)	107	...
Amount of covenant which you actually pay to a charity (but not to anyone else)	269	...

TOTAL NET OUTGOINGS   **M** ...

Multiply **M** by $\dfrac{100}{71}$ **N** ...

ADD **L** + **N**   **O** ...

DEDUCT **O** from **I**, gives taxable income   **P** ...

SECTION 7: THE TAX YOU SHOULD PAY

Tax at basic rate (29 per cent) on £17,200 (or amount **P** if less)   ...

Tax at higher rates on amounts over £17,200

     The first £3,000 at 40%   ...

     The next £5,200 at 45%   ...

     The next £7,900 at 50%   ...

     The next £7,900 at 55%   ...

     On amounts over this, tax at 60%   ...

TAX ON AMOUNT **P**   **Q** ...

ADD Tax deducted from net outgoings **N** – **M**   **R** ...

TOTAL TAX DUE **Q** + **R**   **S** ...

SECTION 8: THE TAX YOU HAVE PAID

Tax already deducted under PAYE (for example, in job, pensions, social security benefits, fringe benefits, etc.) Find this from your P60   144   £ ...

	PAGE NO.	£
Tax already paid on self-employed or partnership income	191	...
Tax credits on dividends or distributions	244	...
Tax deducted from interest received (but excluding interest from building society, bank, licensed deposit-taker, or other interest in composite-rate scheme, p. 244	243	...
Tax deducted from maintenance payments received	107	...

TOTAL   **T**   ...

ADD Amount of interest actually received from: 244
Bank   ...
Building society   ...
Licensed deposit-taker and other interest in composite scheme   ...

TOTAL INTEREST FROM BANK ETC.   **U** ...

Multiply **U** by $\dfrac{100}{71}$ **V** ...

DEDUCT **U** from **V**   **W** ...

TOTAL TAX YOU HAVE PAID: ADD **T** + **W**   **X** ...

SECTION 9: PAID TOO MUCH OR TOO LITTLE TAX?

Total tax due   **S** ...
less Total tax paid   **X** ...
The difference   **Y** ...

If **Y** is a plus figure, you owe that amount of tax.

If **Y** is a minus figure, now work out how much tax you can reclaim.

SECTION 10: HOW MUCH TAX YOU CAN RECLAIM

Enter **Y** as a minus figure   ...
Add **T**   ...
Total   **Z** ...

If **Z** is zero or a plus figure, you can reclaim amount **Y**

If **Z** is a minus figure, you can reclaim amount **T**

Note 1

If you have opted to have the wife's earnings taxed separately, you both go through the above method to find the amount of tax due for each of you separately:

1 The husband completes all sections, except Section 2.

2 The wife completes all sections, except Sections 2 and 3. Wherever it says 'husband', substitute yourself. In Section 8, add up tax paid on earned income, not investment or unearned income, for example, dividends, interest, maintenance payments.

Note 2

If you (or your spouse) is entitled to age allowance, you will need to work out how much you are entitled to.

Enter **C**	£ ...
Enter **G**	£ ...
Enter **H**	£ ...
Enter chargeable gains on life insurance policies (p. 262)	£ ...
ADD UP THESE AMOUNTS	**a** £ ...
Enter **J**	£ ...
Enter **N**	...
ADD up **J** + **N**	**b** £ ...
DEDUCT **b** from **a**, gives 'total income'	**c** £ ...

1 If you are single and your 'total income' **c** is £9,400 or less, enter £2,850 for age allowance. But if **c** is £10,173 or more, enter single person's allowance (£2,335) at Section 5 instead.

2 If you are married and your joint 'total income' **c** is £9,400 or less, enter £4,505 for age allowance. But if **c** is £10,675 or more, enter married man's allowance (£3,655) at Section 5 instead.

But if **c** is more than £9,400, but less than £10,173 if single or £10,675 if married, do the following calculation:

Enter **c**	£ ...
Deduct £9,400	9,400
Leaves	...

Multiply by 2   . . .

Divide by 3   **d** . . .

Enter £2,850 if single, £4,505 if married   **£** . . .

DEDUCT **d**, gives age allowance   **e** . . .

EXAMPLE I

Walter Burns earns £22,000 in his job. He received expense payments of
£150 (£30 of these are not allowable) and has the following fringe benefits: car (taxable value £575), luncheon vouchers (taxable value £351).
He contributes £1,100 to a pension scheme. Walter writes the occasional
article for trade magazines; in 1986/7 this amounted to £450.

Sheila Burns is self-employed. She has worked through the calculation
in Chapter 24, 'The Self-Employed', p. 178, and her taxable income
from self-employment for 1986/7 (based on her accounting year ending
in 1985/6) is £8,100. She contributes £1,200 to a self-employed pension
scheme and pays £85 a year for a Section 226A life insurance policy.

Their investment income is as follows: interest paid on National
Savings Investment Account, £250 (no tax deducted); distributions
received from unit trusts, £130.65 plus tax credits of £53.36; and interest
from a building society account of £37 (£52 grossed-up).

During the year they had the following outgoings: interest paid gross
on a home improvement loan £420, mortgage interest of £2,280 paid
net under the MIRAS scheme and net maintenance payments to
Walter's ex-wife, £3,000.

SECTION I

Walter fills in this section: his income is £22,000 + £150 + £575 +
£351 + £450. The total at **A** is £23,526. He deducts certain of his
outgoings: allowable expenses of £120 and pension contributions £1,100
(**B** is £1,220). The figure at **C** is £22,306.

SECTION 2

Sheila fills in her income and the outgoings she can deduct. This comes
to: **D** £8,100, **E** £1,285. Deducting **E** from **D**, gives **F** £6,815. Sheila can
claim the wife's earned income allowance, which gives a figure at **G** of
£4,480.

SECTION 3

Adding up investment income gives:

$$\mathbf{H} = £250 + £130 + £53 + £52 = £485$$

Walter and Sheila can now find what **I** will be by adding **C**, **G** and **H**. This will come to:

$$£22,306 + £4,480 + £485 = £27,271 \text{ (I)}$$

SECTION 4

They claim tax relief on interest on a home improvement loan paid without basic-rate tax deducted (that is, not under the MIRAS scheme) of £420. The total **J** is £420.

SECTION 5

Walter can claim married man's allowance of £3,655 (**K**). So **L** is £420, plus £3,655 equals £4,075.

SECTION 6

Sheila and Walter pay their mortgage under the MIRAS scheme, net interest of £2,280 in 1986/7. Walter also makes maintenance payments to his former wife of £3,000 after deducting basic-rate tax. **M** comes to £5,280 and **N** is £5,280 × $\dfrac{100}{71}$ = £7,437.

The next sums are:

$$\mathbf{L} + \mathbf{N} = £4,075 + £7,437 = £11,512 = \mathbf{O}$$

Deducting **O** from **I** gives taxable income **P** = £27,271 − £11,512 = £15,759.

SECTION 7

This is where Sheila and Walter work out how much tax they should pay.

Tax at the basic rate on £17,200 or amount **P** if less. **P** is less than £17,200 so calculation is:

$$29 \text{ per cent of } £15,759 = £4,570 = \mathbf{Q}$$

Adding back the tax deducted from net outgoings (**N** − **M**) is £7,437 − £5,280 = £2,157 (**R**). This gives total tax due **Q** + **R** = **S** £6,727.

SECTION 8

Now they add up the tax they have paid. Walter has paid tax under the PAYE system, which has collected tax of £5,448 on his salary, his fringe benefits and his freelance work. Sheila has paid tax of £1,299 on her business income. And the tax credit of £53.36 they get on the unit trusts is treated as tax paid. But tax has not been paid on the National Savings Investment Account nor the unallowed part of Walter's expenses. Amount **T** comes to £6,800. They are treated as having paid basic-rate tax on their building society interest of £15 (amount **W**). Amount **X** is £6,815.

SECTION 9

Total tax due **S** is £6,727 and total tax paid **X** is £6,815, so the difference **Y** is minus £92. Now Sheila and Walter have to work out how much tax they can reclaim.

SECTION 10

Sheila and Walter enter **Y** as a minus figure (− £92) and add **T**, which is £6,800. Amount **Z** is a plus figure, so Sheila and Walter can reclaim amount **Y**, that is, £92. They have overpaid tax because they paid more interest on their home improvement loan than had been allowed for in Walter's PAYE code.

EXAMPLE 2

Jane and Edmund Davidson are in their late sixties. Their income consists of pensions of £8,000 (from the state and a former employer), dividends of £1,420 (plus tax credits of £580) and interest received from a building society of £288 (grossed-up amount £406).

Jane and Edmund need to work out how much age allowance they are entitled to (see *Note 2*). Income (**C**) comes to £8,000, **G** is nil and **H** (investment income) is £1,420 + £580 + £406 = £2,406. This gives amount **a** = £10,406.

They have no outgoings, so **J** + **N** is nil (amount **b**) and amount **c** (total income) is £10,406. This is more than £9,400 but less than £10,675 for a married couple, so they do need to do a further sum to work out how much age allowance they can claim.

Deduct £9,400 from amount **c** (£10,406) = £1,006. Multiply by 2 and divide by 3 gives amount **d** = £671. Deducting **d** from £4,505, gives age allowance **3** of £3,834.

Jane and Edmund should read Chapter 18, 'Retired or Near Retirement Age', p. 124, to find out how to reorganize their investments to keep more age allowance.

11 · APPEALS AND INVESTIGATIONS

Arguments with your Tax Inspector are to be avoided if at all possible. But if you think that an assessment is wrong, you should appeal against it. If you cannot sort it out with your Inspector, this chapter takes you through the appeals process.

You might also wish to claim an allowance or tax relief to which you are entitled and which you haven't claimed before. Claims can be back-dated for some years, so you could reclaim tax paid in previous years. This chapter outlines the time limits for claiming such reliefs, and explains where you stand if the taxman has collected too much tax from you as the result of a mistake. It ends by looking at how the Inland Revenue carries out investigations when it probes the affairs of taxpayers who are thought to have been less than frank in filling in their Tax Returns.

APPEALS

If you get a Notice of Assessment which you think is wrong, you can appeal against it, in the first place to your Tax Inspector. You can also appeal against a PAYE Notice of Coding (p. 141), or any other decision made about your tax affairs by the Inland Revenue.

It may seem a little odd to appeal to the Tax Inspector who issued the notice or whatever in the first place. But the decision may have been issued by a more junior member of staff, or simply made in the absence of the full facts. Most appeals are resolved with little difficulty by negotiation between taxpayer and Inspector. If you cannot reach agreement with your Tax Inspector, you can appeal to the Commissioners, the courts and ultimately the House of Lords.

APPEALS TO THE COMMISSIONERS

The Commissioners provide the first tier of appeal with which you can raise your case. Your Tax Inspector may also refer a case to the Commissioners: this is a way of pressuring you to answer letters or enquiries which the Inspector thinks is a delaying tactic.

There are two groups of Commissioners:

● *Special Commissioners*: These are full-time civil servants who are tax experts and who usually hear cases on their own with only a clerk to keep notes

● *General Commissioners*: These are unpaid lay people, serving voluntarily in the same way as magistrates. They sit in groups of two or more, with a clerk who gives expert advice, to hear cases in their locality.

Certain technical matters such as valuation of shares will automatically go to the Special Commissioners. Arguments over personal allowances or delays always go to the General Commissioners. If your appeal is not covered by any such general rule, it will automatically be heard by the General Commissioners.

But you can opt for it to be heard by the Special Commissioners. This might be worth doing if your appeal is on a point of law. You must make the choice within the time limit for entering the appeal.

Once a case has been referred to the Commissioners, you will get notice of the hearing from the clerk. With delay cases (where you have failed to supply your Tax Inspector with information, say), the hearing may not take place for a year or two. Most such appeals never get as far as a formal hearing since the case will be resolved when the taxpayer comes up with the facts.

You can present your own case to the Commissioners or be represented by a lawyer or accountant (which could be expensive). If you are the party who is appealing, you open the proceedings by seeking to prove that the Inspector's decision is wrong. The Inspector replies, leaving you with a final chance to make your case and reply to the Inspector. The Commissioners' decision (which can be to increase your tax bill, as well as to reduce it or leave it as it is) will be given at the end of the hearing or in writing soon after.

APPEALING AGAINST COMMISSIONERS' DECISIONS

Either you or the Tax Inspector can appeal against the decision of the Commissioners to the High Court, then to the Appeal Court and ultimately to the House of Lords. This becomes an expensive business, since you will need to be represented, and you may have to pay the Inland Revenue's costs if you lose.

Even if you do appeal, you must still pay the tax bill decided by the Commissioners, pending a final decision by the courts. And you cannot normally appeal on a point of fact (for example, what your expenses were), only on a point of law (whether the expense was allowable). If the Tax Inspector appeals, you have a hard decision to make: the tax at stake could be much less than the cost of fighting the case and discretion may be the better part of valour if that is so. Certainly you should try to get financial support for your appeal (for example, from your trade union or professional association).

CLAIMING A TAX REPAYMENT

If you discover that you are entitled to an allowance which you haven't been claiming, or you are entitled to tax relief on some expenditure, you should put in a claim for a tax repayment. You can claim back the tax you have overpaid for up to six complete tax years before the current one – and, perhaps, get interest on the overpaid tax.

Suppose that on reading this Guide in October 1987, you realize that you've been entitled to tax relief on the interest you pay on a loan. You can claim tax relief on interest paid on the loan back to 6 April 1981 – six years before the start of the 1987/8 tax year. If you took out the loan after 6 April 1981, the tax relief runs only from when you got the loan.

Although you have up to six complete tax years to discover an outgoing or allowance to which you are entitled, the time limits are rather shorter in other cases:

● to choose separate taxation of wife's earnings (p. 93), you must tell your Tax Inspector within twelve months of the end of the tax year for which it is to apply

● if you have a new source of income, you must tell your Tax Inspector about it within twelve months of the end of the tax year in which you start to get it

● to have losses from self-employment set off against income from other sources (p. 188), you must tell your Tax Inspector within two years of the end of the tax year in which you want the relief

● to set losses from a new business off against income from tax years before the business was started (p. 189), you must tell your Tax Inspector within two years of the end of the tax year in which the losses arise.

INTEREST ON TAX REBATES

You can get interest on rebates of overpaid tax if both the following conditions are met:

● the rebate is £25 or more

● you get the rebate more than one year after the end of the tax year to which it relates. So you won't get interest on a tax rebate paid to you in the 1987/8 tax year unless it is for tax overpaid before 6 April 1986.

The interest, called repayment supplement, is tax-free, and is paid at the following rates:

● 8.25 per cent from 6 June 1987 onwards

● 9 per cent from 6 April 1987 to 5 June 1987

● 9.5 per cent from 6 November 1986 to 5 April 1987

● 8.5 per cent from 6 August 1986 to 5 November 1986

● 11 per cent from 6 May 1985 to 5 August 1985

● 8 per cent from 6 December 1982 to 5 May 1986

● 12 per cent from 6 January 1980 to 5 December 1982.

Interest is paid for each month (complete or part) from twelve months after the end of the tax year for which it is due until the rebate is paid. But if the tax was originally paid more than twelve months after the year for which it was due, then the interest runs from the end of the tax year in which the tax was actually paid.

EXAMPLE

Susan Barlow paid £1,000 too much tax on her investment income during the 1984/5 tax year. She could claim a rebate up to six complete tax years after the year of the overpayment, that is, as late as 5 April 1991. And she could get interest on the rebate if it is paid more than twelve months after the end of the 1984/5 tax year, that is, after 5 April 1986.

So if Susan got her £1,000 rebate on 25 September 1987, she would get interest for each part or whole month since 5 April 1986 (unless she had paid the tax after this date). This is seventeen whole months and one part month – eighteen months in all. The rate of interest is as follows:

● 11 per cent per annum for the four months from 6 April 1986 to 5 August 1986 £36.67

● 8.5 per cent per annum for the three months from 6 August 1986 to 5 November 1986 £21.25

● 9.5 per cent per annum for the five months from 6 November 1986 to 5 April 1987 £39.58

● 9 per cent per annum for the two months from 6 April 1987 to 5 June 1987 £15.00

● 8.25 per cent per annum for the four months since 6 June 1987 £27.50

So the total interest would be £36.67 + £21.25 + £39.58 + £15.00 + £27.50 = £140.00.

CHASING UP A REBATE

Time can seem to pass remarkably slowly while you await your rebate. If nothing seems to have happened after a few months, send a reminder. Telephone calls should follow up the reminder (ring your local PAYE Enquiry Office if you deal with a far-distant London Provincial office). If you don't feel that you're getting anywhere, write to the District Inspector. If that brings no response, then consider writing to the Regional Controller (get the address from your tax office). As a last resort, you could write to your MP. If there appears to be a case of maladministration, an MP can refer it to the ombudsman (though only a handful of taxpayers end up having to go to these lengths).

Note that replies to claims may take longer from tax offices where computers are being installed. But it is your money, so be persistent.

MISTAKES

If you discover that you have made a mistake in filling in your Tax Return (or in any other communication with your Tax Inspector), come clean quickly. If there's any suggestion that you have delayed telling the taxman, there could be penalties (p. 84).

But what happens if the mistake is the Tax Inspector's? For example, you might have told your Inspector that you were no longer entitled to an allowance, but your PAYE code wasn't altered to collect the extra tax. If the mistake is found six years later, you could be liable for tax for all six years.

Provided you've taken reasonable care to keep the Tax Inspector informed (by filling in Tax Returns, notifying new sources of income, etc.), some or all of the underpaid tax may not have to be paid. You'll be let off all the tax if your gross income is £8,500 or less (£11,000 if you are over sixty-five, or if you get a state retirement pension or a widow's pension). If your gross income is over these limits, the proportion of the underpaid tax which you must pay is as follows:

GROSS INCOME		% OF TAX YOU MUST PAY
Under 65	*65 and over*	
£8,501–£10,500	£11,001–£13,000	25
£10,501–£13,500	£13,001–£16,000	50
£13,501–£16,000	£16,001–£18,500	75
£16,001–£23,000	£18,501–£25,500	90
£23,001 +	£25,501 +	100

If you were first told about the mistake before 23 July 1985, the limits are lower.

INVESTIGATIONS

Your Tax Inspector gets information about you from many sources: your employer, your bank and building societies, companies and unit trusts you invest in and so on (p. 51). If you try to conceal a source of income, the taxman may get to hear of it and decide to make you the subject of an investigation. And information supplied by other bodies is supplemented by a greatly increased effort by the Inland Revenue itself to detect tax evasion:

● local tax offices search out businesses which don't bother to send in Tax Returns (the so-called black economy)

● regional Special Offices coordinate blitzes on hard-to-monitor trades such as builders and contractors

● the Enquiry Office in London, the equivalent of the police flying squad, tackles the really sophisticated tax dodgers.

And the Inland Revenue is backed by some fairly formidable powers to seize papers and search your home or office, and to demand that others hand over documents of yours. Once you have been rumbled on a tax dodge, your Tax Inspector can, in certain circumstances, have you charged in criminal proceedings. In practice, you are likely to avoid such ignominy but only by paying the tax you owe plus hefty penalties and interest.

This heavy artillery is wheeled out in only a limited number of cases each year. But an investigation can be launched into your tax affairs for much more mundane reasons (because you overlook a source of income, for example). And if you are self-employed, you may be the subject of some searching enquiries about your business accounts, even if you have been entirely honest in declaring your income and claiming expenses.

UNDECLARED INCOME

If your Tax Inspector thinks that you haven't disclosed a source of income, the first shot will normally be to send you a brief letter asking you to confirm that the information given in your latest Tax Return is correct. If you get such a letter, check thoroughly that you have put everything in your Tax Return.

Start with your last Tax Return to make sure that you have left nothing out of the latest one. If you are a married man, ask your wife to check that all her income is declared. Investigations are often launched because a wife opens a savings account without telling her husband (perhaps to provide a surprise gift).

If you cannot immediately identify the omission, a discreet phone call to the Inspector might help. He or she might be prepared to give you some general guidance on what sort of income is under review (though he or she does not have to tell you).

If you can't find what has been missed out, don't despair: the information given to the Tax Inspector may be incorrect – for example, there may be a muddle over names. And if you do identify a mistake, come clean and quickly: your Tax Inspector can impose penalties if you have been unhelpful or obstructive.

Once a mistake of this kind has been found, you will be asked to sign a Certificate of Full Disclosure. This confirms that you have now made a full return of your income for the period in question, and should be signed only if you are certain that this is true. You will then have to negotiate what you must pay with your Inspector – this will be the extra tax plus, usually, penalties (see overleaf).

ACCOUNTS INVESTIGATIONS

Investigations into business accounts are now targeted very carefully on areas which seem most promising. For example, businesses which deal mainly in cash or where records are rudimentary are prime candidates for scrutiny. But every business can expect a full once-over sooner or later.

Tax Inspectors monitor a wide variety of businesses and will usually have a pretty good idea of what is reasonable in the way of income for most trades. For example, they will be well-informed about the sort of tips you might get as a taxi-driver or about the profit margin on common product lines. If your income seems suspiciously low, you could be in line for investigation.

Similarly, your Tax Inspector will pay close attention to expenses which are unusually high in relation to your income. And the amount of expenses which you claim for things like the use of your car which is also available for your private use will also be scrutinized. If you are clearly living in a style which cannot be supported by your declared income, expect some searching questions.

The Inspector's first step will probably be to summon you to a meeting to go through your books and records. There may, of course, be good reason for the discrepancies identified: you might have lost income through refurbishments, for example, or have incurred high start-up costs. It is for you to justify the figures in your accounts, and well-kept books with supporting paperwork will be an essential tool in doing this.

If you use an accountant to produce your accounts, initial queries will be raised with the accountant. But if the Inspector suspects that there is more than meets the eye, a face-to-face interview will be sought. You can, of course, bring your professional adviser with you to this interview. If you don't use an accountant, consider employing one to guide you through the investigation.

Ask the Inspector for copies of the notes taken during the interview. If there are any inaccuracies, notify the Inspector immediately – these notes can be used as evidence in an appeal to the Commissioners.

BACK-TAX AND PENALTIES

Where extra tax is found to be payable, the Tax Inspector can go back up to six complete tax years before the current one and include them on the assessment. If there is neglect (that is, you have failed to reply to letters, complete a Tax Return or send in a document requested by the Tax Inspector), the tax can be collected for up to twelve complete tax years before the current one. And there is no time limit if there is fraud or wilful default.

Your Tax Inspector can also charge interest on the tax from earlier years and impose financial penalties. For example, if you have submitted false Returns, you can be charged a £50 penalty for each Return; in cases of fraud, you can also be required to pay *twice* the unpaid tax (that is, a penalty equal to the amount of unpaid tax). Supplying incorrect information attracts a penalty of £250 (double, if fraudulent).

In practice, your Tax Inspector will mitigate these penalties at least to some degree, according to the circumstances of the case. For example, if you are helpful and cooperative, the penalties might be considerably reduced: if the amount of tax involved is large and you concealed the error for many years, mitigation will be less or none at all.

Once an investigation is over and you have signed a Certificate of Full Disclosure, your Inspector will suggest the amount you should pay to settle the investigation. You can either accept the suggestion or make a lower offer if you think the penalty is excessive. Your offer should be put in writing, and it will be referred with the papers to Inland Revenue Head Office. Your Inspector will make a recommendation on your offer (presumably to accept if it is for the amount suggested), but the decision rests at Head Office.

If you get involved in an investigation, you will find useful information to guide you in two new Inland Revenue leaflets:

- IR 72 *The examination of business accounts*

- IR 73 *How settlements are negotiated.*

12 · SINGLE PEOPLE

As far as the tax system is concerned, the term 'single people' spans far more of the population than the conventional image of bachelor and spinster. The Tax Inspector normally includes children and separated, divorced and widowed people, as well as single adults and single parents living on their own. But this chapter deals mainly with the latter two categories.

The other groups which are treated as single for tax purposes should read the appropriate chapter:

HOW SINGLE PEOPLE ARE TAXED

By and large, the taxation of single people does not differ from that of married people. You can claim the same outgoings, for example, mortgage interest relief. And your income is worked out in the same way. The difference emerges in the allowance which you can claim compared to a married person. You can claim:

● the single person's allowance (and not the higher married man's allowance) or

● age allowance for a single person

● and, if you have a child living with you, the additional personal allowance.

SINGLE PERSON'S ALLOWANCE

The amount of the allowance for 1987/8 is £2,425 and for 1986/7 is £2,335. You get this allowance automatically; you do not have to claim it specially in your Tax Return.

AGE ALLOWANCE

If you are, or become, sixty-five during the tax year, you can claim this special larger allowance instead of the single person's. For a single person, the amount of age allowance for 1987/8 is £2,960 and for 1986/7 is £2,850. For the 1987/8 tax year, there is a higher allowance if you are (or become) eighty during the tax year. For a single person it is £3,070. Both age allowances are bigger if you are married. However, with either of the age allowances, once your income rises above a certain level, you will not be able to claim the full allowance (see p. 124 for more details on age allowance).

ADDITIONAL PERSONAL ALLOWANCE

This allowance gives extra tax relief if you have a child living with you and you cannot claim the married man's allowance, because you are single or divorced, for example. You are normally entitled only to the lower single person's allowance, and the additional personal allowance brings what you can claim up to the amount of the higher married man's allowance (Example, p. 88).

The amount of additional personal allowance for 1987/8 is £1,370 and for 1986/7 is £1,320. You can also claim this allowance if you are married but the wife is totally incapacitated throughout the tax year.

To get the allowance, you must have a child (either your own or someone's else's) living with you for the whole or part of the tax year. To be eligible for the allowance, your own child has to be under sixteen at the start of the tax year. But you can also claim it if your child is over sixteen but in full-time education (for example, school, university or college) or is being trained by an employer for at least two years for a trade, profession or vocation. 'Your child' includes a step-child, adopted child or legitimated child. If you are maintaining another child at your own expense, he or she should be under eighteen at the start of the tax year.

It is possible that two people could claim the allowance for the same child because the child lives with each of them for part of the year (who has custody is not the deciding factor). If this applies to you, you can agree with the other what proportion you can each claim. If you cannot agree, the allowance will be divided up according to the amount of time the child lives with each of you during the tax year.

If you are unmarried but living together and have two children, you may each be able to claim the full allowance (p. 101). But each of you can never claim more than one allowance, even if you have five children living with you.

if you are already claiming housekeeper allowance (p. 113), you are not entitled to additional personal allowance.

EXAMPLE

Sally Jones is a single parent with two children living with her. Her income is £10,000. As well as the single person's allowance she can claim the additional personal allowance. Her tax bill will be:

	£	£
Income		10,000
less Allowances		
single person's	2,425	
additional personal	1,370	
	———	3,795
Taxable income		6,205
Tax at the basic rate (27%) is		£1,675

If Sally had not claimed the extra allowance, her tax bill would have been £2,045.

WHAT TO PUT IN YOUR TAX RETURN

You do not have to put anything to get the single person's allowance. For additional personal allowance, put the child's name and date of birth and fill in the other details asked for.

For 1987/8, with Forms 11 and 11P claim age allowance in the ALLOW-ANCES section of the form by ticking the appropriate box. With Form P1 there is no set place to claim the allowance, but in the PENSIONS section give your date of birth if you or your wife was born before 6 April 1928.

Form 11P

Age allowance To claim this you or your wife must have been born before 6 April 1923.

Additional personal allowance

Child's name
(Surname first)

Child's date of birth

If the child was 16 or over on 6 April 1987 and receiving full time education or training, give the name of the university, college, school or type of training.

Does he or she live with you? Yes ☐ No ☐

Is any other person claiming the allowance for the child? Yes ☐ No ☐

If you are claiming because your wife is unable to look after herself, what is her illness or disability?

Is she likely to be unable to look after herself throughout the year ending 5 April 1988? Yes ☐ No ☐

13 · MARRIED

Weddings are still sentimental, emotional occasions. Most people toast the happy couple with a glass of champagne and a glint in the eye, even if for bride and groom it is a second, or even third, attempt at a happy marriage. And for most newly-weds, the taxman will also be adding a gift of higher tax allowances. But for a few couples, marriage means paying *more* tax, not less. So, if tax affairs dominate your life, hesitate before tying the knot and whip out your calculators, along with all your financial papers.

The reason for this odd state of affairs is that husband and wife are normally treated as one person by the taxman. Where, before marriage, there might have been two Tax Returns to fill in, after marriage there is normally one. It is the husband's responsibility to fill it in, giving details of his wife's income as well as his own. He is legally responsible for paying the tax bill, too, although a Tax Inspector can collect the tax due on her extra income from the wife, if the husband does not pay.

This anachronism in our society is a hangover from the days when, on marriage, all a woman's property automatically belonged to her husband. This is no longer so, but the tax system still treats a wife's income as belonging to her husband. This state of affairs is destined to disappear, as there is currently a Green Paper suggesting changes. But nothing will happen until the 1990s. In the meantime, you will have to do the best you can and seize the opportunities which exist for reducing your tax bill.

THE TAX DIFFERENCE MARRIAGE MAKES

The fundamental change which occurs is that you are now considered as one tax unit by the taxman. After the year of marriage, only the husband will be required to fill in a Tax Return. Marriage also means a change in the allowances you can claim – see next page.

Incomes are added together when you are married, but you may be able to save tax by opting for separate taxation of the wife's earnings

(p. 93). A different choice you can make, separate assessment (p. 98), will not save you any money at all.

Marriage also changes the amount of tax relief you can claim on your home (p. 98) and the amount of tax-free capital gains (p. 99) you are allowed.

ALLOWANCES BEFORE AND AFTER MARRIAGE

The obvious change is that instead of two single person's allowances (£2,425 in 1987/8, £2,335 in 1986/7), after the tax year of marriage you can claim the higher married man's allowance (£3,795 in 1987/8, £3,655 in 1986/7) and the wife's earned income allowance (£2,425 in 1987/8, £2,335 in 1986/7) to set against the wife's earnings, but not investment (or unearned) income.

In the tax year in which you marry, these rules do not apply unless you marry on 6 April. If you marry on any other date, the wife will get the single person's allowance and any other allowances she was getting (for example, additional personal allowance). The husband will be entitled to the married man's allowance. He will be able to claim the full allowance if you were married before 6 May. After that date, you lose one-twelfth of the difference between the single person's and married man's allowances for each complete month (that is, ending on 5 May, 5 June and so on) in which you are unmarried.

DATE OF MARRIAGE	AMOUNT OF ALLOWANCE	
before	*1986/7*	*1987/8*
	£	£
6 May	3,655	3,795
6 June	3,545	3,681
6 July	3,435	3,567
6 August	3,325	3,452
6 September	3,215	3,338
6 October	3,105	3,224
6 November	2,995	3,110
6 December	2,885	2,996
6 January	2,775	2,881
6 February	2,665	2,767
6 March	2,555	2,653
6 April	2,445	2,539

In the year you marry, you are allowed to transfer unused allowances from one to the other. So, if your income is too low to use up all your allowances, don't waste them. The husband can transfer any allowance he is entitled to; the wife can transfer the dependent relative allowance, blind person's allowance or allowance for a son or daughter on whose services she depends. If her loan interest, which qualifies for tax relief, is greater than her income, that can also be transferred to the husband after the marriage.

Throughout your marriage, the wife can set all or part of the married man's allowance against her earnings, as well as the wife's earned income allowance, if the husband has no income at all (or less than the amount of the married man's allowance).

EXAMPLE

Patrick Smith is a student living on a grant. His wife Isobel is working as a secretary. There is a small amount of interest from a National Savings Investment Account, £150 a year. Patrick can transfer the unused part of the married man's allowance to Isobel, that is, for 1987/8 £3,795 less £150, £3,645. Adding this to the wife's earned income allowance of £2,425 gives Isobel allowances of £6,070.

OTHER ALLOWANCES

Other changes are:

● the husband can claim the higher age allowance for a married man (p. 124) if he or his wife are aged sixty-five or more during the tax year

● the husband can claim the dependent relative allowance (p. 122) for any of his or his wife's relatives. The wife can claim the allowance to set against her income, but the maximum amount is £100 a year. Before marriage, or if she chooses to have her earnings taxed separately after marriage (see right), the amount of the allowance is up to £145

● you cannot claim the additional personal allowance (p. 87) after the tax year of marriage, unless the wife is totally incapacitated for the whole of the tax year

● you cannot claim housekeeper allowance (p. 113) after marriage.

INCOME BEFORE AND AFTER MARRIAGE

For many, marriage is a tax blessing, as it means lower tax bills because of higher allowances. In 1987/8, for example, you can claim allowances after marriage of £6,220 (married man's and wife's earned income), but before marriage only £4,850 (two single persons'). You can earn an extra £1,370 free of tax simply because of marriage, which is a tax saving of up to £370. But, for higher earners this tax saving can soon be swallowed up because the two incomes are lumped together and thus could pay tax at a higher rate than you otherwise would do.

Higher-rate tax is payable in the 1987/8 tax year once your income, after deducting outgoings (for example, mortgage interest) and allowances, is more than £17,900. But your income needs to be much higher than this before the beneficial effect of higher tax allowances is cancelled out by the detrimental effect of higher tax rates. For the 1987/8 tax year, the figure is a joint income of over £26,870, which must include wife's earned income of at least £6,545. The exact figure for you will depend on what allowances and outgoings you have.

SEPARATE TAXATION OF THE WIFE'S EARNINGS

If you are a married couple whose joint incomes will be over £26,870 for the 1987/8 tax year, it could be worth your while to ask the taxman if you can have your earnings taxed separately (p. 98 for how to ask your Tax Inspector). This will mean returning to the same tax position before you were married. Well, not quite. You cannot opt to have your unearned or investment income taxed separately after marriage. It will always be included with your husband's income, even if, for example, it was income from the wife's investments which she had before marriage or which she bought with her own money.

The Example below shows what happens to the incomes of one couple, before they were married, after marriage (but without separate taxation) and after choosing separate taxation.

Note that the taxman calls separate taxation of your wife's earnings the 'wife's earnings election'.

EXAMPLE

Before marriage: Jim Davidson earns £25,000. He also has a company car (taxable value £525 in 1987/8) and has investment income of £300. He has outgoings of £1,500 (grossed-up mortgage interest; under the MIRAS scheme he pays £1,095, see p. 223). His girlfriend Joanna has an earned income of £12,000. She makes personal pension payments of £500 and has an investment income of £1,000.

Their individual tax bills for 1987/8 are:

Jim

Earned income		£25,000
Company car		525
Investment income		300
		£25,825
less outgoings	£1,500	
less allowances	2,425	
		3,925
leaves a taxable income of		£21,900

Jim's tax bill is £17,900 at 27%		£4,833
2,500 at 40%		1,000
1,500 at 45%		675
		£6,508

Joanna

Earned income		£12,000
Investment income		1,000
		£13,000
less outgoings	£500	
less allowances	2,425	
		2,925
leaves a taxable income of		£10,075

Joanna's tax bill is £10,075 at 27%	£2,720

Together (before marriage) they pay tax of £6,508 plus £2,720 equals £9,228.

After marriage (for 1987/8, assuming this is not the year they married), Jim and Joanna's taxable income and tax bill would look like this:

Earned income (including car) £37,525
Investment income 1,300

£38,825

less outgoings 2,000
less allowances (including
married man's) 6,220

8,220

leaves a taxable income of £30,605

Their tax bill would be:

£17,900 at 27%	£4,833
2,500 at 40%	1,000
5,000 at 45%	2,250
5,205 at 50%	2,602.50

£10,685.50

Their tax bill after marriage would be £10,685.50 − 9,228 = £1,457.50 more than before marriage, despite the higher allowances.

If Jim and Joanna choose separate taxation of earnings:

Jim
Earned income £25,525
Investment income (including
Joanna's' 1,300

26,825

less outgoings £1,500
less single person's
allowance 2,425

3,925

leaves a taxable income of £22,900

The tax bill is:

£17,900 at 27%		£4,833
2,500 at 40%		1,000
2,500 at 45%		1,125
		£6,958

Joanna

Earned income		£12,000
less outgoings	£500	
less wife's earned income allowance	2,425	
		2,925
leaves a taxable income of		£9,075

The tax bill is:

£9,075 at 27% = £2,450.25

With separate taxation of earnings, the tax bill comes to:

£6,958 + £2,450.25 = £9,408.25

This is a tax saving of:

£10,685.50 − £9,408.25 = £1,277.25

However, marriage still costs Jim and Joanna £180.25 for the year, compared to when they were unmarried.

WHAT SHOULD YOU DO?

You need to work out for yourself if you would save tax by opting for separate taxation of the wife's earnings. Use the Example above to see how to do this.

From the husband's earnings (less deductions to employer's pension scheme):

Deduct: ● allowable personal pension payments

● gross amount of outgoings which he pays, such as

qualifying loan interest, enforceable maintenance payments

- allowances he can claim

Add: • taxable value of fringe benefits

- expenses he has to pay tax on

- before-tax investment income for both husband and wife

From the wife's earnings (less deductions to employer's pension scheme):

Deduct: • allowable personal pension payments

- gross amount of outgoings which she pays, such as qualifying loan interest, enforceable maintenance payments

- allowances she can claim. Note that the dependent relative allowance is £145 for the wife, if taxed separately

Add: • taxable value of fringe benefits

- expenses she has to pay tax on

Now work out the tax bills with and without separate taxation to see if you will save anything.

The Table below gives a rough guide to when you should make the choice for the 1986/7 and 1987/8 tax years.

1986/7

Joint income at least £	Lower paid earns at least £
26,521	6,986
30,000	6,048
35,000	5,478
40,000	5,309
45,000	5,127
48,425	4,890

1987/8

Joint income at least £	Lower paid earns at least £
26,870	6,545
30,000	5,851
35,000	5,404
40,000	5,299
45,000	5,117
48,541	4,916

MAKING THE CHOICE

If you want to choose separate taxation of wife's earnings, ask your tax office for Form 14. It must be signed by both of you. You must make this choice not later than 5 April following the tax year in which you want to be taxed separately. If you want to change your mind, you must sign Form 14-1, and send it to the husband's tax office within twelve months after the end of the tax year in which you want to be taxed jointly. Choosing to be taxed separately does not mean you have to fill in two Tax Returns; you will get just the one which the husband is responsible for filling in.

SEPARATE ASSESSMENT

This is not the same thing at all as separate taxation. You will not save any money by choosing separate assessment. It simply divides up the tax bill between the two of you.

However, if you opt for this, you each have to fill in your own Tax Return, which means you may be able to keep your money matters a secret from your better half. And the husband is no longer legally responsible for paying the wife's bit of the tax bill.

To choose separate assessment ask for Form 11S. It can be signed by either of you and you must return it between 6 January and 5 July in the tax year for which you want to be separately assessed. If you want separate assessment for the 1988/9 tax year, choose it before 6 July 1988, but on or after 6 January.

HOME AND MARRIAGE

As a married couple you are entitled to claim tax relief for interest paid on a loan of £30,000 or less to buy or improve your main or only home.

Before you were married you were each entitled to relief for that amount.

If you each have a mortgage to buy a home before you marry, you can carry on getting the tax relief on both of them for up to twelve months. And if you are deciding to buy another home for you both to live in, you can also claim tax relief on a mortgage of £30,000 or less to do so. In all, you could be claiming tax relief on three homes when you first marry.

CAPITAL GAINS

The two main differences which marriage makes are:

● each of you is entitled to a tax-free slice of gains if you are single (£6,300 in 1986/7, £6,600 in 1987/8). As a married couple you are entitled to one slice between the two of you

● there will normally be no capital gains tax to pay if one of you gives an asset to the other.

Although the normal CGT treatment for husband and wife is to add up your gains and losses to work out the bill, you can choose to keep the gains and losses of each of you separate. This is worth choosing only if one of you has made a loss and the other a gain, but within the tax-free limit. Write to your Tax Inspector by 5 July after the end of the tax year you want to do this for.

WHAT TO PUT IN YOUR TAX RETURN

The last section of the Tax Return is where you can claim allowances to set against your income. You do not need to claim wife's earned income relief as you will get this automatically. But you have to claim married man's allowance if you wish to do so.

To claim the allowance, give your wife's name(s) and, if you were married in the last tax year, the date of marriage and your wife's maiden name. You can carry on claiming the married man's allowance if you are separated from your wife, but wholly maintaining her with voluntary contributions.

Form 11P

Married man's allowance	To claim this you must be living with or wholly maintaining your wife
Wife's first name(s)	

| If you were married after 5 April 1986, give – Date of marriage | | Wife's former surname | |

For how to choose separate taxation of the wife's earnings, see p. 98 and to choose separate assessment, see p. 98.

14 · LIVING TOGETHER

Would you be better off living together rather than marrying? There are a number of ways in which the tax treatment of a couple who choose to live together without marrying differs from the taxation of a married couple. The differences are:

- allowances you can claim

- the amount of tax relief on your home

- how investment (or unearned) income is taxed

- the amount of tax-free capital gains

- the treatment of gifts between the two of you (inheritance tax).

ALLOWANCES

Marriage gives you the married man's allowance to set against the husband's income and the wife's earned income allowance to set against the wife's earnings. If the husband does not earn but the wife does, the wife can also claim the married man's allowance. But the reverse is not true; the husband cannot also claim the wife's earned income allowance if the wife does not earn.

If you are not married, each of you is entitled to a single person's allowance to set against your own income. In the case of the woman, it does not matter whether the income is earned or not, unlike for a wife. Additionally, if you have a child either of you can claim the additional personal allowance (p. 87) and if you have two children you can both claim it. The allowance can be claimed even if you are not the child's parent, as long as you are maintaining it.

For 1987/8, the difference can be summarized (assuming the wife's earnings are not taxed separately, see p. 93):

ALLOWANCES YOU CAN CLAIM FOR 1987/8
(SEE CODE BELOW)

	MARRIED		NOT MARRIED	
no children		£		£
both have income (wife's must be earned)	A,B	6,220	2C	4,850
man only has income	A	3,795	C	2,425
woman only has income (if wife's not earned, A £3,795)	A,B	6,220	C	2,425
one child				
both have income (wife's must be earned)	A,B	6,220	2C,D	6,220
man only has income	A	3,795	C,D	3,795
woman only has income (if wife's not earned, A £3,795)	A,B	6,220	C,D	3,795
two children				
both have income (wife's must be earned)	A,B	6,220	2C,2D	7,590
man only has income	A	3,795	C,D	3,795
woman only has income (if wife's not earned, A £3,795)	A,B	6,220	C,D	3,795

CODE: A Married man's allowance
  B Wife's earned income allowance
  C Single person's allowance
  D Additional personal allowance

HOW ONE CAN GIVE THE OTHER AN INCOME

As you can see from the Table above, if you live together the allowances are greater if you both have income and two children. If only one of you has an income, you can increase the amount of allowances you can claim by handing over part of the income from one to the other. There are two ways this can be done:

● *affiliation order*: If you have a child, the woman can ask the courts to make an affiliation order against the man as the father of the child. The maintenance payments will normally be treated as the woman's income and you can set the normal allowances against it. The man will be able to claim tax relief for the maintenance payments

● *covenant*: One of you can covenant an income to the other and claim basic-rate tax relief (for more about covenants, see p. 119). Make the covenant for the difference between the possible allowances and outgoings which could be claimed *less* the amount of the before-tax income. It may be sensible to make a covenant only if you know the other person will have no income for three years, as revoking a covenant can be done but is time-consuming.

EXAMPLE

Harry White lives with Susan Barnes and they have two children, James and Charlotte. The only income is Harry's £15,000 a year, and mortgage interest is £1,500. He claims the single person's allowance and additional personal allowance, totalling £3,795. If only Susan had some income, she could claim the same. Harry covenants an amount equal to the unused allowances to Susan.

Without the covenant		
Harry's income		£15,000
less *outgoings*:		
mortgage interest		1,500
		13,500
less *allowances*:		
single person's	£2,425	
additional personal	1,370	3,795
Taxable income		£9,705
Tax at basic rate (27%)		£2,620
With the covenant		
Harry's income		£15,000
less *outgoings*:		
mortgage interest	£1,500	
gross covenant payments	3,795	5,295
		9,705

less *allowances*:		
single person's	£2,425	
additional personal	1,370	3,795
Taxable income		£5,910
Tax at basic rate (27%)		£1,595
Susan's *income*		£3,795
less *allowances*:		
single person's	£2,425	
additional personal	1,370	3,795
Taxable income		nil

The amount of tax Harry and Susan pay together has fallen from £2,620 to £1,595, simply by using a covenant. Susan could also have made an affiliation order against Harry, as he is the father, and asked for maintenance of the same amount, giving the same tax result.

YOUR HOME

A married couple can claim tax relief on interest paid on loans of £30,000 or less to buy your home. An unmarried couple buying a home together can each claim tax relief on loans of £30,000 or less (£60,000 or less in total). This applies as long as you are both paying the interest.

INVESTMENT (OR UNEARNED) INCOME

Marriage creates a difference in the treatment of a woman's investment income. A married woman cannot set the wife's earned income allowance against investment income, but an unmarried woman can set the single person's allowance against it.

A further difference occurs when it comes to what rate of tax you may have to pay. An unmarried couple will pay basic-rate tax for the 1987/8 tax year on the first £17,900 of income received by each of you. This applies whether the income is earned or not.

A married couple's incomes are added together and you pay basic-rate tax on the first £17,900 of joint income. You can choose to have the wife's earned income taxed separately (p. 93), increasing the amount of income taxed at basic, rather than higher, rate. But, you cannot choose to have the wife's investment income taxed separately.

CAPITAL GAINS

Between them, a husband and wife can make net capital gains of up to £6,600 free of tax in the 1987/8 tax year (£6,300 in 1986/7). But an unmarried woman and man can each have the same amount free of tax.

There are, however, a couple of disadvantages to the unmarried state. Giving something to your partner may mean a CGT bill, although you can make a 'holdover' election (p. 287); this would not be necessary if you were married. And you cannot set off any losses one of you has made against any gains of the other.

INHERITANCE TAX

The rules of inheritance tax will apply to any gifts or transfers between an unmarried couple, see p. 291. So if you give something to someone who is not your spouse and die within seven years, there may be some tax to pay.

WHAT TO PUT IN YOUR TAX RETURN

You will fill in your Tax Return as a single person. You do not need to claim single person's allowance as you get it automatically. For how to claim additional personal allowance, see p. 88.

15 · SEPARATED AND DIVORCED

Separation and divorce can be a messy business, both financially and emotionally. Sadly, it is also a time when you should be clear-thinking and well-organized. Your split may be amicable and you may both cooperate to try to maximize the income of the two new households. But that may not be the case. Instead, one or both of you may be determined to come off better financially than the other. In this case, you need your wits about you to make sure no mistakes are made when it comes to maintenance agreements and other arrangements.

When you separate, as far as the taxman is concerned you become two single people again (with one exception, see p. 111). From now on, you must each complete your own Tax Return and after separation your incomes are no longer added together. In the tax year you separate, a married woman will need to apportion her income between the marriage and the period when she is treated as a single person. Earnings, dividends and interest are split according to when she receives them. Other income, such as profits from self-employment or rent, is apportioned on a time basis.

The main changes caused by divorce or separation are:

- allowances (see below)

- the need for one of you to pay maintenance to the other (see right)

- what happens to your home (p. 110)

- capital gains tax (p. 111)

- inheritance tax (p. 111).

WHO GETS WHICH ALLOWANCES

The husband is entitled to the married man's allowance for the whole of the tax year in which you separate. But he will not get it after this (reverting instead to the single person's allowance), unless he is wholly maintaining the wife by voluntary payments while separated. After divorce, he will not be allowed the married man's allowance. The wife can claim the full single person's allowance for the year of separation, as well as a wife's earned income allowance if she is earning before separation.

If there are children, one or both of you will probably be able to claim the additional personal allowance (p. 87). The husband will not if he is still getting the married man's allowance. The wife will be able to claim a full additional personal allowance in the year of separation.

PAYING MAINTENANCE

Much the same rules apply whether husband or wife pays the maintenance and, in most cases, whether you are separated or divorced.

TYPES OF MAINTENANCE

Maintenance can be:
Either
● voluntary (you cannot be forced to pay it). You do not get any tax relief on this, and there is no tax to pay by your spouse or former spouse
Or
● enforceable (you can be made to pay up). They can be enforceable because you have some formal agreement with your spouse or because there is a Court Order or separation deed which specifies the maintenance payments.

HOW ENFORCEABLE MAINTENANCE IS TAXED

You get tax relief on any enforceable maintenance you pay at your highest rate of tax. You also act as tax collector for the taxman (unless the payments are small, see p. 108). What happens is that you deduct basic-rate tax (27 per cent for 1987/8; 29 per cent for 1986/7) from what you pay and hand over the difference as maintenance. You get your tax relief on the payments by keeping what you have deducted, as long as your tax bill is at least this amount. If you are a higher-rate taxpayer, extra relief is paid by a rebate or through the PAYE system. On the other hand, if you do not pay as much tax as you have deducted, you will have to pay the surplus to the Inland Revenue.

If you are receiving the enforceable maintenance payments (unless they are small, see overleaf), you receive them with basic-rate tax already deducted. So, depending upon your total income and allowance, you may have to pay higher-rate tax, or if your income is small you may get a tax refund.

You should have got Form R185 (see below) from your spouse or former spouse who is making the payments. To get any tax refund due, ask your Tax Inspector to let you have Form R40. Complete this, and send it together with Form R185.

Form R185

Certificate of deduction of income tax *for payments under Deed of Covenant please use form R185(AP)*

Only use this form if income has been deducted from the payment

I certify that on paying to _____

of _____

the amount shown in column 3 below I deducted the income tax shown in column 4, and that this tax has been or will be paid by me either directly or by deduction from other income when received by me.

Nature of the payment e.g. bond, mortgage or loan interest, annuity, maintenance, rent, payments from a discretionary trust etc. 1	Profits or other source out of which paid 2	Gross payment 3	Income tax deducted by me 4	Net payment see Note b. 5	Period for which payment was due see Note c. 6	From to
		£	£	£	Date on which payment due see Note c. 7	Day Month Year

	– Payer's name and address see Note a.	Date payment actually made 8
Enter here in CAPITAL letters please	Postcode	

	– If you are employed, your
	   employer's name and address
	       or
	   If a company or if you are in
	   business the business address	

	Postcode	*Please do not write in the spaces below*

	– District and reference to which
	   Tax Returns are made
	   if known
		District stamp

Signature _____ Date _____
This form should be signed by the person deducting the tax and responsible for accounting for it to the Revenue. If that person is deducting tax on behalf of his employer, e.g. as secretary, cashier, etc., this should be stated.

Notes

"Duty assessed" stamp

a. Where the payment is made by a trustee give the full name of the trust together with the Tax District and reference.

b. In the case of a payment made by trustees of a discretionary trust in exercise of their discretion, enter in column 5 the actual amount paid, in column 4 the amount of tax treated as deducted at a rate equal to the basic rate and the higher additional rate for the year of payment, and in column 3 the corresponding gross amount i.e. the total of the amounts in columns 4 and 5.

c. Do not complete where payment is made upon the exercise of a trustee's discretion.

The person receiving the payments should keep this form.
It will be needed if a claim for repayment of income tax is made.

R185   809555 Dd 8961978 900m 10/85 StS

IF THE MAINTENANCE IS SMALL

Maintenance counts as *small* for tax purposes if the payments are made under a Court Order and meet the following rules:
Either
● it is paid directly to the individual (your husband, or wife, or children, if aged under twenty-one, for their own benefit, maintenance or

education) and, from 6 April 1986, if it is not more than £48 a week or £208 a month

Or

● it is paid for the benefit, maintenance or education of a child under twenty-one years of age, but not directly to the child and, from 6 April 1986, it is not more than £25 a week or £108 a month.

If you make small maintenance payments, you make them without deducting any tax, that is, you hand over the payment in full. You will receive your tax relief through your PAYE code by letting your Tax Inspector know or at the end of the tax year by filling in your Tax Return.

If you are receiving a small maintenance payment and are a taxpayer, you will have to pay tax on it.

WHO GETS THE MAINTENANCE?

Making payments to a child can be very tax-efficient, because the child may have unused personal allowances to set against the income (p. 118). The payments must be

under a Court Order and paid direct to the child,

otherwise they will not be regarded as the child's income. Making the payment to the spouse *for* the child will mean it is treated as the parent's income.

EXAMPLE 1: MAINTENANCE PAID TO SPOUSE

James and Jenny Rawlinson separate. They have two children, who will live with Jenny. After separation, Jenny will be entitled to a single person's allowance and additional personal allowance (£2,425 + 1,370 for 1987/8 = £3,795). James agrees to pay maintenance of £9,000 (he would actually hand over £9,000 less 27 per cent of £9,000 = £6,570). If the maintenance is payable to Jenny (who has no other income), the amount of tax she should pay is:

$$27\% \text{ of } (9,000 - 3,795) = £1,405$$

and her after-tax income should be:

$$£9,000 - 1,405 = £7,595.$$

Jenny will claim back the difference between what James actually hands over (£6,570) and what she should be getting (£7,595) by asking the taxman for a rebate of £7,595 − £6,570 = £1,025.

James keeps the tax deducted of 27 per cent of £9,000 = £2,430 to give him his basic-rate tax relief. Any higher-rate tax relief due will come through the PAYE system once his code is changed.

EXAMPLE 2: MAINTENANCE PAID DIRECT TO CHILDREN

In the above example, if James paid some of the maintenance direct to each of his children (up to an amount equal to the single person's allowance), the after-tax income for his ex-family will be increased without costing James a penny extra himself.

James makes enforceable maintenance payments direct to each of his children under a Court Order of £2,425; to Jenny, he pays £9,000 − £2,425 = £4,150.

He actually hands over to each child £2,425 less 27 per cent of £2,425 = £1,770 and keeps the basic-rate tax deducted, £655. But each child can set the single person's allowance against the maintenance and thus should pay no tax. They claim back the tax deducted (£655 for each) from the taxman, giving each an income of £2,425.

To Jenny, James actually hands over £4,150 less 27 per cent of £4,150 = £3,029.50. But Jenny has allowances of £3,795 and her after-tax income should be:

$$£4,150 \text{ less } 27 \text{ per cent of } (£4,150 − £3,795) = £4,054$$

so she claims back the difference (£4,054 − £3,029.50) from the taxman.

Jenny's and the children's after-tax income is:

$$£2,425 + £2,425 + £4,054 = £8,904$$

Without costing James anything, their after-tax income has increased by:

$$£8,904 − £7,595 = £1,309$$

YOUR HOME

Once you are separated or divorced, you are likely to need two homes instead of one. You can each get tax relief on loans of up to £30,000 to buy a home. But if only one of you is paying the interest for both homes, the limit stays at £30,000. So the best financial arrangement is for each of you to pay the mortgage for the home you are living in.

If one of you cannot afford this, the other could make bigger enforceable maintenance payments. This would mean a bigger income for the one receiving the payments, but no more tax to pay because of the tax relief on the mortgage. The one who pays the maintenance will be able to claim more tax relief on the maintenance payments.

CAPITAL GAINS TAX

You can carry on making gifts to your spouse free of CGT in the year of separation. After this, CGT may be payable, unless you agree to sign a holdover election. To make sure that you do not sign an election to your disadvantage, get professional advice.

For the tax year of separation, the husband will have to include the wife's gains up to the date of separation in his tax-free limit (£6,600 in 1987/8; £6,300 in 1986/7). But the wife can have the full tax-free limit for any gains she makes in the rest of the tax year after separation.

If one of you moves out of the family home and gives it or sells it to the other, any gain you make will be free of CGT as long as the transfer happens within two years of the date of separation. Even if the transfer occurs after that, there may still be no CGT to pay as long as your ex-spouse is still living in the family home and you have not claimed that any other property is your main home.

INHERITANCE TAX

If you are separated, any gifts the one makes to the other are free of inheritance tax. But once you are divorced, IHT may be payable, unless the gift is for the maintenance of an ex-spouse and any children.

WHAT TO PUT IN YOUR TAX RETURN

If you receive maintenance or alimony, you will find the slot to put this information in the 1987/8 Form 11 and Form 11P at the end of the INCOME section under the heading *All other profits and income*, and in Form P1, *Maintenance, alimony or aliment received*, in the INVESTMENTS, SAVINGS, ETC. section.

Form 11P

All other profits or income enter gross amounts		
	Self	Wife
Maintenance, alimony, or aliment received	£	£
Any other income not entered elsewhere eg: accrued income charges and taxable gains on life assurance policies	£	£

What you have to put is the before-tax amount of the enforceable maintenance payments you get during the tax year. Unless it is a small maintenance payment (p. 108), you will have received your payment after the deduction of basic-rate tax, so you will have to gross up what you receive before you enter the amount in the Tax Return – see p. 318 for how to do this.

If your former wife or husband pays you something on a voluntary basis, you do not need to pay tax on it and so you do not need to enter it in your Tax Return.

If the boot is on the other foot and you are paying the maintenance, you are entitled to tax relief at your highest rate of tax, but not on voluntary contributions. You should enter in the Tax Return the before-tax enforceable amount you pay in the tax year, plus the name and address of the person to whom you are paying it. Put this in the OUT-GOINGS section of the Return, under *Other outgoings* in Form 11 and Form 11P and *Maintenance, alimony or aliment paid* in Form P1.

Form 11P

Other outgoings	enter gross amounts before deduction of tax	Self	Wife
Covenants, bonds of annuity, settlements, covenanted payments to charities, accrued income purchased etc.			
Details		£	£
Alimony, aliment or maintenance paid	Details	£	£
UK property rents or yearly interest paid to persons abroad	Details	£	£

If you have a child or children living with you and are either separated or divorced, you may be able to claim an additional personal allowance (p. 87). Claim for this in the ALLOWANCES section of the Return.

16 · WIDOWED

Sorting out your finances may seem like the last thing you want to do when you are first widowed. But knowing what your tax position will be and how much income you are going to have is very important. So do not neglect to find out this essential information.

As far as the taxman is concerned, your marriage is ended once you are widowed, whether man or woman. But there is a special allowance which can be claimed by a widow to ease the financial burden.

WIDOWS

Until your husband died, you would be entitled to the wife's earned income allowance (up to £2,425 in 1987/8; £2,335 in 1986/7) and the married man's allowance (£3,795 in 1987/8; £3,655 in 1986/7) to set against your joint income. After the death of your husband, you can claim the full single person's allowance for the remainder of the tax year plus the widow's bereavement allowance (£1,370 for 1987/8, £1,320 for 1986/7) which you can set against your own income, either earnings or investment income.

What this all means is that for the tax year in which you are widowed, it is possible to have the full married man's allowance, the full wife's earned income allowance, the full single person's allowance and the full widow's bereavement allowance. If you tell your Tax Inspector you have been widowed you may get a large tax rebate.

In the following tax year, you can also claim the widow's bereavement allowance as well as the single person's allowance, unless you have remarried before the start of the tax year. In subsequent years, you claim the single person's allowance unless you remarry.

If you have children living with you, you can claim the full additional personal allowance (p. 87) in the tax year your husband dies and for subsequent years. If you have a living-in housekeeper, you may be able to claim the housekeeper allowance (£100 in 1986/7 and 1987/8), but you cannot claim this as well as the higher additional personal allowance. If the housekeeper is a relative, you are not entitled to housekeeper allowance if someone else is already claiming an allowance for the relative (for example, married man's).

EXAMPLE

Rosalind Smith's husband, Simon, dies in September 1987 leaving two young children, aged seven and nine. He had earned £11,000 since 6 April. Rosalind has a part-time job and had earned £1,300. She also received investment income of £3,500.

After his death and before the start of the next tax year, Rosalind earns another £1,500 and receives investment income of £4,000. She also receives income of £2,000 from Simon's pension scheme.

Tax relief on their mortgage interest is given through the MIRAS scheme.

Before death		
Simon's earnings		£11,000
Rosalind's investment income		3,500
Rosalind's earnings		1,300
Total income		15,800
less allowances:		
married man's	3,795	
wife's earned income (not the full £2,425)	1,300	5,095
Taxable income		10,705
Tax at 27%		£2,890

But by the time Simon dies, they will not have received the full allowances they are entitled to for this period through the PAYE system and there will be a tax rebate due for Rosalind.

After death		
Rosalind's earnings from job		£1,500
investment income		4,000
pension		2,000
Total income		£7,500
less allowances:		
single person's	£2,425	
additional personal	1,370	
widow's bereavement	1,370	5,165
Taxable income		£2,335
Tax at 27%		£630

WIDOWERS

Before your wife's death, you would claim the married man's allowance and the wife's earned income allowance if your wife had earnings. After your wife's death, for the rest of the tax year you carry on claiming the married man's allowance, but you cannot claim housekeeper or additional personal allowance (unless you were already entitled to it because of your wife's incapacity).

In subsequent tax years, until you remarry, you claim single person's allowance. If you are entitled to it because you are responsible for bringing up children, you can claim the additional personal allowance (p. 87). If you have a living-in housekeeper, you may be able to claim housekeeper allowance (£100 in 1986/7 and 1987/8), but you cannot claim this as well as the higher additional personal allowance. If the housekeeper is a relative, see WIDOWS on p. 114.

WHAT TO PUT IN YOUR TAX RETURN

You do not claim the widow's bereavement allowance on your Tax Return. Instead, when you are widowed you should write to your Tax Inspector asking for the allowance. You should get it automatically in the next tax year if you remain entitled to it.

There is nowhere to claim housekeeper allowance on Form 11P or

Form 11, so put a tick in the box at the end of the ALLOWANCES section and you will be sent another form. Fill in the details asked for on this additional form. Form P1 has a space for you to put the details in ALLOWANCES.

Form 11P

To claim any of the following allowances, tick the box that applies and I will send you the appropriate claim form.

☐ Son or daughter whose services you depend on	☐ Housekeeper allowance	☐ Friendly Society and Trade Union Death and Superannuation benefits

17 · CHILDREN, STUDENTS AND DEPENDANTS

The idea that your newborn infant could be a taxpayer might strike you as laughable. Nevertheless, a child, no matter how young, is treated as a single person. Your child is entitled to personal allowances and may have to fill in a Tax Return.

As far as the taxman is concerned, your offspring is a child until marriage or the eighteenth birthday intervenes, whichever is the earlier.

This chapter looks at how children's income is taxed (see below), what allowances can be claimed (p. 118) and what happens to any capital gains (p. 118). The taxation of a student's income is described on p. 118. Using covenants to increase income is described on p. 119. Finally, what allowances can you claim for a dependent relative? Find out on p. 122.

A CHILD'S INCOME

INCOME FROM A JOB

Income which your child earns from a job, for example, as a paper-boy or -girl, is treated as earned income and could be taxable. But as the single person's allowance can be set against it (see overleaf) your child will probably not have to pay any tax on it.

If your child receives a grant or scholarship, it will not be income. However, if your employer gives your child a scholarship as one of your fringe benefits, you can be taxed on it (p. 154).

INCOME FROM INVESTMENTS

Most children will be non-taxpayers, because their income is unlikely to be large and they can claim the single person's allowance to set against it. The best investment for a child to make may not be in a bank or building society account. These pay interest with tax deducted which cannot be claimed back. Instead, from a tax point of view, your child should consider National Savings Investments, unit trusts or shares.

For the income to be your child's, the money to make the investment should be, for example, a gift from a relative or earnings from a job.

But an investment from money you give your child will produce income considered to be yours, apart from the first £5 each year. Your child should invest your gifts in investments which are treated as tax-free, such as National Savings Certificates.

If a relative or godparent wishes to give your child money, paying it under a deed of covenant can be a tax-efficient way of doing it. The person giving the money deducts basic-rate tax from the payment; you can claim it back for your child. So, for example, your child can receive £100, which costs the giver only £73 in 1987/8. But, if you make a deed of covenant payable to your child aged seventeen or less, you will pay tax on it (and at higher rates, if you are a higher-rate taxpayer). How to make a covenant is explained on p. 121.

ALLOWANCES FOR CHILDREN

Your child can claim the single person's allowance (£2,425 in 1987/8; £2,335 in 1986/7) to set against earnings or income from investments. The allowance can also be set against maintenance payments paid direct to a child under a Court Order (p. 109).

If you are divorced, separated, widowed or unmarried you can claim the additional personal allowance for a child who lives with you and is maintained by you. You may also be able to claim if you are a married couple and the wife is totally incapacitated during the whole of the tax year. Additional personal allowance is described in more detail on p. 87.

CAPITAL GAINS

You can give an asset to your child (as long as under eighteen and unmarried) and any gain on the asset will be your child's, not yours. However, if your child (while under eighteen and unmarried) sells the asset and invests it to produce an income, the income will be yours.

Note that your gift may be considered a disposal by you and capital gains tax might be payable.

STUDENTS

A STUDENT'S INCOME

A student's income is taxable and includes:

- earnings from a holiday job. If it is the student's only income and will not be more than the single person's allowance, it can be paid without tax deducted. Ask for Form P38S from the tax office

● what is earned while at work, if the student is sponsored

● earnings from part-time jobs

● income from investments

● income received under a deed of covenant (see below), but not if paid by a parent to a student aged seventeen or less and unmarried. In this case, it counts as the parent's income.

However, a student may also receive the following and these are normally not part of a student's taxable income:

● grants from a local education authority

● what you give your student child if not paid under a deed of covenant

● if the student is sponsored, what is received from the sponsor while at college. To qualify as tax-free, the course must last an academic year and involve full-time attendance of at least twenty weeks. The amount of the payment should be £5,000 or less or the amount which would be received as a grant whichever is higher

● post-graduate grants from a research council

● other awards and scholarships may be tax-free.

A STUDENT'S ALLOWANCES

A student can claim the usual personal allowances to set against taxable income, that is, single person's, married man's, wife's earned income or additional personal.

COVENANTS

If you give money to someone whose income is too low to pay tax, you can get tax relief on the payments if you make them under a deed of covenant. But you can't get tax relief on covenant payments to your husband or wife, or your own children unless they are married or aged eighteen and over.

So you can use a covenant to get tax relief on gifts to an ageing relative with too little income to pay tax. You can also get tax relief on covenant payments to young children provided they are not your own (grandchildren or godchildren, for example).

And you can take advantage of covenants if you have children aged eighteen and over in full-time education. They are likely to have too little income to pay tax, and you can get tax relief on covenant payments to them. Covenant payments from a student's parents will not affect the amount of grant with most first-degree courses (though they may affect the amount of supplementary benefit the student can claim in the summer holidays).

Students can claim supplementary benefit in the summer holidays only. If the parent hands over net amounts under covenant which do not exceed the parental contribution, the covenant payments will not be counted as part of the student's resources during the summer holidays.

If the parent hands over net covenant payments greater than the parental contribution, the excess is divided by fifty-two and the result added to the student's weekly resources. Up to £4 of this excess may be disregarded, however.

WHAT IS A COVENANT?

A deed of covenant is a legally binding agreement to make a series of payments. You can get tax relief at the basic rate only on covenant payments, as long as neither you nor your spouse nor any unmarried child of yours under eighteen benefits.

The covenant must be worded so that the payments have to continue for more than six years. But you can still get the tax relief if the payments are set to continue for seven years or until the child stops full-time education; this form of wording is used in covenants for students where payments are likely to be required for three or four years only.

Note that there are different rules for covenants to charity (p. 209).

HOW IT WORKS

The deed of covenant will normally be worded so that you agree to give a fixed *gross* amount each year (all in one go or in set instalments). When you make each payment under the covenant, you deduct tax at the basic rate from the gross amount and hand over the *net* amount. So if you agree to hand over a gross amount of £100 to your student child, for example, and the basic rate of tax is 27 per cent, you deduct £27 from the £100, and hand over the net amount of £73 (that is, £100 − £27).

You can keep the tax you deduct from the gross amount provided you pay at least that much basic-rate tax on your income. And provided your child's income (including the gross amount of the covenant payments) is too low to pay tax, your child can reclaim the £27 you have deducted. So your child ends up with the gross amount of your gift of £100, at a cost to you of just £73.

If the child pays some tax, but less than the amount you have deducted, only the difference can be claimed back. In deciding whether the person receiving the covenant payments pays tax or not, you must include the gross amount of the covenant payments (and the income of their spouse if married).

DRAWING UP A COVENANT

A deed of covenant is a legally binding document and should be drawn up with proper legal advice. But for covenants to students, you can use the pre-printed Form IR47 drawn up by the Inland Revenue. Ask your tax office for the student covenant kit which includes the deed and other forms you will need to claim the tax relief. Simply fill in the gaps on the pre-printed form with details about yourself, the child, the amount you want to give and the dates you want to give it on.

A covenant must contain the words 'signed, sealed and delivered' to be valid in England and Wales. It must be signed and dated before the first payment is due; you cannot backdate the covenant to cover payments already made. And the signing must be done in the presence of a witness who must also sign the deed (the witness should not be a relation). The deed should technically be sealed by sticking on a disc of paper but the Inland Revenue has said that it won't insist on this. You 'deliver' the deed once you have completed these steps by giving it to the child (keeping a photocopy for reference).

If you are drawing up a covenant in Scotland, you do not need to seal or deliver the deed, nor is a witness required. But you must write the words 'Adopted as holograph' in your own handwriting above your signature, and at the bottom of previous pages if the deed covers more than one sheet.

The child should send the completed covenant to the tax office, where it will be registered. You and the child may be asked to complete Form R110 or R111: this says there is no agreement to end the covenant early.

MAKING THE PAYMENTS

It is important to fulfil the promises in the deed of covenant to the letter, handing over the net amount on the stated date. When you make each payment, you should also hand over a completed Form R185(AP): you can get a supply of these from your tax office.

Form R185(AP) sets out the gross payment, the tax deducted and the net payment. Once you have made all the payments due under the covenant in the tax year, the child should send these to his or her tax office with Tax Claim Form R40(S).

Student children will find all the necessary forms in the Inland Revenue covenant kit. If you make payments to a student child in instalments each term, it may be possible to reclaim the tax deducted after each payment; check with the student's tax office.

EXAMPLE

Sally Bing is expected to make a parental contribution of £1,260 a year towards the student grant her son Eric gets at university. She uses the Inland Revenue's pre-printed covenant form to make the payments in three equal instalments of £420 at the start of each term.

When each payment is due, Sally deducts tax at the basic rate (27 per cent for 1987/8) from the £420. Twenty-seven per cent of £420 is £113.40, so Sally hands over £420 − £113.40 = £306.60 to Eric.

Apart from the £1,260 of gross covenant payments each year, Eric's only other taxable income is £26 of building society interest and £360 he earned in the summer holidays. So Eric's income for the tax year is £1,260 + £26 + £360 = £1,646. This is well below the single person's allowance for 1987/8 of £2,425, so Eric can reclaim all the tax Sally has deducted from the covenant payments.

At a cost to Sally of £919.80, therefore, Eric has received £1,260.

OTHER DEPENDANTS

You may be able to claim an allowance for a dependent relative called dependent relative allowance. You are entitled to it if you help to support or look after a relative, either the husband's or the wife's. The relative would have to be old (sixty-five during tax year), disabled or permanently ill *or* you can claim it for your mother or mother-in-law if widowed, separated or divorced.

The amount of the allowance is £100 for both the 1986/7 and 1987/8 tax years. However, if you are a single woman (including separated, divorced or widowed and in the year of marriage) or a married woman who has your earnings taxed separately, the amount of the allowance is £145. If someone else also helps to support the relative, the amount of the allowance will be split between the two of you in the proportion you each contribute.

You can claim the allowance:

● if the relative's income is small, that is, income less outgoings comes to no more than the single person's basic retirement pension, and

● either the relative lives with you or you contribute at least £75 to their upkeep. If it is less than this, the allowance will be reduced to the amount you contribute.

Married women, who qualify for the invalid care allowance (a social security benefit) because they look after severely disabled people at home, can now claim the wife's earned income allowance to set against it. The change has been backdated to the 1984/5 tax year, so if you have paid tax on the allowance at some time since 6 April 1984, write to your Tax Inspector and ask for a rebate.

WHAT TO PUT IN YOUR TAX RETURN

You do not enter your child's income or claim your child's allowances in your Tax Return. These should be put in the child's own Tax Return. However, any income your child receives as a result of your gift should be put in your Return as it is treated as your income (unless £5 or less). Put this income under *Settlements* in the INCOME section.

Form 11P

Settlements Include income and capital from settlements, parental gifts, etc. and transfers to be treated as your income	Self £	Wife £

Claim additional personal allowance (see p. 89) and dependent relative allowance by entering the details asked for in the ALLOWANCES section.

Form 11P

Dependent relative allowance	What is the dependant's annual income (excluding voluntary contributions) from:
Dependant's name	State pension or benefit £
Dependant's date of birth	Other pension £
Does he or she live with you? Yes No	Other income £
What is the dependant's relationship to you or your wife (if mother, say if widowed, divorced or separated)?	If the dependant does not live with you, enter the weekly amount you contribute £
What is the dependant's illness or disability (if any)?	If any other relative contributes, enter the weekly amount contributed £

18 · RETIRED – OR NEAR RETIREMENT AGE

How does your taxation change when you get older? Your income will alter, the amount and its source. Few of you will be working a 35-hour week for a salary or what you earn from your own business. Instead, you will be receiving a pension from the state and perhaps a pension from your former employer or from your own personal pension plan. To supplement the income, you may have money invested which pays you an income in the form of interest or dividends. And if your income is too low, you may be looking to earn some extra money from a part-time job. Another source of income you could consider if you own your own home is a home income scheme. All these alterations in the pattern of income inevitably mean that you may be taxed in different ways from formerly. And there may be new forms to fill in and send to your Tax Inspector.

Another change occurs in the allowances you can claim as you get older. Age allowance is specially for the elderly and there are a couple of other allowances which you may be more likely to claim as you age.

This chapter includes details on:

● allowances (see below)

● income (p. 126 – pensions p. 126, investments p. 127, annuities p. 127, a job p. 128, home income scheme p. 128)

● covenants (p. 128)

● what you put in your Tax Return p. 129.

ALLOWANCES

AGE ALLOWANCE

This is an allowance which you can claim if you or your spouse are aged sixty-five during the tax year and your income is below a certain level. The amount of the allowance is larger than the normal single person's or married man's allowances. And if you are aged eighty or more during the tax year, the allowance is even bigger.

	1987/8		1986/7
	65-plus	*80-plus*	
Single person's	£2,960	£3,070	£2,850
Married man's	4,675	4,845	4,505

Once your income (strictly 'total income', see below) has reached £9,400 in 1986/7 or £9,800 in 1987/8, your age allowance will be reduced. The allowance is reduced by £2 for each £3 over the income limit. So, for example, in 1987/8, if you are single and your income is £10,100 (that is £300 over the limit), your allowance is reduced by £200, that is, an allowance of £2,760.

By the time your income has reached £10,603 (if you are single, less than eighty, but more than sixty-five) or £11,120 (if you are a married couple), the level of the allowance will have been cut to the normal personal allowance (in 1987/8 £2,425 for a single person, or £3,795 for a married couple). For those aged eighty or over, the benefit of age allowance will not run out until £10,768, if you are single, or £11,375, if you are married. If your income is in the region where you are losing age allowance, you should choose your investments carefully (p. 127).

Broadly, to find your 'total' income you have to add up your gross income for the year and deduct your outgoings. Gross income includes gross interest; for example, you have to gross up the interest you receive from a bank or building society. You also have to include in gross income any taxable gain you make on a life insurance policy, for example, a property bond. You don't have to include any income which is tax-free, such as the return from a National Savings Certificate.

The outgoings you deduct include mortgage interest, pension contributions and half Class 4 National Insurance contributions but not investments in the Business Expansion Scheme.

OTHER ALLOWANCES

There are some other allowances which you may be able to claim:

● *housekeeper* allowance may be claimed by a widow or widower of any age (p. 113)

● *son's or daughter's service allowance* may be claimed if you are ill or elderly (sixty-four or over) and you are cared for by your son or daughter, who lives with you and is maintained by you. It can be claimed by a married man, but not if the wife is under sixty-four and healthy. This allowance cannot be claimed as well as housekeeper's or blind person's allowance

● *blind person's allowance* may be claimed by a registered blind person of any age. If you are married and both of you are registered blind, you can claim two allowances.

INCOME

PENSIONS

There are a few tax-free pensions (p. 171) but the following pensions are taxable:

● state retirement, including the earnings-related bit

● old person's

● from your former employer

● from your own personal pension plan

● from a partnership of which you were a partner.

A married woman who receives her own pension will, in most cases, be able to claim the wife's earned income allowance to set against it, as a pension is earned income. However, in the case of a state retirement pension, this applies only if the pension is based on her own rather than her husband's National Insurance contributions. The pension is part of her husband's income if it is based on his contributions, so the wife's earned income allowance cannot be claimed.

Although the state retirement pension is taxable, it is paid without any tax being deducted – and if it is your only income, there will be no tax to pay because it will be less than age allowance.

However, if you have other income as well as the state retirement pension, for example, a pension from your employer or income from investments, there will be tax to pay. This will be collected through the PAYE system if your other income is an employer's pension. It may appear that too much tax is deducted from this pension, but this is because tax has not been deducted from the state one.

If your other income is from investments, tax will be collected on this and the state pension by a Notice of Assessment.

Pensions from abroad are taxed slightly differently. Normally you pay tax on 90 per cent of the pension and it is taxed on a preceding-year basis.

INVESTMENTS

If your income is in the region where you lose age allowance (p. 125), each extra £ of income you receive is effectively taxed at a high rate.

EXAMPLE

Susan Webster is seventy. Her income for the 1987/8 tax year is £10,150, which is £350 over the income limit for age allowance. The allowance will be reduced by £2 for each extra £3 of income:

$$(£10,150 - £9,800) \times \tfrac{2}{3} = £233.33$$

Susan can claim age allowance of £2,960 − £233.33 = £2,726.67. The extra tax paid as a result of the extra £350 income is 27 per cent of £350 income plus 27 per cent of £233.33 lost age allowance, that is, £94.50 plus £63 equals £157.50 extra tax.

Extra tax of £157.50 on extra income of £350 means an effective tax rate of 45 per cent.

If your income is in this region and you have investments, it makes financial sense to invest in investments which are tax-free, such as National Savings Certificates.

If you are a non-taxpayer, you may find that investments such as banks and building societies do not give you the best return. The interest from these is paid with no more basic-rate tax to pay, but non-taxpayers cannot claim any tax back. Better investments for non-taxpayers will probably be those that pay interest without any tax deducted, for example, some National Savings investments. Or you could consider investments which are paid with basic-rate tax deducted but which can be claimed back, such as interest from some British Government stocks or dividends from unit trusts and shares.

If you regularly have to claim tax back, ask for Tax Claim Form R40 rather than a Tax Return. Fill it in and you should get a rebate if you have paid too much tax. You can do this before the end of the tax year if you have already received all your income of this type.

ANNUITIES

One way of increasing your income if elderly (say, seventy plus) could be to buy an annuity from a life insurance company. In return for a lump sum, the company will guarantee to pay you an income for the rest of your life, for example. There are many different variations on the theme and you should ask for advice on the best sort for you.

If you choose to buy an annuity as an investment, the tax treatment is different from an annuity which is bought as part of an employer's or personal pension scheme. If it is part of the pension scheme, the whole of it is treated as earned income (and the wife's earned income allowance can be set against it). With an annuity which you buy separately, part of the income is thought to be a return of the money you have invested (and is tax-free) and part is interest. Only the interest part is taxed, but it is taxed as investment income (and the wife's earned income allowance cannot be set against it).

A JOB

Once you reach retirement age, you do not have to pay any more National Insurance contributions, but if you are in a job your employer does.

However, until you reach the age of seventy (if a man) or sixty-five (if a woman), there is little point in earning more than £70 a week, as for every extra £1 you earn over the limit, your pension is docked £1. You can defer drawing your pension and, if you do, it will be increased when it is paid to you.

HOME INCOME SCHEME

You can increase your income by using a home income scheme if you are aged sixty-five or more and own your own home. A life insurance company gives you a mortgage on your home and you use the lump sum raised to buy an annuity (see above). You get tax relief on the mortgage interest payments.

COVENANTS

Covenants can be used as a tax-efficient way of increasing your income or by you to increase someone else's income.

If you are a non-taxpayer, someone (for example, a relative) could make a covenant payable to you. For example, you could receive an income of £500 at a cost to the giver of £365. The giver hands over the £365 to you and you claim back the basic-rate tax deducted (see p. 119 for more details).

On the other hand, you may want to give money to someone else if you are a taxpayer. If your income is in the region where you are losing age allowance, making covenant payments is even more tax-effective for you, because it will mean a higher age allowance, that is, it will increase by £2 for each £3 of gross covenant payments. There are more details on covenants in Chapter 17 'Children, Students and Dependants', p. 117.

WHAT TO PUT IN YOUR TAX RETURN

You have to make two extra entries. You need to give the information about any pensions you are receiving, and you may want to claim your higher personal allowance, called age allowance. You can claim age allowance if you or your wife or husband are sixty-five or more during the tax year (and for 1987/8, you get a higher amount still if you are aged eighty or over during the tax year). For the 1987/8 returns, Forms 11 and 11P, you claim the allowance in the ALLOWANCES section of the Form. Tick the appropriate box.

Form 11P

> ☐ **Age allowance** To claim this you or your wife must have been born before 6 April 1923.

But in Form P1, the allowance is claimed under the PENSIONS section. At the end of this section there is a space to give your date of birth if born before 6 April 1928 (for the 1987/8 tax year).

You also need to give some information about pension in your Tax Return. If you have the 1987/8 Form P1, give the details required in the section headed PENSIONS. With Form 11 and Form 11P, give details about the state retirement pension, widow's and other pensions in the INCOME section under the heading *Social Security pensions and benefits*

Form 11P

Social Security pensions and benefits		Self	Wife
Retirement or old person's pension. If wife's pension (or part of it) is paid by virtue of her own contributions, enter an 'X' here ▶		£	£
Unemployment or Supplementary benefits *enter the full taxable amount*		£	£
Give the amount of taxable benefit (if any) you have already included in the 'Earnings' column above		£	£
Widows and – *say what type* other benefits *(from order book)*		£	£
Pension from former employer and other pensions		Self	Wife
Name and address of payer(s)		£	£

and details about a pension from an employer's scheme in *Pension from former employer and other pensions*. Put the name and address of the payer and the amount received. With Form 11P, you are also asked for information on the front page.

To claim the allowance for a son or daughter whose services you depend on, tick the box on the last page of Forms 11 and 11P.

Form 11P

To claim any of the following allowances, tick the box that applies and I will send you the appropriate claim form.

☐ Son or daughter whose services you depend on	☐ Housekeeper allowance	☐ Friendly Society and Trade Union Death and Superannuation benefits

The allowance is claimed in the ALLOWANCES section of Form P1.

EMPLOYEES:
19 · EARNINGS AND EXPENSES

Employees may feel helpless when it comes to dealing with the tax system. A common view is that it is all handled by your employer and so there is nothing for you to do. And many of you may have little communication with your Tax Inspector and so feel divorced from the whole taxing process.

Whatever your view about the influence you can bring to bear on your tax bill, there is no need to pay more than you have to, even if it is only small sums that you can save. Both your Tax Inspector and your employer are fallible human beings and make mistakes. And so do you. You may have forgotten to claim some deduction against tax which would be allowed or to tell your Tax Inspector as quickly as you can about a change in circumstances which means less tax. To satisfy yourself that you are not paying too much tax, you have to follow up the information which you receive about the tax you are paying. This chapter should help you to do this.

As an employee, you need to know what is the income from your job (called earnings, or emoluments in tax jargon) (p. 132). You also need to know what expenses the tax system allows you to deduct from this earned income (p. 135). You may receive fringe benefits as part of your remuneration package; how these are taxed are explained in Chapter 20, 'Employees: Fringe Benefits', p. 151.

You can find the information you need to check the tax you pay on the earnings from your job in your:

● payslip (p. 143) which your employer must give you by law each time you are paid

● Form P60 (p. 144) which your employer must give you at the end of the tax year

● Notice of Coding (p. 140), although you may not receive one every year. This will be sent to you by your Tax Inspector

● in some circumstances, your Tax Inspector will send you a Notice of Assessment (Form P70) when your tax bill is sorted out after the end of the tax year. This includes information about all your income, not just the income from your job. Chapter 9, 'The Forms', p. 55 tells you how to check this.

Income tax on your earnings is not the only tax you pay; you will also find that National Insurance contributions (p. 144) will be deducted from your wage or salary.

EARNINGS

Earnings are payments or rewards you receive for the work you do in your job. Not everything your employer pays you will be treated as earnings; genuine personal gifts (for example, wedding presents) are not taxable. On the other hand, payments received from someone else besides your employer can be earnings. The deciding factor in determining whether a payment or a reward is part of your earnings is whether it is received because of your job.

Payments and rewards do not necessarily imply only money; what is called money's worth can be treated as earnings. The commonest example of this is if you receive fringe benefits as part of your pay package.

Your Tax Inspector can take as your earnings for the tax year the amount you actually earned during the year, not necessarily the same figure as the amount you received. In practice, for the vast majority of taxpayers, the amount paid during the tax year will be substituted. It will probably only be in the cases of employees who receive bonuses at the end of the year that the different calculation for earnings will be made.

From the 1987/8 tax year, it was proposed in the March Budget that you can get some extra pay free of tax if part of your pay in linked to your employer's profits in a registered scheme. Half of the pay linked in this way will be free of tax, up to a maximum of pay linked of £3,000 a year or 20 per cent of your total pay, whichever is less.

To be registered, it is proposed that a scheme must include at least 80 per cent of employees, last for at least one accounting year, the amount of pay linked must be at least 5 per cent of the total pay for employees and pay must go up and down with yearly audited profits.

WHAT ARE EARNINGS?

The following would all normally be treated as earnings by your Tax Inspector:

● wages and salaries

● bonuses, including Christmas ones

● commission

● profit shares

● fees

● overtime pay

● holiday pay

● cost-of-living allowances

● tips

● advances made on any of the above

● long-service awards (but tax-free if not money, if paid after twenty years of service, if the cost is £20 or less for each year of service and if you have not received a similar award within the last ten years)

● cash allowances, for example, meals or mileage allowance, over and above the amount of your allowable expenses (p. 135)

● pension from your former employer (p. 126)

● sick pay, including statutory sick pay

● maternity pay, including statutory maternity pay

● payments made under a permanent health insurance policy (but if you have paid the premiums yourself, the payments received are tax-free until the end of a full tax year)

● the taxable value of fringe benefits (p. 151)

● payment made on becoming an employee ('golden hellos')

● payment made on leaving a job ('golden handshakes') or payment in lieu of notice (p. 164)

● payment made to compensate for giving up membership of a trade union

● the amount of any debts settled for you by your employer

● the amount of your share of National Insurance contributions paid for by your employer (that is, not the employer's share)

● Job Release allowances capable of beginning earlier than a year before pensionable age.

Earnings from a job are taxed under what's called Schedule E (p. 34). Other income which comes under Schedule E are the state retirement pension (p. 126) and other taxable social security benefits such as unemployment or supplementary benefit (p. 168).

WHAT ARE NOT EARNINGS

Gifts or payments made only for personal reasons are not earnings and normally not taxable. To be treated as not taxable, these items must be unexpected and non-recurring, for example:

● wedding presents

● prizes for passing external exams

● gifts by way of a testimonial.

Board, lodging, uniforms, etc. which are provided by your employer are not taxable as these cannot be turned into money. However, if you get a cash allowance for these items, what you do not spend on these expenses will be taxable. As an exception, miners who get cash allowances instead of free coal do not pay tax on the amount.

WHEN YOU ARE SICK OR ON MATERNITY LEAVE

Nearly all employees are entitled to receive statutory sick pay for up to twenty-eight weeks. This is paid through the PAYE system and both income tax and National Insurance contributions are deducted.

Once the period for claiming statutory sick pay has run out, you can claim sickness benefit and then invalidity allowance from the state. Both of these are tax-free.

Some employers operate their own sick pay scheme, which pays between two-thirds and three-quarters of your normal pay after an initial period. This will be taxed in the same way as normal earnings. If you have paid the premiums yourself for an insurance policy to do a similar task, the income is taxed slightly differently. There is a 'tax-free holiday' which finishes at the end of the first full tax year after you start to receive it. After this, the income is taxed as unearned income.

This could be a problem for married women, as they cannot set off the wife's earned income allowance against it.

There is a change this tax year in the way you are paid while on maternity leave. If your baby was due before 21 June 1987, you carried on getting taxable maternity pay from your employer and you may also have received maternity allowance from the state, which was tax-free. But for babies expected on or after 21 June 1987, this is replaced for employees by statutory maternity pay. This is payable for up to eighteen weeks and is taxable in the same way as statutory sick pay.

EXPENSES

The rules about what employees can claim for expenses are much more stringent than the rules for the self-employed. From your taxable earnings, you can deduct expenses *which are incurred wholly, exclusively and necessarily in the performance of your duties*. In practice, this means that there is relatively little which can be deducted. If an expense is not allowable, the amount is added to your earnings and taxed in the normal way.

Wholly and *exclusively* do not mean that you will not be able to claim an expense if it is not all used in your job. For example, if you need an office in your house to be able to do your job (that is, in the performance of your duties, see below), you will be able to claim part of the house expenses.

Necessarily means that the expense must be necessary for any suitable holder of the job to be able to do it, not that it is necessary for you personally. You can't, for example, claim the cost of travelling from your home to the office. But you can claim the cost of travelling between offices if your job involves you working in two different locations.

Finally, the words *in the performance of your duties* do not mean that you can claim expenses which allow you to do the job in the first place (for example, child-minding expenses cannot be claimed). Nor do the words mean that expenses which allow you to do your job better can be claimed.

These rules about expenses apply regardless of who paid the money. So it makes no difference to what you can deduct from earnings if:

- you paid for the expenses, or

- you paid and your employer paid you back, or

- your employer paid for them in the first place.

The fact that you employer insists that certain expenses are made does not alter the rules about what you can claim.

There are, however, some expenses which the law allows, regardless of whether they meet the rules above in your particular case. These include:

● certain flat-rate deductions for tools and special clothing. The amounts are agreed between the Inland Revenue and the trade union. For example, if you are an agricultural worker, you can claim a flat-rate deduction of £45. If you would be entitled to a bigger deduction than the agreed amount, you can claim the larger. Ask for leaflet IR1

● subscriptions, but not entrance fees, to certain societies approved by the Inland Revenue.

EXPENSES WHICH ARE NORMALLY ALLOWED

These include:

● what you spend for meals and lodging while temporarily working away from home. In theory, it is supposed to be the extra amount, but in practice, you will not have to deduct your home expenses if you can show that you still have to pay these. If your job involves travelling all the time, for example, lorry driver, you can also claim the cost of meals. Keep all your receipts to back up your claim

● the cost of travel between two places of work for the same employer

● car expenses, or a proportion, if you have to use your car in the performance of your duties; you may also be able to claim a capital allowance for buying the car (p. 184)

● cost of keeping your name on a register if it is a condition of your job, for example, chemist, optician

● subscriptions (see above)

● cost of maintaining and replacing tools which you have to provide in your job, see above for flat-rate expenses agreed. You may be able to claim a capital allowance (p. 184), for buying the tools in the first place

● if you have to work at home, you may be able to claim a proportion of the cost of heating, lighting, cleaning, telephone and insurance. If part of the house is used exclusively for work you may have capital gains tax worries (p. 181)

● the cost of special clothing which you have to have for work and which you have to provide, for example, helmet for safety reasons

● the cost of books which you have to provide as part of your employment, but this may only be special reference books

● the interest on loans (but not overdrafts or credit card debts) which you need to buy capital equipment qualifying for a capital allowance (for example, tools, car). You can claim only the interest for the tax year in which the loan begins and the following three tax years

● the cost of entertaining some overseas customers

● under very strict rules, the expenses of a wife or husband accompanying you on a business trip may be allowable. This would apply if he or she had special qualifications needed on the trip, or if your health was very poor and you needed to be accompanied.

EXPENSES NOT NORMALLY ALLOWED
These include:

● the cost of travel between your home and your work and the cost of travel between two different jobs (that is, two different employers)

● the cost of getting a job in the first place, for example, travel cost to go to an interview, payment to an employment agency

● books you buy to help you do your job better

● the cost of a housekeeper, nanny, childminder to enable you to do the job in the first place

● clothing you wear for work which you could also wear out of working hours

● entertaining expenses for UK customers. However, if your employer refunds what you have paid and does not claim the amount as an allowable expense of the business, you will generally not be taxed on the amount.

HOW YOUR TAX INSPECTOR FINDS OUT ABOUT EXPENSES
There are three ways your Tax Inspector receives information about expenses which have been reimbursed by your employer. First, your Tax Inspector may not know all the details because your employer

arranges with your Tax Inspector to give what's called a *dispensation* for expenses. The Tax Inspector will agree to this only if the expenses are allowable for tax relief; they will not be added to your earnings and so will not be taxed. If there is a dispensation, your employer does not need to give details of the expenses paid and you do not have to put them in your Tax Return.

Second, if a dispensation has not been agreed, and you are treated as a higher-paid employee (p. 152), your employer will fill in Form P11D with the amount of expenses and fringe benefits (p. 151). You need to give details of all your expenses (even the allowable ones) in the INCOME section of your Tax Return and claim the amount of the allowable expenses in the OUTGOINGS section. Make sure that what you put in your Tax Return agrees with what your employer has put in Form P11D. You will be taxed on expenses which have been reimbursed by your employer but which are not allowable as the taxman will classify those as earnings.

Finally, if you are not higher-paid (p. 152), your employer fills in Form P9D.

If your expenses have not been reimbursed, the only way your Tax Inspector finds out about any which are allowable (that is, you can deduct them from your earnings and so get tax relief) is if you give the information in your Tax Return. So don't forget to do so.

HOW YOUR EMPLOYER WORKS OUT YOUR TAX

Your employer operates the PAYE system for the government. This system is designed to deduct tax from your earnings on a regular basis, for example, monthly if you are paid once a month. The intention is that at the end of the tax year, you should have paid the right amount of tax on your taxable earnings for the year. It is only common sense to check that this is so.

There are two forms which your employer will give you which should tell you what tax has been deducted:

● your payslip. You should get a payslip with each wage or salary payment (see p. 143 for how to check)

● Form P60. You will be given this at the end of each tax year (see p. 144).

THE PAYE SYSTEM

All employers operate this system including those employing people in the home (for example as a nanny). Your employer will have:

- your tax code, which is sent by your Tax Inspector

- tax tables.

Using these two things together tells your employer how much tax should be deducted every time your wage or salary is paid.

Your tax code reflects the amount of allowances and outgoings it is estimated you can set against your earnings in the current tax year. This is the amount of pay which will be free of tax in the tax year. If your code, for example, is 422H, you are entitled to £4,229 free of tax.

Your employer is given two sets of tax tables. One set tells your employer how much of the free-of-tax pay you will get each time you are paid. If you are paid monthly, you should get $\frac{1}{12}$ of your free-of-tax pay each month; if you are paid weekly, it is $\frac{1}{52}$. So, with a tax code of 422H, a weekly-paid employee would receive £81.33 pay each week free of tax, that is, £4,229 divided by 52. The second set of tables tells your employer how much tax should be deducted from the rest of your pay, less any contributions to approved pension schemes.

The PAYE system is cumulative. This makes it easy for the tax you pay to be adjusted if you become entitled to more or less tax-free pay during the year. Suppose, for example, you get married at some stage in the tax year. If you tell your Tax Inspector you should get a new Notice of Coding with a bigger number in the code. In your next pay packet you should find less tax deducted.

On the other hand, if you have been paying too little tax, your code will be adjusted so that you pay the right amount of tax from now on. But your Tax Inspector may allow you gradually to repay any tax owing during the next tax year rather than in one big lump now.

YOUR PAYE CODE

Your code is made up of a number and a letter. The number tells your employer how much pay you get free of tax, see above. The letters are as follows:

L: you have been given the single person's or wife's earned income allowance

H: you have been given the married man's allowance or the additional personal allowance

P: you have been given the full single person's age allowance

V: you have been given the full married person's age allowance.

These letters mean that if these allowances change during the tax year the changes can be made automatically to your salary. However, if you have the letter T after your number, changes cannot be made automatically and you may have to wait longer for any rebate to come through. You may have the letter T if you have asked your Tax Inspector to give you it because you do not want your employer to know what allowances you have or if you are getting the age allowance, but not the full one.

You may have a letter before the number instead of after. If you have a second job you may have D; this tells your employer to tax all your earnings from your second job at a higher rate. The letter F means that the taxable state benefits you get come to more than the amount of your tax-free pay. Other codes are:

BR: your earnings from your second job are taxed at the basic rate

OT: you are not entitled to any tax-free pay

NT: your earnings should be paid without any tax deducted.

Once you have been given a code, this is what will be used to work out your after-tax pay unless your Tax Inspector issues a new one. Changes in allowances, for example, an increase in the married man's allowance, which are made in the Budget, will be sent automatically to your employer. But if you have other changes, for example, if you get married during the tax year, you should let your Tax Inspector know so that you will be given a new PAYE code. Otherwise, at the end of the tax year you will have paid too much tax and will have to claim a rebate, which can take quite a time.

YOUR NOTICE OF CODING

You may not receive a Notice of Coding each year. You may receive one only if you inform the Tax Inspector of some change. Otherwise, your employer will be told to carry on using the code you had for last year. This is what a typical Notice of Coding might look like, although more computer-printed ones are being issued these days.

EXAMPLE

Sanjay Patel has received a Notice of Coding for 1987/8 (see right) and decides he should check it.

The first item on the Notice is *Expenses*. Sanjay has paid £45 subscription for membership of a society which the Inland Revenue accepts as relevant for his job.

Form P2

**A form P3 (PAYE coding guide) is enclosed or was
sent to you with a previous notice of coding**

How your PAYE code is calculated

Expenses	45
Death and Superannuation Benefits	
Interest payable	250
Personal allowance	3,655
Age allowance (estimated total income £............)	
Wife's earned income allowance	
Additional personal allowance	
Dependent relative allowance	
Widow's bereavement allowance...	
Total allowances	**3,950**

Less allowances given against other income

Untaxed interest...	50	
Occupational pensions		
Social security benefits		
Car benefit	525	
		575
Net allowances		**3,375**

Less adjustments for

....

Tax unpaid for earlier years 198**5**-8**6** £...**85**.........	293	
equivalent to a deduction of		
198 -8 (estimated £..................)		
equivalent to a deduction of		293
Allowances given against pay etc.		**3,082**

Your code is shown overleaf

Printed in the UK for HMSO. Dd. 8400946 10/84 99829.X

If Sanjay paid for funeral or life insurance through a trade union or friendly society, the amount would be under *Death and Superannuation Benefits*.

Sanjay pays for his mortgage through the MIRAS scheme (p. 223) and so it is not included here, but he expects the interest on a home improvement loan to be £250 for the 1987/8 tax year and this interest is paid gross.

The next few lines are where any allowances to which Sanjay would be entitled are entered. He can claim the married man's allowance. As the Notices are sent out in January or February 1987, this is before the rate of the allowances for 1987/8 are set in the Budget in March. So the figure here is for 1986/7. Sanjay will not receive a new Notice of Coding after the Budget. Instead, Sanjay's employer will be instructed what to do to give Sanjay the right amount of tax relief for the new rate of allowance.

Beneath the list of allowances are some spare lines where Sanjay's tax office could enter any other items which are not specified. At the bottom is the figure for *Total allowances*; in Sanjay's case this comes to £3,950.

The next set of entries are those which will reduce the size of Sanjay's code to give him less tax relief. Under *Untaxed interest*, the tax office has put £50, which is the amount Sanjay receives in 1986/7 in a National Savings Investment account which Sanjay opened a few years ago; this is taxed on a preceding-year basis (p. 250). The next line would be where the tax office would enter the amount of any pension from a former employer; in Sanjay's case this is none. And if Sanjay had received any unemployment benefit, for example, this would be entered here.

The next few lines are spaces where the taxable value of fringe benefits would be put. Sanjay has a company car, so the figure of £525 appears.

If Sanjay were a higher-rate taxpayer, an adjustment would be made on the next lines to show the amount of higher-rate tax relief Sanjay would be entitled to on his mortgage.

Sanjay underpaid tax in 1985/6; he owes the taxman £85. As he is a basic-rate taxpayer, that would need a deduction of 293 to repay the tax owed. The final figure for Sanjay of allowances given against pay is £3,082. Knocking off the last figure gives a code of 308 H (see p. 139 for why the letter is this one).

YOUR PAYSLIP

Each time you are paid by your employer by law you should receive a written statement (usually a payslip) which shows the amount of your pay and the amount of any deductions. Below is an example of a pay-slip.

Payslip

NAME . . . . 1 . . . .   W/E . . . . . 2 . . . .

WORKS/DEPT. No. . . . 3 . . . .   Code No. . . . 4 . . . .

Tax Week No. . . 5 . . . .

GROSS WAGES TO DATE		TAX DEDUCTED TO DATE	
£ 6	p	£ 7	p

WAGES DUE FOR WEEK	£	p
BASIC		
HRS. O/T @		
HRS. O/T @		
HRS. O/T @		
BONUS, HOLIDAY, SICK PAY, S.S.P. S.M.P.		
OTHER		
GROSS	8	
DEDUCTIONS	11	
INCOME TAX REFUND		
NET £	12	

DEDUCTIONS

	£	p
Company Pension.		
National Insurance . . 9 .		
Standard Rate at . . . . . %		
Reduced Rate at. . . . . . %		
. . . .		
INCOME TAX. . . 10 . . .		
OTHER DEDUCTIONS. . .		
. . . .		
. . . .		
Form P100	11	

The entries are:

1 The employee's name

2 The date of this salary payment

3 The name or number of the department

4 The employee's PAYE code

5 The week of the tax year. For example, the pay period is the first week in January which is the thirty-ninth weekly pay period in the tax year. So the number 39 would be entered here

6 The gross amount of pay paid to date in this tax year

7 The total amount of tax deducted to date in this tax year

8 The amount of your gross wage for this pay period

9 The amount of the employee's National Insurance contributions. This payslip does not show the amount of the employer's National Insurance contributions

10 The amount of tax deducted in this period

11 Total deductions in this pay period

12 The employee's net pay in this period.

This payslip does not include all the items which are sometimes seen in payslips. For example, it does not tell you the total amount of your National Insurance contributions which you have paid in this tax year.

If you are a basic-rate taxpayer, you can easily check that your employer has deducted the right amount of tax for the 1987/8 tax year:

STEP 1   Work out how much gross pay you should get each month (if paid monthly) or each week (if paid weekly)

STEP 2   Find the amount of tax-free pay. Do this by taking the number in your code and adding 9 to the end. (For example, turn 385 into 3859). If you are paid monthly, divide this figure by 12; if weekly, divide by 52.

STEP 3   Add this figure of free-of-tax pay to the amount of any pension contributions to an approved scheme.

STEP 4   Deduct the figure in STEP 3 from the amount of gross pay you found in STEP 1.

STEP 5   Find the amount of basic-rate tax by multiplying the figure from STEP 4 by 0.27 for the 1987/8 tax year.

The figure this calculation gives you may differ by a few pence from the figure in your payslip. This will probably be caused by the rounding differences in working out free-of-tax pay.

FORM P60

This is a form (or its equivalent) which your employer has to give you at the end of each tax year. It shows your gross and net pay, tax and National Insurance contributions for the year. Sometimes the figure for gross pay is given as pay after any contributions to an employer's approved pension scheme.

You will need Form P60 to enable you to fill in your Tax Return.

NATIONAL INSURANCE CONTRIBUTIONS

Both employer and employee have to pay Class 1 National Insurance contributions. These are a percentage of your earnings, but not worked out in quite the same way as pay for income tax purposes. The differences are:

● NI contributions are worked out on earnings before deducting any pension contributions to an approved scheme

● tips and fringe benefits are not included in earnings for calculating NI

● outgoings and allowances are not deducted before working out the amount of any contributions

● it is proposed that any profit-related pay which will be free of income tax will *not* be excluded in working out the amount of NI contributions.

WHAT CONTRIBUTIONS DO YOU PAY?

Class I contributions are paid by employees and employers; the self-employed pay a different class. Certain groups of people are said specifically to be employees for contribution purposes. These include:

● office cleaners

● most agency workers, including temps but not outworkers

● wives employed in their husbands' businesses and vice versa

● certain part-time lecturers and teachers.

There are also some groups of employees who do not pay Class I contributions. These include:

● employees whose earnings are less than the weekly lower-earnings limit (£38.00 for 1986/7; £39.00 for 1987/8)

● people of under sixteen

● people over retirement age, that is, women over sixty and men over sixty-five (but employers still pay the normal contributions)

● people employed outside Great Britain and its Continental Shelf

● in some circumstances, married women or widows pay a reduced rate, see below.

Employees who are 'contracted-out' still pay Class I contributions, but at a lower rate. You can be 'contracted out' if you contribute to your employers' 'approved' pension scheme. If you are contracted out, when it comes to your retirement you will receive the basic state retirement pension, but not the additional pension from the state.

HOW MUCH ARE THE CONTRIBUTIONS?

The Table below shows both the employee's and the employer's contributions for 1987/8. If your earnings are less than the lower-earnings limit (£39 a week in 1987/8), neither you nor your employer pay any contributions. However, if your earnings are above this limit, contributions are payable on all your earnings, not just on your pay over the limit. Once your earnings pass an upper-earnings limit (£295 a week in 1987/8), the amount of your contributions do not increase but your employer's do.

TABLE: CONTRIBUTION RATES FOR 1987/8

If you are not contracted out

WEEKLY EARNINGS	EMPLOYEE'S CONTRIBUTION (% on all pay) (1)	EMPLOYER'S CONTRIBUTION (% on all pay) (1)
less than £39	nil	nil
£39–£64.99	5	5
£65–£99.99	7	7
£100–£149.99	9	9
£150–£295	9	10.45
over £295	–(2)	10.45(3)

(1) These rates apply to the full amount of earnings, not just the excess over the previous limit. For example, if you earn £70 a week, the amount of your and your employer's weekly contribution is 7 per cent of £70, that is, £4.90.

(2) The employee's maximum contribution, regardless of earnings, is 9 per cent of £295, that is, £26.55 a week.

(3) There is no maximum contribution for employers.

If you are contracted out

WEEKLY EARNINGS	EMPLOYEE'S CONTRIBUTION		EMPLOYER'S CONTRIBUTION	
	on first £39 %	*on amount over* £39 %	*on first* £39 %	*on amount over* £39 %
£39.00–£64.99	5	2.85	5	0.9
£65.00–£99.99	7	4.85	7	2.9
£100.00–£149.99	9	6.85	9	4.9
£150.00–£295.00	9	6.85	10.45	6.35
over £295.00	–(1)	–(1)	10.45	(2)

(1) The maximum employee's contribution is what you pay if your earnings are £295, that is, £21.05 weekly contribution.
(2) The employer's contribution is 10.45 per cent up to £39, 6.35 per cent on earnings between £39 and £295 and 10.45 per cent on earnings over £295.

REDUCED RATE OF CONTRIBUTION

If you were a married woman or a widow on 6 April 1977, you had the right to choose on or before 11 May 1977 to pay Class 1 contributions at a reduced rate. For 1987/8 the rate is 3.85 per cent on earnings up to £295 a week. The rate is the same whether you are contracted out or not. If you are paying this rate, you are not entitled to receive benefits like a pension. However, you can claim certain benefits, like pension, death grant and widow's benefit on the contribution record of your husband.

There are three circumstances in which you lose the right to pay at this reduced rate:

● divorce, or

● non-payment of your Class 1 contributions at this reduced rate, or no earnings from self-employment, for two consecutive tax years, or

● being widowed and not being entitled to widow's benefit or industrial or war widow's pension.

TWO OR MORE JOBS

You pay Class 1 contributions for each job. But there is a maximum amount you can be required to pay each year. For 1987/8, this is £1,407.15 for all jobs if you are not contracted out. If you are contracted out, the maximum contribution is £1,115.65 and if you pay reduced rate contributions it is £601.95. If you have one job which is contracted out and another which is not, the contracted-out contributions are converted to the non-contracted-out level to see if your contributions are over the maximum yearly level.

If you have paid too much (must be at least £1.77 more than the maximum), you can claim a refund. Get Form CF28F from a DHSS office. Send it, together with evidence of overpayment (for example, your P60 forms from your jobs) to Refunds Groups, Records Division, Newcastle-upon-Tyne NE98 1YX. Refunds of £19.51 or more should be received automatically. If you know you will be paying more than the maximum, you may be able to defer payment (rather than pay now and reclaim later). See DHSS leaflet NP28 *'More than one job?'*

WHO IS AN EMPLOYEE?

You cannot just decide to call yourself employed or self-employed. It depends on what you do in your work and how you do it. You are probably an employee if some of the following apply to you:

● you have to carry out your work personally, that is, you cannot employ someone else to do it

● you can be told what, when and how to do your work

● you get a pension, holiday pay, sick pay or overtime pay from someone else

● you work a certain number of hours a day, a week or a month

● you work mainly or completely for one business

● you have to work at a place decided by the person you are working for.

WHAT TO PUT IN YOUR TAX RETURN

In the INCOME section of your Tax Return, you will need to give details of what you earned from your job (or jobs) for the tax year. Enter your total earnings from your job less contributions to your employer's pension scheme. You will get this information from Form P60, which your employer gives you at the end of each tax year. There is a separate entry for the amount of any tips you may receive in your job.

Form 11P

As well as the amount of your earnings from each of your jobs, you have to give the name and address of your employer or employers, plus what your job is. You have to give the information about employer and earnings for yourself, and your wife, if you are a married man.

In the INCOME section, under the heading *Benefits/expense allowances* for Form 11P and Form 11, or in the EARNINGS section under the heading *Value of benefits in kind from your work* on Form P1, you have to give details about any fringe benefits your employer gives you – see Chapter 20, 'Employees: Fringe Benefits', p. 151, for what to put for these. You also have to give information about expenses. If you are not higher-paid (p. 152), and you have been given a fixed expense allowance to cover expenses, say £25 a day if you are away from home on business, enter what you *have not* spent on allowable expenses. If you are higher-paid, you have to put the total amount of any expenses your employer gave you, unless your employer has a dispensation for all your expenses (p. 137).

Form 11P

Benefits/expense allowances	Details	£	£

Turn to the OUTGOINGS section of the Tax Return. Put here the amount of the expenses you are claiming for your employment. Give the details of what the expenses are for (see p. 135 for what you can claim).

Form 11P

Expenses in employment		Self	Wife
Details of expenses		£	£

There is a separate box for fees for subscriptions to a professional body. You have to put in the name of the organization and the amount you are claiming.

Form 11P

Fees or subscriptions to professional bodies	Name of professional body	£	£

20 · EMPLOYEES: FRINGE BENEFITS

While employees may cast an envious eye over what the self-employed can charge up in expenses, the reverse happens, too. The self-employed may look longingly at fringe benefits which employees may receive as part of their pay package. Typical examples are company cars, luncheon vouchers or interest-free loans to buy your season ticket for the railway.

Fringe benefits can sometimes be a tax-efficient way of being paid. The value of fringe benefits is part of your taxable earnings, but sometimes the value placed on them can be relatively low, less than it would cost you to pay for the benefit yourself. And some fringe benefits are tax-free. So a fringe benefit from your employer can be more valuable to you than an increase in wages.

Fringe benefits are usually paid for by your employer, but if anyone gives you a benefit because of your work, it may be taxable.

HOW FRINGE BENEFITS ARE TAXED

To find out how any benefit will be valued by your Tax Inspector (and hence how much tax you will pay on it), you have to look at both yourself as a taxpayer and the nature of the benefit. These simple rules should help you sort out how you will be taxed:

RULE 1: As far as fringe benefits go, taxpayers are divided into two categories: the lower-paid and the higher-paid or directors (p. 152).

RULE 2: Some fringe benefits are tax-free, regardless of what you earn (p. 153).

RULE 3: There is a general rule for valuing benefits paid to the lower-paid and another general rule for valuing benefits paid to the higher-paid, or directors (p. 154).

RULE 4: Some fringe benefits are valued in special ways:

- cars and petrol (p. 156)

- cash vouchers, credit tokens, credit cards and charge cards (p. 158)

- cheap loans (p. 158)

- living accommodation (p. 159)

- property, other than cars, which you are lent (or have now been given) (p. 160)

- employee share schemes (p. 161).

THE LOWER-PAID, THE HIGHER-PAID AND DIRECTORS

A crucial distinction in the taxation of fringe benefits is whether the tax system treats you as higher- or lower-paid. For 1986/7 and 1987/8, the watershed between the two categories is an income of £8,500 or more a year, which by today's standards is not a very high income at all. If you are treated as higher-paid, the tax rules for fringe benefits are harsher than if you are treated as lower-paid.

The figure of £8,500 includes all your earnings from your job, together with the taxable value of any fringe benefits you receive (valued as if you are higher-paid), but after deducting the yearly contributions to an approved pension scheme. You also have to include the amount of any expenses you paid for but which are reimbursed by your boss, although you will not have to include those for which there is a dispensation. You have to include the amount of these reimbursed expenses *even if* these are allowable.

EXAMPLE

Toby Townsley earns £8,200. He also has the use of a company car for his private mileage. Does Toby count as lower- or higher-paid? To check how he will be taxed he has to add the taxable value of the company car, valued as if he is higher-paid, to his salary. The value set for his car for 1987/8 is £525 (p. 157). Adding this to £8,200 gives an income of £8,725 which makes Toby a higher-paid employee.

The rules for taxing fringe benefits if you are treated as being higher-paid normally also apply if you are a director. If you are a director, you will escape the harsher tax treatment only if:

- you earn less than £8,500 *and*

- you own or control 5 per cent or less of the shares and either work full-time for the company or are employed by a non-profit-making organization or a charity.

BENEFITS WHICH ARE TAX-FREE

These benefits are generally tax-free regardless of whether you are treated as higher- or lower-paid:

● perks which you get while doing your job, for example, a carpet in your office, more secretarial help

● luncheon vouchers of up to 15p each working day

● contributions to an approved or statutory pension scheme, which also provides life insurance

● meals, if provided for all employees on your employer's premises, even if in different canteens

● tea or coffee

● reasonable removal expenses, if you have to move for your job

● entertainment provided for all staff, if cost is modest, for example, Christmas party costing £30–35 a head

● the cost of medical insurance for treatment needed while abroad in your job

● the cost of an insurance policy to pay you an income while sick (p. 134)

● long-service awards (but not of money) in certain circumstances. The award will be tax-free if given after twenty years of service, if the cost is £20 or less for each year of service and if you have not received a similar award within the last ten years

● special clothes needed for work

● cheap or interest-free loans, but if higher-paid only if below a certain amount or if interest would qualify for tax relief (p. 158)

● shares in your employer's company obtained through an approved employee share scheme (but there may be CGT to pay when you sell the shares)

● subscriptions paid to professional societies, if approved by the Inland Revenue

● your employer can let you have goods and services cheap, if it does not cost your employer anything

● the cost of books and fees (and possibly expense of living away from home and additional travelling) incurred while attending educational courses.

Note that if you are lower-paid, there will be other fringe benefits which are tax-free for you, although taxable for the higher-paid (see below).

THE GENERAL RULES: HOW FRINGE BENEFITS ARE TAXED

These general rules do not apply to all benefits or perks; some of them have special rules for calculating the *taxable value* to be added to your earnings (p. 156). Nor will these rules apply if you give up part of your pay in exchange for a fringe benefit, for example, a car. Your Tax Inspector will tax you on the amount of pay you have given up if it is more than the taxable value which would normally be put on the benefit.

THE LOWER-PAID

The general rule for working out the value to be added to your earnings is:

the taxable value of a benefit is its second-hand value.

The consequence of this rule is that many benefits are tax-free, or very lightly taxed, for the lower-paid as a lot of perks have no, or very low, second-hand values. As the following have no second-hand value, these benefits are tax-free for the lower-paid, but not for the higher-paid:

● the use of a company car

● insurance to pay the cost of going for private medical treatment

● board and lodging, but not if you are paid cash

● the use of a day nursery or crèche provided by your employer

● any fees or subscriptions paid for membership of a society

● hairdressing service provided at work

● the use of property lent to you by your employer

● educational scholarships given to your children by your employer.

The second-hand value of other items can be low. For example, a suit which costs £200 might have a second-hand value of only a third of that, say £70. If you were lower-paid, your employer could give you a suit costing that amount and you would pay tax at the basic rate on only £70. For the 1987/8 tax year, this would be tax of 27 per cent of £70, that is, £18.90. But if your employer had given you a pay rise of £200, you would have paid tax of 27 per cent of £200, that is, £54. A fringe benefit can leave you much better off than an equivalent salary rise.

THE HIGHER-PAID

The general rule for putting a taxable value on fringe benefits, if you are treated as higher-paid or you are a director (p. 152), is:

what it costs your employer less what you pay towards the cost.

In the example of the suit above, you would pay tax on the £200 it cost your employer to buy the suit, that is, for a basic-rate taxpayer in the 1987/8 tax year, 27 per cent of £200, or £54. In this case, there is no advantage for the higher-paid to be given a fringe benefit rather than an equivalent rise in salary.

EXAMPLE

Rita Bernard earns £13,000 and is a higher-paid employee. She checks what will be the taxable value added to her earnings for the year 1987/8. She gets the following perks:

● a 2.3 litre company car costing £15,000

● a pension scheme including life insurance of four times her salary

● luncheon vouchers of £1 a day

● free tea and coffee

● she can buy toiletries manufactured by the business she works for at a discount on the shop price of 30 per cent (but still more than it costs her employer to make them)

● six suits costing her employer a total of £750 (but she has paid back £50).

First, Rita looks up to see which of the benefits will be tax-free. This applies to the pension scheme, life insurance, the first 15p of her luncheon vouchers, the free tea and coffee and the discount on the goods she can buy from her employer (as it does not cost the employer anything).

Second, she looks to see what will be added for the taxable benefits, the car, the suits and the remaining 85p a day of luncheon vouchers. These come to:

company car (see below)	£1,100
suits (£750 less £50)	700
luncheon vouchers	
(£1 less 15p for each working day)	221
Total	£2,021

THE SPECIAL RULES FOR VALUING BENEFITS

Some fringe benefits are valued in special ways. These include:

● cars and petrol

● cash vouchers, credit tokens, credit cards and charge cards

● cheap loans

● living accommodation

● property, other than cars, which you are lent (or have now been given)

● employee share schemes.

CARS AND PETROL

The taxable value of a car for a higher-paid employee is set by the government, which increases it each year in the Budget. Despite this, a company car remains a valuable fringe benefit for the higher-paid (and it is tax-free for the lower-paid, p. 154).

In the Example on p. 155, Rita Bernard is a basic-rate taxpayer with a company car. The car is valued at £1,100 and she will pay tax of 27 per cent of £1,100 on this, that is, £297. But it could cost her ten times this, that is, £3,000 plus, to buy and run this car herself.

The taxable values for a car and private petrol provided by your employer for 1986/7 and 1987/8 are given in the Tables below. If you pay your employer anything for using the car, you deduct the amount from the value in the Table. And if you don't have the car for the whole tax year, the taxable value put on your use is a proportion of the figure in the Table.

If you are higher-paid, you will be taxed on the figure for petrol if your employer pays for any petrol you use privately, no matter how small an amount. Always check your Notice of Coding carefully; unless you specifically tell your Tax Inspector that you pay for all your petrol, the taxable value is often included in your code. If you are lower-paid, as long as your employer pays directly for petrol, it is a tax-free benefit.

TABLE 1: TAXABLE VALUES FOR 1986/7

ORIGINAL MARKET VALUE	AGE OF CAR AT END OF YEAR		PETROL
	under 4 years	4 years or more	
Up to £19,250	years		
Size of engine:	£	£	£
up to 1300 cc	450	300	450
1301–1800 cc	575	380	575
1801 cc or more	900	600	900
£19,251 to £29,000	1,320	875	900
£29,001 or more	2,100	1,400	900

TABLE 2: TAXABLE VALUES FOR 1987/8

ORIGINAL MARKET VALUE	AGE OF CAR AT END OF YEAR		PETROL
	under 4 years	4 years or more	
Up to £19,250	years		
Size of engine:	£	£	£
up to 1400 cc	525	350	480
1401–2000 cc	700	470	600
2001 cc or more	1,100	725	900
£19,251 to £29,000	1,450	970	900
£29,001 or more	2,300	1,530	900

Note there are some exceptions to these figures. These include:

● you pay $1\frac{1}{2}$ times the above figures for the car, but not petrol, if you use the car for your job for 2,500 miles or less

● you pay $\frac{1}{2}$ the above figures for the car and the petrol if you use the car for your job for 18,000 miles or more

● if you have two company cars, you pay $1\frac{1}{2}$ times the above figure for the car which you don't drive so much on business. The figure for petrol and the figures for the first car are unchanged.

The taxable values in the Tables include what your employer pays for costs such as business petrol, repairs or insurance. If you pay for these and your employer reimburses you, you make two entries in your Tax Return, one in the INCOME section for the reimbursed expenses and one in the OUTGOINGS section for allowable expenses.

Using a pool car is not a fringe benefit and there will be no tax bill. To be a pool car, a car must:

● be included in the pool for the year and be used by more than one employee

● not usually be kept overnight near an employee's house

● be used privately only in an incidental way, for example, as part of a business trip.

CASH VOUCHERS, CREDIT TOKENS, CREDIT CARDS AND CHARGE CARDS

All employees, lower- or higher-paid, are taxed on the value of cash vouchers which they receive and which they could exchange for goods. This also applies to credit tokens, credit cards and charge cards. The value is what it costs your employer less anything you contribute towards it less any allowable expenses.

CHEAP LOANS

You may have a cheap or interest-free loan from your employer to help you buy:

● your railway season ticket

● your home

● some other item.

If you are lower-paid, any of these loans would be a tax-free fringe benefit. If you are higher-paid, the loan could still be tax-free, depending on what the loan is for and how big it is.

If the loan is for something which would entitle you to claim tax relief, for example, a loan of £30,000 or less to buy your home, the loan from your employer is a tax-free fringe benefit. However, should the loan from your employer be more than £30,000, the amount over the £30,000 limit is taxable. The value is worked out in the way described below.

If you have a loan from another source to buy a house, for example, from a bank or building society, and an interest-free loan from your employer takes you over the £30,000 limit, that part of your employer's loan is a taxable fringe benefit. This applies even if you had your employer's loan before you took out the other one.

EXAMPLE

Betty Barrow already has a £25,000 interest-free mortgage from her employer to help her buy her house. She now borrows from her bank another £10,000 to carry out some home improvements. This takes her loans over the £30,000 limit of loans eligible for tax relief. Despite the fact that she had the loan from her employer first, her Tax Inspector will now value as a taxable fringe benefit that part of her employer's loan which is over the £30,000 limit.

If the loan is not eligible for tax relief, your Tax Inspector will value it as a benefit, using the following calculation. The value is the difference between the amount of interest you pay your employer and the amount of interest at the *official rate*, currently 10.5 per cent. You will only pay tax on the value if it is more than £200; if it is £201 or more, you pay tax on £201, not just the £1 which is over £200.

EXAMPLE

William Bland borrows £4,250 from his employer to buy a car. He pays interest at 5 per cent on the loan. The taxable value of William's loan is:

$$(10.5 - 5) \text{ per cent of } £4,250 = £233.75.$$

William will pay tax on the full £233.75, not just the amount over £200.

LIVING ACCOMMODATION

Whether you are higher- or lower-paid, if your employer provides you with living accommodation, you will normally pay tax; the bill will be based on the 'annual value' (the gross rateable value of the property less any rent you pay). Note that there are special calculations for

Scotland, because the 1985 rating revaluation produced figures out of line with the rest of the country.

There are some special circumstances in which living accommodation could be a tax-free benefit. This applies if:

● it is necessary for you to do your job properly, or

● it is customary for your sort of job to be provided with living accommodation to help you do your job better, or

● it is necessary for security reasons.

Unless the living accommodation is for security reasons, it will not be tax-free for a director who owns more than 5 per cent of the share capital or who does not work full-time for the company or for a company which is a non-profit-making or charitable body.

If the accommodation is not a tax-free benefit and costs more than £75,000, the tax bill will be higher than one based on the gross rateable value. It is worked out as:

cost of living accommodation less £75,000 × official rate of interest (p. 159) less any rent you pay on the 'annual value' (p. 159).

The higher-paid will always have to pay tax on what your employer pays for heating, lighting, cleaning, decorating or furnishing, even if the living accommodation is tax-free. There is, however, a limit put on the value of these, that is, 10 per cent of your earnings without including these benefits.

PROPERTY, OTHER THAN CARS, WHICH YOU ARE LENT (or have now been given)

If your employer lends you something, like furniture or a painting, you have to pay tax each year on 20 per cent of its market value at the time it was first loaned to you (less anything you pay to your employer for using it).

If your employer gives you the item you have been borrowing, you are taxed on the greater of:

● the market value at the time you were given the item, less anything you have paid, or

● the market value at the time you were lent the item, less what you have paid less the amount you have already paid tax on. The rules are slightly different for items first lent to you before 6 April 1980.

EMPLOYEE SHARE SCHEMES

There are several different sorts of employee share schemes. Some of them are 'approved' by the Inland Revenue, which means that they receive favourable tax treatment. The approved ones are:

● share option schemes

● savings-related share option schemes

● profit-sharing schemes.

Share option schemes

A share option scheme is a way of buying into your employer's company. You have the right to purchase shares at some future date. The price you pay is fixed at the time of the option. Since 6 April 1984, the Inland Revenue now approves schemes which meet certain conditions, although unapproved ones are far more common. To be approved, the scheme must meet these conditions (among others):

● the option must be for a maximum of £100,000, or four times this or last year's earnings, if greater

● the price you pay to buy the shares should at least be the market value at the time of the option

● the option to buy should be for at least three, but not more than ten, years from the date of the option. You will be able to exercise the option once every three years

● you can be in the scheme only if you work at least twenty hours a week for your employer (and if you are a director, this should be twenty-five hours).

If the scheme is approved, you pay capital gains tax on the profit you make when you sell your shares. Provided the conditions about the price to pay are kept, there is no income tax to pay when you are granted the option nor when you exercise it.

Savings-related share option schemes

With this type of approved scheme, you buy the shares using what you have saved in a special Save-As-You-Earn scheme, which runs for five or seven years. To be approved, the scheme must meet these conditions:

● the most you can save in the SAYE scheme is £100 a month (£50 a month before 1 September 1984). The minimum saving required by the scheme cannot be more than £10 a month

● the price fixed to buy the shares in the future cannot be less than 90 per cent of the market value at the time the option was given by your employer.

If the scheme is approved, there will normally be no income tax to pay but there could be capital gains tax when you sell the shares. Note that at the end of the saving period, you do not have to buy the shares, you can simply take the proceeds of your saving.

Profit-sharing schemes

If it is an approved scheme in which your employer provides money to trustees to buy shares, there will be no income tax to pay, except on dividends, unless you take out the shares before five years are up. The following conditions, among others, should be met:

● you are not allocated shares worth more than 10 per cent of your earnings each year, but there is a minimum of £1,250 and a maximum of £5,000 a year

● you do not withdraw your shares from the trust within five years of getting them

● the scheme must be open to all employees who meet certain re-quirements.

After the five-year period, if you sell or give away the shares, there could be capital gains tax to pay.

WHAT TO PUT IN YOUR TAX RETURN

You have to enter what's called the *taxable value* (p. 154) of the fringe benefits you get from your employer. For example, in the 1987/8 Tax Return you are asked to give this information in Form 11P and Form 11 in the INCOME section under *Benefits/expense allowances*. In Form P1 it goes in the EARNINGS section under *Value of benefits in kind from your work*. You do not have to include benefits for which your employer has a *dispensation* (p. 138). Find this out from your employer and check the details he or she gives in Form P11D (p. 138).

Form 11P

| Benefits/expense allowances | Details | £ | £ |

You also have to tell the taxman if you have received a taxed sum from an approved profit-sharing scheme. You do not have to enter the amount, simply put a cross in the appropriate box. If you have already included the amount you receive elsewhere on Form 11P, but not on Form P1, you should put a cross in the box below.

Form 11P

| If you or your wife received a taxed sum from the trustees of an approved profit sharing scheme, enter an 'X' here | ▶ | Self | | Wife | |
| If the sum is included in the income shown above, enter an 'X' here | ▶ | Self | | Wife | |

EMPLOYEES:
21 · STARTING AND
LEAVING JOBS

Starting work, changing jobs and being sacked are all difficult and
stressful periods of your life. The stress is magnified by the necessity to
keep an eye on the tax side of these changes. You may need to fill in
forms; you certainly need to check the forms you are given. Failure to
do so may mean paying too much tax and having to claim a tax refund
later.

LEAVING A JOB

When you leave a job, your boss should fill in Form P45; you should
get two copies and your Tax Inspector a third. This should show your
PAYE code, the total amount of pay received and the total tax paid so
far in the tax year. When you start your new job, you hand over the
P45 to your new employer.

If you do not have another job to go to and will be claiming unemployment benefit, your employer should also give you Form P50
which will let you claim tax refunds during your unemployment. You
should give your Form P45 to the DHSS. If you are not going to claim
unemployment benefit, ask for a tax refund.

WHAT HAPPENS IF YOU GET A LUMP SUM FROM YOUR BOSS

It depends on what the lump sum is. If it is wages or salary owed to
you, holiday or overtime pay, commission or bonus, these are taxed as
earnings in the normal way under the PAYE system. However, if your
employer gives you money in lieu of notice or any additional payment
over and above the earnings due to you, it will be tax-free if the payment:

● is not specified in your contract of employment

● is unexpected

● totals £25,000 or less.

allowances or if you have not been earning so much, an emergency code means you will be paying too much tax. Once your employer has your code, you will get a tax refund in your wage packet.

If you have been unemployed before starting this job and claiming unemployment benefit, the DHSS should have given you the P45 to hand to your new employer.

WHAT TO PUT IN YOUR TAX RETURN

There is a section in the three Tax Returns, P1, 11P and 11, in which to put the amount of any leaving payments and compensation you have received. What you have to put is: your former job, the name and address of your former employer and how much you were paid as a leaving payment or compensation. Note that this does not include any earnings your employer owes you.

Form 11P

22 · UNEMPLOYMENT AND OTHER BENEFITS

It may seem a paradox that you should need to worry about your tax position when you are unemployed, but unemployment benefit is taxable. And so are some other benefits which you get from the state. The fact that they are taxable does not automatically mean that if you are unemployed *you* will pay tax on them; but it does mean that you need to keep an eye on whether you have paid too much or too little tax during the tax year while you are unemployed, on strike or laid off.

There is, however, a wide range of benefits which are tax-free whatever the size of your income and which do not have to be entered in your Tax Return. There are more details of these on p. 57.

UNEMPLOYMENT

WHAT SHOULD YOU DO WHEN YOU ARE UNEMPLOYED?

You must give your Form P45 from your old job to the benefit office when you first sign on. If you have not regularly had a job since leaving school or college and do not have a Form P45, ask to fill in Form P187.

WHAT MONEY DO YOU GET WHILE UNEMPLOYED?

Any unemployment and supplementary benefit you get, because you are unemployed, for yourself and another adult you are supporting, is taxable in the same way as your wage or salary is. But this does not mean that tax is deducted from the benefit. Instead, the benefit is included in your taxable income for that tax year and the amount of tax you pay will be sorted out either when you get a new job or at the end of the tax year. This means that you will not get a tax rebate while unemployed and claiming benefit.

If, however, you are unemployed and not claiming benefit, you can claim a tax rebate once you have been out of work for four weeks. Claim on Form P50; ask your tax office for one.

WHAT HAPPENS WHEN YOU GET A JOB?

Fill in card UB40 and return it to your benefit office. The office will check how much tax you have paid. If you have paid too much tax you will get a refund either from the benefit office or from your new employer. If you have paid too little tax the extra you should pay will be included in your PAYE code and collected probably in the next tax year.

The benefit office will give you two documents:

● Form P45 which you give to your new boss

● a statement of taxable benefits which must be kept safe as it cannot be replaced. Check this at once and if you disagree with it, write to your tax office within sixty days saying why it is wrong.

WHAT HAPPENS AT THE END OF THE TAX YEAR IF YOU DO NOT HAVE A JOB?

Your benefit office will send you a form P60U which includes a statement of taxable benefit (see above for what to do if it is wrong).

If you have paid too much tax the benefit office will give you a refund.

IS ALL THE BENEFIT TAXABLE?

No, there are some people for whom supplementary benefit received while unemployed is not taxable:

● a man aged sixty-five or over

● a woman aged sixty or over

● a single parent with a child aged under sixteen

● a man aged sixty or over who is entitled to the long-term scale of supplementary benefit

● someone who has to stay at home to look after a severely disabled person.

And you may receive some supplementary benefit which is not taxable, regardless of whether you are in one of the categories above. The tax-free bit is any extra supplementary benefit you receive over the standard weekly amount of unemployment benefit.

ARE YOU LIKELY TO PAY TAX ON THE BENEFIT?

If you are unemployed and living on benefits for the complete tax year, the amount you receive is likely to be below your allowances and so there will probably be no tax due. But if you are unemployed for a short time, you may well find yourself paying tax on any benefit you receive.

EXAMPLE

Richard Parkes loses his job at the end of 1987 and signs on for unemployment benefit at the beginning of January 1988. He's received £12,000 in wages so far this tax year; tax deducted is £2,471. Unemployment benefit of £50.85 a week is paid to him, and no tax is deducted, although it is taxable. Richard is still unemployed at the end of the tax year.

The benefit office gives him a statement of taxable benefits showing that he has received taxable benefits of £711.90 in the tax year. His income, allowances and tax due for the year are as follows:

Earnings	£12,000
Benefits	712
Total	12,712
less married man's allowance	3,795
Taxable income	£8,917

The tax due at 27 per cent is £2,407. But Richard has had tax deducted under PAYE of £2,471 and so is due a refund of £64.

ON STRIKE

You cannot get any benefit for yourself while on strike or considered to be directly interested in a strike. But if you are a man, you can get supplementary benefit for a wife and this is taxable. The taxable bit is the smaller of either the weekly rate of supplementary benefit for her or what you actually receive. But the tax is not deducted from the benefit when paid; instead it is included in your taxable income for the year (see p. 169 for how this will be collected). If you have paid too much tax you will get the refund when you return to work.

When the strike is over, the benefit office will give you a statement of taxable benefit (see p. 169 for what to do).

LAID OFF OR ON SHORT-TIME WORKING

Any benefit you receive for yourself and one adult dependant is taxable, but the benefit office pays it without tax deducted. The part of the benefit which is taxable is the same as for unemployment (p. 169).

When work returns to normal, the benefit office will send you a statement of taxable benefits (see p. 169 for what to do). Any tax due will be collected in the same way as if you were unemployed.

Sometimes your employer pays any benefit along with your wages. Normally, in this case, tax will be deducted from your benefit (if it is due) under the PAYE system. If your employer does not deduct tax, the benefit office will send you a statement of taxable benefit and tax due will be collected at a later date.

CHECKLIST OF BENEFITS

Benefits which are taxable are treated as earned income under Schedule E, the same Schedule as earnings from a job or a pension from your employer.

FOR CHILDREN

TAX-FREE: ● family income supplement

● maternity allowance and maternity grant

● industrial death benefit child allowance

● student grants

● child benefit

● child dependency additions paid with widow's allowance, widowed mother's allowance, retirement pension, invalid care allowance, unemployment benefit or supplementary benefits

● child's special allowance

● one-parent benefit

● war orphan's pension

● guardian's allowance.

TAXABLE: ● statutory maternity pay.

FOR WIDOWS

TAX-FREE: ● war widow's pension.

TAXABLE: ● widowed mother's allowance

● widow's allowance

● widow's pension.

FOR THE SICK AND DISABLED

TAX-FREE: ● sickness benefit

● war disablement benefits

● disablement benefit

● attendance allowance

● invalidity allowance when paid with invalidity pension

● invalidity pension (contributory or non-contributory)

● mobility allowance

● death grant.

TAXABLE: ● invalid care allowance. The tax treatment of invalid care allowance has recently changed. You can now set the wife's earned income allowance against it if you are a married woman. This applies to any invalid care allowance you have received since 6 April 1984. If you have paid tax on it during this period, ask your tax office for a rebate

● invalidity allowance, when paid with retirement pension

● statutory sick pay

● industrial death benefit (if paid as a pension).

FOR THE ELDERLY

TAX-FREE: ● Christmas bonus for pensioners

● Job Release allowance (within one year of pensionable age).

TAXABLE: ● retirement pension and old person's pension

● Job Release allowance, if paid earlier than one year before retirement age.

OTHER BENEFITS

TAX-FREE: ● housing benefit

● rent and rate rebates

● supplementary benefit, but see p. 168

● TOPS training allowance and grants under similar government schemes for those undergoing training.

TAXABLE: ● supplementary benefit paid to the unemployed, those on strike and short-time working

● unemployment benefit (p. 168). From the 1987/8 tax year, note that this will be treated as earnings for separate taxation of the wife's earnings.

WHAT TO PUT IN YOUR TAX RETURN

Do not enter any of the benefits which are tax-free. But you will have to enter details of taxable benefits. In Forms 11P and 11, give the details for unemployment or supplementary benefit and for widow's and other benefits under SOCIAL SECURITY PENSIONS AND BENEFITS. In Form P1, there are two separate entries; *Unemployment or Supplementary Benefit* is in the EARNINGS section and the space for the other benefits is in the PENSIONS section. Enter the full taxable amount in Forms 11 and 11P, but simply tick the appropriate box in Form P1.

Form 11P

Social Security pensions and benefits

	Self	Wife
Retirement or old person's pension. If wife's pension (or part of it) is paid by virtue of her own contributions, enter an 'X' here ▶	£	£
Unemployment or Supplementary benefits *enter the full taxable amount*	£	£
Give the amount of taxable benefit (if any) you have already included in the 'Earnings' column above	£	£
Widows and — *say what type* other benefits *(from order book)*	£	£

23 · WORKING ABROAD

There is one group of individuals who can receive their earnings free of tax. To include yourself in this select band you need to meet certain conditions which would radically alter your lifestyle, that is, work abroad for a period of 365 days. The exact rules are explained in this chapter.

You can qualify for this special treatment even if you are resident and ordinarily resident in the UK, although in general the UK tax system seeks to tax *all* the earnings of people who fall into that category, whether earned in the UK or abroad. What *resident* and *ordinarily resident* mean is explained below.

The tax laws actually aim to spread the net wider still by taxing the income of people who live abroad and are paid income from the UK, as well as those who live here but receive income from abroad. But the tax treatment of those who live abroad is beyond the scope of this Guide and you should take professional advice, for example from your bank or an accountant.

What happens to income from investments abroad if you live in the UK is explained in Chapter 30, 'Investments', p. 241.

RESIDENT AND ORDINARILY RESIDENT

If you are both of these, according to your Tax Inspector, all your earnings are subject to the UK tax laws. You can be resident and ordinarily resident for one tax year, and not necessarily for the next; a fresh decision is taken each year.

You are *resident* for a tax year if
either:
● you are in the UK for at least six months (in practice taken to be 183 days, ignoring the day you arrive and the day you leave)
or:
● you visit the UK yearly and stay for a long period. Your Tax Inspector would take a visit of three months to be a long period and you

would be regarded as resident if you had been doing this for the last four years, say

or

● you have a home in the UK, whether owned or rented does not matter, and you come to the UK in that tax year for a visit, no matter how short. This rule can be ignored if you work full-time abroad, either in a job or running your own business

or:

● you are a British or Irish subject, ordinarily resident in the UK (see below) who is occasionally resident abroad.

You are *ordinarily resident* if you intend to be in the UK on a more permanent basis, although this is rather ill-defined. You can be resident but not ordinarily resident, for example. But if you have been resident for a number of years, or plan to be when you first arrive in the UK, your Tax Inspector will probably classify you as ordinarily resident.

GETTING TAX RELIEF ON ALL YOUR EARNINGS

Your Tax Inspector will try to tax all your worldwide earnings if you are resident and ordinarily resident. However, if you can qualify for the 100 per cent deduction on earnings from abroad, it means that all your earnings from abroad will be free of UK tax. The basic rule is that you must be working abroad for a qualifying period of 365 days or more; this period can straddle two tax years. You can meet this basic rule in two ways:

● *either* you are abroad for the whole of the qualifying period

● *or* you can return for short visits to the UK. No intervening period in the UK can be longer than sixty-two days *and* the total number of days in the UK cannot be more than one-sixth of the total number of days in the new qualifying period. The new qualifying period consists of the days in the continuous period so far (abroad and in the UK), plus the number of days you now spend abroad until your next return to the UK. You can have a succession of periods in the UK and periods abroad and still qualify for the 100 per cent deduction, as long as the above conditions are met for each absence.

A day of absence from the UK means one where you are not in the UK at the end of the day, so your travelling days to the UK will not count as part of the qualifying period. However, the travelling days from the UK are days of absence.

EXAMPLE

Christine Barber gets a job working abroad for her employer. Her trips to the UK and the number of days working abroad are as follows:

abroad	95 days
UK	60 days
abroad	120 days
UK	30 days
abroad	180 days.

None of the trips to the UK break the 62-day rule, but what about the one-sixth rule? At the end of her second trip abroad of 120 days, Christine has spent 60 days in the UK out of a period of 95 + 60 + 120 = 275 days. This is more than one-sixth of the total and so can't count towards the continuous period for the 100 per cent deduction.

The counting can start again from the beginning of Christine's second trip abroad. At the end of her third trip abroad, Christine has spent 30 days in the UK out of a total of 330 days (120 + 30 + 180) in this period. This is less than one-sixth of the total and would count towards the continuous period; but it is not long enough. It needs to be a continuous period of 365 days. If Christine now returns to work in the UK, she will not be able to claim the 100 per cent deduction on any of her earnings.

However, if she returns abroad for a fourth trip of 90 days after spending 20 days in the UK, and starting from the beginning of her second trip abroad, she has spent:

$$30 + 20 \text{ days} = 50 \text{ days in the UK, and}$$
$$120 + 180 + 90 = 390 \text{ days abroad,}$$

that is, 440 days in total in the continuous period.

This period now meets all the conditions for getting the relief on her earnings, starting with her second trip abroad, the 120 days. None of the trips in the UK is longer than 62 days, the continuous period is more than 365 days and the trips to the UK come to less than one-sixth of the continuous period.

Residents in the UK can claim the usual personal allowances. So, if you are entitled to the 100 per cent deduction on your earnings for work abroad, you can set the allowances off against any other income, for example, investment income.

WHAT TO PUT IN YOUR TAX RETURN

If you have worked abroad during the year, you have to give details in your Tax Return. In Forms 11P and 11, for employees, there is space in the INCOME section, under *Duties performed abroad*. Give your occupation, your employer's name and address and the earnings for which you are claiming a deduction. You also have to state the dates you left and returned to the UK during the year (attach a separate sheet if you cannot fit them in). There is no special place for all this information in Form P1; instead there is a box to tick at the end of the EARNINGS section. Do this and attach the details given above.

Form 11P

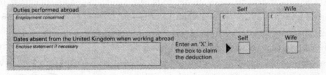

24 · THE SELF-EMPLOYED

Being in business for yourself can be a fairly traumatic experience. One of the extra difficulties you face will be that you are responsible for much more work on your tax affairs than if you were employed, where quite a lot of the work is done by your employer. Just because you work for yourself does not mean that you have to do the tax work yourself; you can employ someone, like an accountant or bank, to do it for you. However, if you do this, you should certainly try to understand how your tax bill is worked out, so you can keep an eye on what your adviser does.

Getting your adviser to present your tax affairs to your Tax Inspector gives them an air of greater credibility. But even if you do this, your accounts are only as solid as the records on which they are based. If you do not keep accurate records, you or your adviser will have difficulty producing accurate accounts and tax calculations. And if your Tax Inspector is not happy with the figures you submit, you will not have the records to back them up.

Being self-employed has tax advantages. There are more expenses you can deduct from your income than if you are an employee. You will also find that you are not paying tax on your income as you earn it, as you do if you are an employee paying tax under the PAYE system; indeed, there can be a considerable delay between earning the money and paying tax on it.

You can be in business for yourself in three ways:

● you can be self-employed. This chapter explains your tax treatment. Note that you cannot just 'go' self-employed; you have to convince your Tax Inspector that you are in business for yourself (p. 196). In tax jargon, as a self-employed person you are taxed under Schedule D Case I or Case II

● you can be in partnership with someone else. The tax treatment is explained briefly in Chapter 26, 'Partners', p. 202

● you can work for your own company as a director. You are treated as an employee with some extra special rules. Your detailed tax treatment is beyond the scope of this Guide.

If your earnings are only occasional and consist of the odd bit of freelance work, you may find that your Tax Inspector wants to tax you in yet another way, not as a self-employed person (see Chapter 25, 'Freelance – and Other Odd Bits of Income', p. 199).

HOW TO WORK OUT TAXABLE PROFIT

Your first step in working out your tax bill is to transform what you have got in your accounts into what your Tax Inspector needs. If you only had a magic wand it would be easy, but as you do not, instead you have to add on a bit here and take away a bit there to turn the figure you have for profits from your accounting records into taxable profits. Broadly:

1 *start* with accounting profit

2 *deduct* any expenses which are allowable for tax, but which are not in your accounts (p. 180)

3 *add* any expenses which you have claimed in your accounts which are not allowed for tax purposes (p. 183)

4 *deduct* money which you have received which is not income, such as proceeds from the sale of an asset. Chapter 4, 'Income', p. 25, explains in more detail what is and what is not income. You should also deduct the amount of any Enterprise Allowance you have included.

5 *add* any items taken from stock for own use and not in the accounting figure. Include them at your usual selling price

6 *gives* you business profits. The next stage is to:

7 *deduct* the amount of capital allowances you are claiming for capital expenditure (p. 184)

8 *deduct* losses on which you are claiming tax relief against profits from the same business (p. 187)

9 *deduct* half your Class 4 National Insurance contributions for the year (p. 190)

10 *add* any balancing charges or *deduct* any balancing allowances (p. 186)

11 *gives* you taxable income from self-employment.

There may well be other deductions you can make from this figure, that is, outgoings and allowances, such as married man's allowance or personal pension payments, before you arrive at the final figure for working out your tax bill. Chapter 10, 'Checking Your Income Tax Bill', p. 67, shows you how to do this.

EXAMPLE

Rupert Bainbridge is calculating his taxable income for the year:

1 His accounting profit is £16,753, but he needs to work out how much he will pay tax on:

2 and 3 First, he scrutinizes expenses. Depreciation of £444 is not allowable and he adds that back. However, he has forgotten to claim anything for the cost of cleaning his office, and he deducts £120 for that.

4 and 5 He has not included anything but income in his accounts and he hasn't received any Enterprise Allowance. Nor has he used anything from stock without paying for it.

6 His business profits are £17,077, that is, (£16,753 + £444 − £120)

7 He can claim capital allowances on the equipment he is buying of £520

8 There is no loss relief to claim

9 His Class 4 National Insurance contributions come to £654, and he can claim relief on half this amount, that is, £327 (see p. 191 for how to work this out)

10 He has not sold any business asset on which he has claimed a capital allowance, and so there is no balancing charge or allowance

11 Rupert's figure for taxable income from self-employment is £17,077 − £520 − £327 = £16,230.

EXPENSES

You can get tax relief on a business expense if it is incurred 'wholly and exclusively' for the business. Claiming business expenses, which are allowable for tax relief, reduces the amount of tax you have to pay. So this is an area of your accounts to which you should pay close attention.

It is worth noting that different expenses are allowable for different businesses; and different amounts of the same expense can be allowable for one but not another. There is no definitive ruling which applies to all businesses; you have to show that an expense is justified in your case.

Just because you use something in your private life does not also mean that it is not an allowable expense for the business. It may well be, and it is always worth claiming something just in case it is allowed. Common examples of items used for both private and business purposes are use of your car and use of your home as your office. As long as your car is sometimes used wholly for business purposes, you can claim a proportion of the car expenses, for example, a proportion based on a ratio of the number of business miles to total miles.

But you may have difficulty claiming as allowable an expense which happened jointly for business and private reasons. For example, a trip abroad to see a customer which you combine with a holiday means that none of the expenses of the trip are strictly allowable.

Part of the running costs of your home, such as part of your gas and electricity bill for heating and lighting, burglar alarm maintenance, insurance and telephone, will be allowable if it is also your office. You can claim rent and rates, but if you own your home be wary of claiming for part of your home used exclusively for your business. This could have an effect when it comes to selling, as you may find your Tax Inspector taxing you for the capital gain made on the part of your home used exclusively for work. Instead, you could claim for the 'non-exclusive use of a room at home' and don't restrict your activities to one room alone. It would be wise to check with your Tax Inspector first, before claiming.

If you cannot claim back VAT, for example, because you are not registered, the VAT included in the cost of an item is part of the allowable expense. If you can claim back VAT, it is not allowable and you will not get tax relief on that part of the cost.

CHECKLIST OF EXPENSES YOU CAN NORMALLY CLAIM

General business

You can claim the normal business expenses of running a business, such as:

● cost of goods you sell or use in your product

● selling costs, such as advertising, sales discounts, gifts costing up to £10 a year (if the gift advertises your business or product), reasonable entertainment of overseas trade customers

- office or factory expenses, such as heating, lighting, cleaning, security, rates, rent, telephone, postage, printing, stationery, normal repairs and maintenance

- proportion of home expenses, if used for work (see p. 181)

- books, magazines, professional fees and subscriptions to professional and trade organizations which are of use to your business

- travel expenses (but not between home and work, or, usually, meals), running costs of car (see p. 181), delivery charges, charge for hiring capital equipment, such as cars

- replacing small tools

- accountancy and audit fees.

Staff expenses

- wages, salaries, bonuses, redundancy and leaving payments, contributions to approved pension schemes, pensions to former employees and their dependants (but not your salary or your partner's salary)

- cost of employing your wife or husband (p. 196)

- employer's National Insurance contributions (but not all your own, see p. 191)

- staff entertainment, for example Christmas party

- gifts to staff

- subscriptions and contributions for benefits for staff.

Financial expenses

- bank charges on business accounts

- interest on loans and overdrafts for business purposes, and cost of arranging them (but not interest on capital paid or credited to partners, or interest on overdue tax)

- the interest part of hire purchase payments (that is, the amount you pay less the cash price)

- premiums for insurance for the business (but not your own life insurance, or sickness insurance)

- specific bad debts (but not a general reserve for bad or doubtful debts)

- contributions to local enterprise agencies, if approved by the government, but not if you receive any benefit from the agency

- contributions and trade or professional subscriptions which secure benefits for your business or similar payments to societies which have arrangements with the Inland Revenue (sometimes only part of the payment will be allowed)

- incidental cost of obtaining loan finance, but not stamp duty, foreign exchange losses, issue discounts or repayment premiums.

Legal expenses

- legal charges such as debt collection, preparing trading contracts, employee service contracts, settling trading disputes and renewing a short lease (that is, fifty years or less)

- premium for grant of lease, but limited to the amount assessed on the landlord as extra rent spread over the term as the lease is paid

- fees paid to register trade mark or design, or to obtain a patent.

EXPENSES WHICH ARE NOT NORMALLY ALLOWED

- your own income and living expenses, most of your National Insurance contributions (p. 191), income tax, capital gains tax, inheritance tax, fines and other penalties for breaking the law (but you could pay a parking fine for an employee), costs of fighting a tax case

- depreciation or initial cost of capital equipment, buying a patent, vehicles, fixed advertising signs, buildings and the cost of additions, alterations or improvements to them. However, you may be able to claim capital allowances (p. 184)

- legal expenses on forming a company, drawing up a partnership agreement, acquiring assets such as leases

- business entertaining expenses (except overseas customers), gifts to customers (but see p. 181), normal charitable subscription and donations, donations to political parties

- reserves or provisions for expected payments, such as repairs, general reserve for bad and doubtful debts (but see above).

CAPITAL ALLOWANCES

What you spend on plant, machinery and vehicles is not an allowable expense. But this does not mean that you are unable to get any tax relief for spending on capital equipment for your business. You can, but by claiming what's called a capital allowance. You deduct the amount of the allowance you claim from your profits and thus pay less tax. The normal allowance you will claim is called a writing-down allowance.

To be able to claim a capital allowance, the rule is the same as for allowable business expenses; the expenditure must be *wholly and exclusively* for your business. But, as with expenses, if you have bought something which you use in your business as well as privately, you can claim a proportion of the allowance.

WHAT ARE THE RATES OF ALLOWANCE?

The maximum writing-down allowances for plant and machinery, cars, patents and know-how are 25 per cent. But, apart from the first year you own one of these assets, it is not 25 per cent of the cost; instead it is worked out on the value as it is written-down over the years you own it. But with industrial buildings, agricultural buildings, and hotels with ten or more bedrooms, the rate is worked out each year on the original cost at a rate of 4 per cent.

These rates are maximums. You do not have to claim the whole amount. If your profits were fairly low one year, and you had outgoings and personal allowances which you could claim and which would wipe out your tax bill, the effect of the allowance would be wasted, because there would be no extra tax saving. Instead, you can defer claiming an allowance (or part of it) and carry forward the value of the asset as it is to the next year.

Before 1 April 1986, there was another sort of capital allowance (called a first-year allowance) which could be claimed on plant and machinery, industrial and agricultural buildings and hotels. The rates of first-year allowance for plant and machinery purchased in the years up to then are:

up to 13 March 1984	up to 100%
from 14 March 1984 to 31 March 1985	up to 75%
from 1 April 1985 to 31 March 1986	up to 50%
from 1 April 1986	nil

You can still claim first-year allowances of 100 per cent on buildings in enterprise zones and expenditure on scientific research.

IF YOU HAVE ONE BUSINESS ASSET

Capital allowances work something like this. If you have only one piece of capital equipment, in the first year you own it, you deduct the amount of the allowance you are claiming from the original cost of the asset. The amount you have deducted is used to reduce your taxable profits. The value of the asset which you carry forward to the next year is the initial cost less the allowance claimed.

EXAMPLE

Paula Barber has been in business in a small way for a number of years. She currently has only one item of capital equipment which she bought a year ago for £500, an electronic typewriter. Last year, she claimed the full writing-down allowance; in this case, 25 per cent. The amount of the allowance she deducted from profits was 25 per cent of £500, that is, £125. The value of the typewriter which she carried forward to this year was £500 − £125 = £375. She can claim a further allowance on the typewriter for this year, that is 25 per cent of £375 = £94. And the value she carries forward is £375 − £94 = £281.

MORE THAN ONE ASSET

If you have more than one asset, capital allowances are not worked out on each individual piece of equipment you have. Instead, you put the values of all the assets (with a few exceptions, see below) in what is called a *pool of expenditure*. And each year you work out the writing-down allowances for the year on the value of your pool of expenditure at the end of the year. You deduct the amount of the allowance you are now claiming from the value of the pool and carry the new value of the pool forward to the next year.

EXAMPLE

David Simonsen has been in business for a number of years. At the start of the current accounting year, the value of his pool of expenditure is £33,658. During the year, he buys a new printing machine, costing £15,000. He adds this to the value of the pool and at the end of the year works out how much he can claim in capital allowances. This is 25 per cent of £33,658 + £15,000 = £12,165. The value of the pool at the start of next year is £33,658 + £15,000 − £12,165 = £36,493.

There are two categories of assets which have their own separate pool:

● cars bought after 31 May 1980 *must* have their own pool, separate from the rest of your equipment. For cars costing more than £8,000 and bought after 12 June 1979, you will have to create a separate pool for each car, with a writing-down allowance of no more than £2,000 each year

● any item of capital equipment (not cars, but it could be calculators, tools or computers, for example) which you expect to sell or scrap within five years can be put in a separate pool. These are known as short-life assets. Being in a separate pool can be an advantage when you sell one of these assets, see below.

WHAT HAPPENS WHEN YOU SELL ASSETS?

When you sell an asset, you have to deduct it from the pool of expenditure. You do this before you work out what capital allowances you can claim for that year. The amount you deduct from the pool is the smaller of either the original cost of the asset or the money you receive when you sell it. Occasionally, especially with assets in their own pool such as cars, the proceeds are greater than the value of the pool. The excess, the *balancing charge*, is added to your profit, see Example below.

If you sell or scrap assets, which you have put in a separate pool because you expect them to have a short life (see above), and the proceeds come to less than the value, you can deduct the difference, the *balancing allowance*, from your profit for the year.

EXAMPLE

Roderick Whittaker has a car he uses in his business. It forms its own pool and the value at the start of the current accounting year is £3,450. During the year, Roderick sells the car for £3,700. This is more than the value in the pool, so Roderick has to add the difference, known as the balancing charge, of £250 to his profit, increasing the size of his tax bill. If he is a basic-rate taxpayer in 1987/8, his tax bill goes up by 27 per cent of £250 = £67.50.

LEASING AND HIRE PURCHASE

With machinery which you lease rather than buy, you do not get a capital allowance. Instead, the leasing payment counts as an allowable expense.

If the machinery is being bought using hire purchase, you can claim a capital allowance when you first use the equipment. The interest part of the hire purchase payment can be claimed as an allowable expense, not as a capital allowance.

WHEN YOU START IN BUSINESS

When you start up on your own, and you take into the business a piece of capital equipment which you already own, you can claim a capital allowance on the value. The Tax Inspector will accept market value as the original value for working out the capital allowance.

During the first years of a business, when you buy an asset, it can be tricky working out when you are going to get the capital allowance on it. This is because you may find in the opening stage that the profits of one accounting year are taxed twice, while the profits of another year are not taxed.

If your first period of business starts midway through a tax year, the writing-down allowance will be restricted to that proportion of 25 per cent which your trading period bears to the tax year ending on 5 April. For example, if you start business on 5 September, you will be entitled to a writing-down allowance of $\frac{7}{12}$ of 25 per cent.

A capital allowance is claimed once. You can claim the allowance for the first year in which it is eligible for tax relief. If the same profits are taxed again, you cannot claim the allowance based on its original cost but on its value after being written down.

LOSSES

Businesses do not always make profits; you may face the situation one day when you have made a loss. The tax system allows you to set off the loss to reduce other tax bills. You can choose to set it against:

● other income for the same tax year

● other income for the next tax year, as long as you are still carrying on the business in which you made the loss (a different business does not count) *or*

● future profits from the same business (but not a different one).

In the early years of the business, losses (which are calculated in the same way as profits) have to be apportioned on a strict basis to 5 April. If the loss is an isolated one, occurring after your first four years of business, your Tax Inspector may accept a claim for a loss for an accounting year ending in the current tax year.

SETTING THE LOSS AGAINST OTHER INCOME

If you have other income, it will improve your cash flow to set the loss against it rather than future profits (and, in any case, these may be uncertain). However, you must set the loss off before any other personal allowances or reliefs (for example, married man's allowance, tax relief on mortgage interest). As you cannot carry forward unused personal allowances from one tax year to the next, making this choice may mean losing part of your allowances if the income is not big enough to cover both the loss and the allowances. Consider setting the loss against:

● future profits, see right

● only the husband's other income for the same tax year, and not the wife's, see STEP 3 below

● other income for the next tax year, see STEP 4 below.

Choosing to set the loss against other income, means setting off the losses in a certain order:

STEP 1 Set the loss first against the husband's earned income (for example, from a job) for the same tax year. This could also include profits made from the same self-employed business in the preceding year

STEP 2 If this earned income is not big enough to set off the whole of the loss, you can set off the excess loss against the husband's unearned income (for example, from investments) for the same year

STEP 3 Set the loss against the wife's earned income first, and then unearned income. You can miss out this step and set the loss against other income for the next tax year (see STEP 4) or future profits of the business (see below).

STEP 4 Any part of the loss on which you have not yet got tax relief can be carried forward and set against other income for the next tax year. The order is the same: the husband's earned income, then unearned income, and, if you choose, the wife's earned income and then unearned income.

You can miss out STEPS 1, 2, and 3 and do this straightaway if you choose.

STEP 5 Any loss still not set off? You can set it against future profits from the same self-employed activity, but not other income for any further years. You can carry forward the loss until you have got tax relief on it all.

In tax jargon, setting losses off against other income is known as claiming under Section 168. To get this relief, claim within two years after the end of the year in which you make the loss.

SETTING THE LOSS AGAINST FUTURE PROFITS

If you decide not to set the loss against other income for the same or the next tax year, you can choose instead to set it against future profits for as many years as you need to get tax relief on it all. It must be profits from the same self-employed activity, and not any other.

In tax jargon, this is known as claiming under Section 171. To get this relief, you must claim within six years of the year in which you want it; the amount of the loss must be claimed within six years of the year of the loss.

LOSSES IN A NEW BUSINESS

If you make a loss during the first four years of your business, you can carry it back and set it against other income in the previous three years, starting with the earliest year. You will be allowed this tax relief only if there is some prospect that the business could be profitable.

To get this relief, you must claim within two years after the end of the year in which you made the loss.

LOSSES IN A CLOSING BUSINESS

A loss made in the last twelve months of a business can be:

● set against other income, *or*

● set against the profits of the same business which you made in the three tax years before you close it, starting with the latest first.

NATIONAL INSURANCE CONTRIBUTIONS

You may have to pay two different lots of National Insurance contributions:

● for yourself, that is, Class 2 and perhaps Class 4 contributions

● for an employee, that is, employer's contributions.

CONTRIBUTIONS FOR YOURSELF: CLASS 2

Most self-employed people will pay Class 2 contributions. Some self-employed will also have to pay Class 4 contributions.

Class 2 contributions are flat-rate – £3.85 for 1987/8 and £3.75 for 1986/7. They are paid weekly, or you can pay them each month by using a direct debit. Paying these contributions gives you access to most social security benefits, with some exceptions. You cannot claim unemployment benefit, widow's benefit, invalidity pension or the earnings-related part of a state pension.

You do not have to pay Class 2 contributions for the tax year if:

● you are aged sixty-five or over, if a man, or sixty or over, if a woman

● your earnings are 'small', that is, you earned £2,075 or less in 1986/7 and there has been no real change in your earning power, or you expect to earn less than £2,125 in 1987/8. If this applies to you, you should not have to pay Class 2 contributions. Get leaflet NI27A from the DHSS and fill in Form CF10, to get your Certificate of Exemption. Do not delay doing this, as your claim cannot normally be backdated more than thirteen weeks

● you chose on or before 11 May 1977 to pay reduced-rate Class 1 contributions or no Class 2 contributions because you are a married woman and you hold a certificate of election CF383

● you are not 'ordinarily' self-employed, for example, you are an employee and your earnings from your part-time self-employment are not likely to be more than £800 in a tax year. See leaflet NI27A.

You do not have to pay Class 2 contributions for any particular week, if for a full week:

● you are incapable of working *or*

● you are receiving sickness, invalidity or industrial injury benefit or the maternity allowance *or*

● you are receiving the unemployability supplement to the industrial disablement benefit or to a war disablement pension *or*

● you are getting invalid care allowance *or*

● you are working outside the UK *or*

● you are in legal custody or in prison.

CONTRIBUTIONS FOR YOURSELF: CLASS 4

Class 4 contributions are earnings-related and paid, at the same time as your income tax bill, on profits you earn between an upper and lower limit:

> 1986/7   6.3% on profits between £4,450 and £14,820
> 1987/8   6.3% on profits between £4,590 and £15,340

This gives a maximum contribution of £653 for 1986/7 and £677 for 1987/8.

Profits for contribution purposes are worked out in much the same way as profits for income tax purposes, except that:

● losses can be set only against your future profits from the same self-employed activity (p. 189)

● any Enterprise Allowance payments are included (p. 196).

You can deduct one-half of your Class 4 contributions from your profits before working out your income tax bill. Class 4 contributions do not increase the amount or range of social security benefits you can claim.

You do not have to pay Class 4 contributions if, among other exceptions, you are:

● aged sixty-five or over, if a man, or sixty or over, if a woman

● not 'ordinarily' self-employed (see left)

● non-resident (p. 174)

● not yet sixteen during the tax year.

EMPLOYER'S CONTRIBUTION

There is no limit on the amount of employer's contribution you have to pay for an employee. The amount of the contribution for 1987/8 is given in the Table on p. 146.

Note that if you employ someone over the normal retirement age, and so they do not pay employee's contribution, you still have to pay employer's contribution.

PAYING YOUR TAX BILL

Working out the figure for taxable profits is not the end of the story. To know what your tax bill is going to be, you need to know which are the profits to be taxed in this tax year; this is not always as easy to work out as it may seem. This is because once your business has been going at least three years, you are normally taxed on what is known as a *preceding-year basis* (see next page for what happens in first few years). So you will be taxed on the profits you earn in the accounting year ending in the previous tax year.

Being taxed on a preceding-year basis means there can be quite a delay between earning the profits and paying the tax due on them. If your profits are rising year by year, you will be earning a higher income while paying tax on lower profits earned earlier. This delay is one of the major tax advantages of self-employment.

You can choose any year-end you like for your business. Just because you start your business on 1 November, say, does not mean your accounting year has to end on 31 October of the following year. Nor does your accounting year have to be a calendar year, that is, 1 January to 31 December. By carefully choosing your accounting year-end, you can maximize the delay between earning profits and paying tax on them. For example, if your accounting year ends on 30 April 1987, you will find that you will not be paying tax on the profits earned in that accounting period until 1989 (see Example below).

You can change your year-end if you want, but think twice as it is a complicated procedure (see Inland Revenue leaflet I R26).

Whereas employees pay their income tax each month or each week, the self-employed have to pay in two equal instalments. The first half is due on 1 January and the second on 1 July.

EXAMPLE

Joanna White becomes self-employed on 1 January 1987 and is considering what date she should choose for her accounting year-end. She would like to choose a year-end which will give the longest period between earning the profits and paying tax on them, as she expects her profits to rise steadily over the years. This is a year-end shortly after 6 April. She compares this with a calendar year-end, that is, 31 December. After the first few years, this is what it would look like:

YEAR-END	PAY TAX ON:	NUMBER OF MONTHS DELAY
30 April 1991	1 January 1993	20 months
	1 July 1993	26 months
31 December 1990	1 January 1992	12 months
	1 July 1992	18 months

Joanna should review the situation in December 1987 and make her decision at that time.

STARTING AND CLOSING YOUR BUSINESS

When you start your business, the normal rule about paying tax on the profits you earn in the accounting year ending in the previous tax year cannot apply for the obvious reason that there is no previous year. So there are special rules about how you are taxed when you are starting a business – and when you are closing it. You have some freedom to choose which profit you are taxed on in the second and third tax years of your business; your Tax Inspector has the choice when it comes to closing the business.

STARTING YOUR BUSINESS

Tax year 1 Your tax bill is worked out using the profit you actually earned before 6 April. Finding out your actual profit may mean that you need to split profits between tax years – the section on p. 194 shows you how to do this.

Tax year 2 You can choose. You can make it the profit you earned in your first twelve months of business. Or, if you do this for both years 2 and 3, you can make your choice the profit you actually earned in tax year 2 (see how to split profits between tax years on p. 194).

Tax year 3 You can choose. You can make your tax bill be based on your profit in your accounting year ending in the previous tax year (but if your first accounting period is more than twelve months, normally the profit you make in your first twelve months of business). Or, if you do this for both years 2 and 3, your tax bill will be based on the profit you actually earned in tax year 3 (see how to split profits between tax years on p. 194).

Tax year 4 Your tax bill will be worked out on your profit in your accounting year ending in the previous tax year (but if your first accounting period is more than twelve months, normally the profit you make in your first twelve months of business).

Tax year 5 etc. You will be taxed on your profit in your accounting year ending in the previous tax year.

CLOSING YOUR BUSINESS

Your Tax Inspector now can make the choice. For the tax year which is two tax years before you close, your tax bill will be worked out on your profit in your accounting year ending in your previous tax year. Or, if your Tax Inspector chooses for both this and the next tax year, the profit you actually earned in this tax year (see how to split profit between tax years on p. 194).

For the tax year before you close, your tax bill is based on your profit in your accounting year ending in the previous tax year. Or, if your Tax Inspector chooses for both this and the previous tax year, the profit you actually earned in this tax year (see how to split profits between tax years on p. 194).

Finally, in the tax year you close, the profit you actually earned in this tax year (see how to split profits between tax years below).

MAKING THE CHOICE

These opening rules mean that some profits may be taxed more than once. This could be an advantage if your profits in the opening year are low compared to subsequent years (see Example 2 on the right). If you are claiming capital allowances in these opening years, however, you can claim only for the first year; you cannot claim a capital allowance twice (p. 187).

To make the choice of being taxed on actual profit in the second and the third tax years, you must tell your Tax Inspector within six years after the end of the third year of assessment.

The closing rules mean that some profits may not be taxed at all. But if you have capital expenditure in those years, you will be able to claim your allowance. For what you spend on capital equipment in the period of profits which are not taxed, you can claim as if it was spent in the next period, unless that is the last tax year. In this case, you can claim as if it was spent in the previous period.

HOW TO SPLIT PROFITS (AND LOSSES) BETWEEN TAX YEARS

To check whether you should make the choice of being taxed on actual profit, you need to work out what profit figure this would give you. Actual profit is the proportion of profit earned during the tax year and is calculated on a time basis. Start with the profit figure for the accounting period and multiply by the number of months of the period in the tax year and divide by the number of months in the accounting period. Note that your Tax Inspector strictly could ask you to apportion profits on a day-by-day basis, not just monthly.

Losses are apportioned in the same way as profits.

EXAMPLE I

Joshua Thwaites starts his business on 1 January 1986 and his first accounting period ends on 30 April 1987. His first tax year is 1985/6 and three months and a few days of his first accounting period falls in that year. Profits for the first accounting period are £10,000. His actual profit for the tax year 1985/6 is likely to be accepted by his Tax Inspector as:

$$\frac{3 \text{ months}}{16 \text{ months}} \times £10,000 = £1,875$$

EXAMPLE 2

Peter Smith starts his business on 1 January 1984 and chooses to make his accounting year run to 31 December. His profits for the first few years are:

ACCOUNTING YEAR	PROFITS
1984	£10,000
1985	12,000
1986	3,000

The opening rules mean that Peter's income to be taxed could be as follows, if his Tax Inspector will accept splitting profits by month rather than by day:

TAX YEAR	TAXABLE INCOME	
1983/4	3 months of £10,000 = $\frac{3}{12} \times £10,000$ =	£2,500
1984/5	first 12 months	= £10,000
1985/6	previous year	= £10,000
1986/7	previous year	= £12,000
	Taxable income for the first four years	= £34,500

Peter works out what the income would be for the first four tax years if he chose to have his tax bill based on the actual profit for both tax years 2 and 3:

TAX YEAR	TAXABLE INCOME	
1983/4	3 months of £10,000 = $\frac{3}{12} \times £10,000$ =	£2,500
1984/5	actual profit = ($\frac{9}{12} \times £10,000$) plus ($\frac{3}{12} \times £12,000$) = £7,500 + £3,000	= £10,500
1985/6	actual profit = ($\frac{9}{12} \times £12,000$) plus ($\frac{3}{12} \times £3,000$) = £9,000 + £750	= £9,750
1986/7	previous year	= £12,000
	Taxable income for the first four years	= £34,750

Peter would be better off if he does not choose to be taxed on actual profits. If Peter's profits had been lower in the first year than in later years, he would probably have been better off making the choice to be taxed on actual profits.

WHAT YOU SPEND BEFORE YOU START YOUR BUSINESS

You may find that you have to spend money before you start trading, for example for rent and rates. As long as it is a normal business expense and it occurs not more than three years before your business starts, it is *pre-trading expenditure*. You can claim it as a loss in your first year of trading and claim loss relief; see p. 189 for how you can do this.

ENTERPRISE ALLOWANCE

This is not taxed in the same way as your business profits. You will pay tax only once on the allowance, if any tax is due, whereas with profits in the opening years, you may be taxed more than twice on them. The allowance will be taxed in the current year, in tax jargon under Schedule D Case VI (see p. 35), but still treated as earned income so the wife's earned income allowance can be set against it. Do not include it in the figure for business profits which you put in your Tax Return (p. 198).

If you were receiving Enterprise Allowance before 18 March 1986 (and received no more payments after that date) it was included in your business profits.

INCOME YOU RECEIVE AFTER YOU CLOSE YOUR BUSINESS

If you receive income from your self-employed business within six years of closing it (*post-cessation receipts*), you can choose to have it treated as income received on the last day of your business. Otherwise it will be treated as earned income when you receive it and taxed in the current year (in tax jargon, under Schedule D Case VI).

You must tell your Tax Inspector within two years of the end of the tax year in which you receive the income if you wish to make this choice.

WHO IS SELF-EMPLOYED?

Whether you are self-employed or an employee is not just a question of your convenience. You are probably self-employed if some of the following apply to you:

● can you determine what work you do, whether you or someone else does it, how you do it and when and where you do it?

● do you pay for the capital equipment of your business?

● have you put your own money into the business?

● if the business makes a loss, do you have to cover it?

● if work is unsatisfactory, do you have to put it right in your own time and out of your own pocket?

EMPLOYING YOUR FAMILY

You would need to establish that your family actually carry out the work you say and that they are paid the going rate for the job, if you wish to employ your wife or husband or your children in your business. You will also have to satisfy your Tax Inspector that they actually receive the money you say you pay them.

If the husband employs the wife in the business, he can claim the wife's earned income allowance to set against her earnings, that is, pay her up to £2,425 in the 1987/8 tax year without paying income tax. But if he pays her more than the lower-earnings limit for National Insurance contributions, £39 a week for 1987/8, both husband and wife will have to pay contributions (p. 146).

Even more tax-saving will occur if paying the wife a high salary can be justified. With your joint income exceeding a certain amount, it can be worthwhile to choose to have the wife's earnings taxed separately (p. 93).

WHAT TO PUT IN YOUR TAX RETURN

If you are self-employed, the Tax Return you will probably be getting is Form 11. With this Tax Return for 1987/8, for example, you are asked for details of your income from your business on the first page, under the heading *Trade, profession or vocation*. You have to give details of what sort of business you are in (for example, barrister, boat-builder and so on). You must also state your business address and the name you trade under, if it is not your own.

Form 11

Trade, profession or vocation		Self	Wife
Business name and address	Type of income	£	£
	Enterprise allowance	£	£
	Balancing charges	£	£
	Deductions for Capital Allowances	£	£
Deduction for Class 4 National Insurance Contributions enter 'X' here		▶ ☐	
If your profits for Class 4 National Insurance Contributions purposes are affected by interest paid, certain capital allowances or losses not given in the assessment, give details on a separate sheet and enter 'X' here		▶ ☐	

197

In the column headed 'Self', you have to put the profits you have earned during the accounting year ending in the tax year to 5 April 1987 (see p. 191). Put the figure for profits after deducting allowable business expenses (see p. 180), but before other deductions; the figure for profits should not include Enterprise Allowance. If you are a married man and your wife is self-employed, you should enter the same information in the column headed 'Wife'.

If your business is carried on abroad, you have to put:

either the figure for profits earned in the year to 5 April, whether you have received the income or not.

or you can put the figure for profits for your accounting year ending in the tax year to 5 April. You have to stick to the same choice in all your later Returns.

Below this, if you have received any Enterprise Allowance (p. 196), you should put how much you received by 5 April 1987.

The next heading says *Balancing charges*. This occurs if you have sold something for which you had claimed a capital allowance and you made a profit when you sold it (p. 186).

Under *Deductions for capital allowances* enter the amount you are claiming for capital expenditure (p. 184). And if you pay Class 4 National Insurance contributions, put a cross in the box marked for this.

If you have Form 11P, you will find the space to enter the same information on the third page of the Tax Return for 1987/8. If you have Form P1, you enter the figure for taxable income (p. 179) in the space on the first page of the Tax Return under the heading *Profits from a trade or profession*.

FREELANCE – AND
25 · OTHER ODD BITS
OF INCOME

The odd bit of freelance or other income from writing an article or doing a bit of dressmaking, for example, can come in handy. For employees it can be an extra bit of work you undertake in the evenings or at weekends. For the housebound it can be fitted in among other family commitments. But knowing how it will be taxed is not straightforward. The income could be taxed as if:

● it is casual income (in tax jargon, this will be taxed under Schedule D Case VI)

● you are self-employed (p. 178)

● you are an employee, where the work is carried out for one business, for example. On p. 148 there is a list of some of the points your Tax Inspector will look for in deciding if you are an employee for that extra bit of income.

HOW CASUAL INCOME IS TAXED

If your Tax Inspector decides your income is casual, your earnings may be taxed on a current-year basis, that is, you will pay tax on your casual income in the same tax year as you receive it. In practice, if you get casual income every year, you may find your Tax Inspector working out your tax bill on what you earned in the previous tax year. If you are also an employee, you may find that tax is collected on this casual income through the PAYE system, that is your PAYE code includes an estimate of your casual income.

Any expenses which you necessarily incurred in getting the income can be deducted before arriving at the figure on which tax will be based. The tax is due on 1 January of the tax year or thirty days after the assessment is received, if this is later.

If you have made a loss, you can set it only against other income being taxed in the same way (that is, under Schedule D Case VI) in the current or future years. It cannot be set against income from a job, for example.

Income taxed in this way is normally regarded as unearned or investment income. Strictly, if you are a married woman, the income will be regarded as your husband's. This would mean that you could not set the wife's earned income allowance against it, although in practice your Tax Inspector will normally allow this.

CAN YOU COUNT AS SELF-EMPLOYED?

It is in your financial interest if your income is treated as income from self-employment and not casual income. First, income from self-employment, after the first few years, will be taxed on a *preceding-year basis* (p. 192) which can help your cash flow if your income from this activity is rising. Second, the treatment of losses is more generous for self-employed income.

There are a number of actions you can take which may help to influence your Tax Inspector. For example, you should always describe your activities as a business or profession and never as occasional. Using headed notepaper for your correspondence and keeping your accounting records carefully can also be an indicator of self-employment. Note that you can be regarded as self-employed as well as employed, so the fact that you have a paid job should not deter you.

WHAT YOU MUST DO WHEN YOU RECEIVE CASUAL INCOME

You must tell your Tax Inspector when you start getting this income (within one year of the end of the tax year in which you first receive it). This still applies if you are making a loss rather than a profit. Failing to receive a Tax Return does not absolve you from this duty.

OTHER ODD BITS OF INCOME

There are some other odd bits of income taxed under Schedule D Case VI. These include:

● income from furnished holiday accommodation, which is treated as earned income (p. 237)

● Enterprise Allowance payments, if you were receiving them on or after 18 March 1986. These are treated as earned income (p. 196)

● income received after you close a business (p. 196)

- income from guaranteeing loans, dealing in futures and some income from underwriting

- certain capital payments from selling UK patent rights.

WHAT TO PUT IN YOUR TAX RETURN

Enter the amount of casual income received and what it is for at the end of the INCOME section under *All other profits or income* for Forms 11 and 11P and under *Any other income or gains* in Form P1, at the end of INVESTMENTS, SAVINGS, ETC.

Form 11P

All other profits or income *enter gross amounts*		
Maintenance, alimony, or aliment received	Self	Wife
	£	£
Any other income not entered elsewhere *eg: accrued income charges and taxable gains on life assurance policies*		
	£	£

For where to enter in Forms 11 and 11P the amount of any Enterprise Allowance you have received, see p. 198.

26 · PARTNERS

A partnership can be a burden shared: the difficulties and the traumas of a business shouldered by two or more of you. But this sharing of obligations may prove to be illusory. What you must look for in a partnership is complete trust that your partner will fulfil your partnership agreement.

When it comes to income tax, this trust in each other is especially important. If your partner does not pay what is due, you will have to cough up for the whole of the partnership income tax bill. The moral is choose your partner carefully; you do not want to be left holding the tax bill (or any other bill).

This chapter outlines the basic tax rules which may be helpful to you if you are thinking of forming a partnership or if your partnership is very simple. If your affairs are at all complicated, you should consult your tax adviser.

BRIEF GUIDE TO TAX FOR PARTNERS

1 The figure for taxable income for the partnership is worked out in the same way as if you were in business on your own (p. 178). So you can deduct expenses, capital allowances, losses and half the Class 4 National Insurance contributions which the partnership pays.

2 The tax bill on the partnership profits is worked out for the partnership as a whole and is in the partnership name. Although the bill will be shared between the partners (see 7), each partner is liable to pay all of the bill. So, if your partner does not pay up, you can be made to cover the whole amount of tax due.

3 If the partnership has any non-trading income (for example, income from investments) or any capital gains, you are not responsible for the full amount of any tax due on it, as you are with the partnership profits. Instead you are responsible only for your share.

4 Profits are taxed on a preceding-year basis, that is, in the current

tax year, you are paying tax on profits earned in the accounting year ending in the previous tax year. But as far as your Tax Inspector is concerned, the profits are divided as you are dividing them in the current tax year, regardless of what happened in the previous year. So the taxman can assume a quite different share out of the profits from the one that actually happens.

5 Once your Tax Inspector has divided up the profits for tax purposes, the tax bill for each partner is worked out. This takes account of the rate of tax each partner is paying, for example, one of you could be paying tax at the basic rate and the other at 60 per cent.

6 The Tax Inspector tots up the tax for each partner and sends the partnership one tax bill to be paid for the total amount, with a separate memorandum account showing how the tax bill should be split between partners.

7 You and your partner may decide to share out the tax bill in quite different proportions from those assumed by your Tax Inspector.

8 If a new partner joins you and you sign a *continuation election* (p. 204), your Tax Inspector will apportion your new partner part of the profits earned before joining. If you do not sign this election, it is assumed that the existing partnership has ceased and the closing rules apply (p. 193).

9 The partnership tax bill is due to be paid in two equal instalments on 1 January and 1 July.

EXAMPLE

Joe Johnson and David Lock have been partners for several years. In the accounting year ending 31 December 1986, they share profits of £20,000 equally between them. From 1 January 1987, they agree that Joe will take three-quarters of the profits and David a quarter.

For the tax year 1987/8, their tax bill will be based on the profits of £20,000 (profits of the accounting year ending in the preceding tax year), but their Tax Inspector will assume a profit split of 3:1. It will be assumed that:

Joe has £15,000
David has £5,000

What actually happened is that those £20,000 profits were shared equally between them, that is, £10,000 each.

When the taxman works out the partnership tax bill, it is done by looking at the tax rates paid by Joe and David. For 1987/8, Joe pays tax at the basic rate, that is 27 per cent, and David at a higher rate 50 per cent (he has other income as well as from the partnership). Both are entitled to a married man's allowance of £3,795.

The tax due is:

$$27\% \text{ of } (£15,000 - £3,795) = £3,025$$
$$50\% \text{ of } (£5,000 - £3,795) = £\ \ 602.50$$

$$£3,627.50$$

The partnership will pay tax of £3,627.50 How the bill is divided between the two partners depends upon what they have agreed.

A PARTNER JOINS OR LEAVES

Either a partner leaving or a partner joining means that for tax purposes the business has ceased and the closing rules apply (p. 193). However, if at least one partner before and after the change is the same, you can sign a *continuation election* which means that the partnership will carry on paying tax on the normal preceding-year basis. To make this choice, all partners before and after the change have to sign the election. It must be made within two years of the change.

If you could make a continuation election but choose not to do so, the tax bills for the first four years of the new partnership are based on the actual profits made (p. 194). You can choose for both years five and six that the tax due is worked out on the actual profits rather than the preceding-year basis. You must make this choice within six years of the end of the sixth year of assessment of the new partnership.

For partnership changes before 20 March 1985, the new partnership was treated in the same way as if you had started on your own in self-employment (p. 193).

IF THE PARTNERSHIP MAKES A LOSS

You get tax relief for losses in the same way as if you were self-employed (p. 187). The loss is split among the partners in the same ratios as the profits would have been shared in the period covered by the accounts. Each of you can decide to treat your share of the loss in the way that suits you the best; you do not all have to make the same decision on how you will get tax relief for the loss.

PUTTING CAPITAL IN A PARTNERSHIP

You can get relief on a loan of any size which you use to buy a share in or make a loan to a partnership. But you can get the relief only if you

are an active partner yourself; that is, if you are a limited partner you
are not eligible.

WHAT TO PUT IN YOUR TAX RETURN

You enter much the same things as you would do if you were self-
employed and on your own (p. 197). But, if you are a partner, you
enter only your share of the profits.

Form 11P

Trade, profession or vocation		Self	Wife
Business name and address	Type of income	£	£
	Enterprise allowance	£	£
	Balancing charges	£	£
	Deductions for Capital Allowances	£	£
Deduction for Class 4 National Insurance Contributions enter 'X' here		▶ ☐	
If your profits for Class 4 National Insurance Contributions purposes are affected by interest paid, certain capital allowances or losses not given in the assessment, give details on a separate sheet and enter 'X' here		▶ ☐	

To claim tax relief on a loan, see above, you enter the details in the
OUTGOINGS section. With Forms 11 and 11P, the heading is *Interest
on other loans*; with Form P1, enter the details under *Other loan interest
paid*. Put the lender's name and the amount of interest you paid in the
tax year. You should be able to obtain a certificate of loan interest paid
from your lender. Enclose it with the Tax Return.

Form 11P

Interest on other loans *enclose certificates*	Self	Wife
Name of lender	£	£

27 · PENSIONS

It's hard when you're in the prime of life to start worrying about pensions and retirement. But there are two good reasons for even the youngest and most active to give some thought to that far-off day of retirement.

First, the earlier you start, the easier it is to provide for your old age. If you've neglected your pension in your twenties and thirties, you may still be able to catch up in your forties and fifties. But the cost will be high and the later you leave it, the higher it gets.

Secondly, the government offers handsome tax incentives to encourage you to provide for your retirement. This chapter begins by looking at the tax reliefs for people who pay into an employer's scheme. It tells you how you can get tax relief on contributions to a personal pension scheme if you are self-employed or do not belong to an employer's scheme. And it looks at the changes to the pension system in the pipeline and the new personal pension schemes to be introduced in early 1988.

For details of how pensions are taxed once you start drawing them, see Chapter 18, 'Retired – or Near Retirement Age', p. 126.

EMPLOYERS' PENSIONS

Employers' pension schemes vary considerably, but typically provide a pension in some way linked to your earnings before retirement (a *final pay* scheme). And most offer some or all of the following benefits: life insurance cover before you retire; a tax-free lump sum when you retire; and a widow's pension (even, occasionally, a widower's pension).

Employers' pensions and other retirement benefits are paid for out of a fund built up from contributions made by the employer and, except with non-contributory schemes, the employees. There are valuable tax incentives to encourage this form of saving for old age:

● there is tax relief on contributions to the pension scheme, for both the employer and the employee (within limits)

● the fund in which the money goes pays no income tax or capital gains tax, so that the return is tax-free (and certainly ought to be higher than what you could earn investing the money yourself and paying tax on profits and income)

● the pension you draw on retirement is taxed as earnings, not investment income (this is important for married women who can claim wife's earned income allowance to set against earned income but not investment income, see p. 91)

● you can take a substantial tax-free lump sum when you retire in lieu of some pension.

THE BENEFITS PAYABLE BY AN EMPLOYER'S PENSION SCHEME

The tax incentives mentioned above are available only for pension schemes which are approved by the Inland Revenue. Because the tax benefits are so great, almost all pension schemes are designed to fit the requirements for approval. The following are the most important:

● you can get a pension from the scheme of no more than 1/60th of your final salary for each year of service, up to a maximum of forty years' service, that is, the maximum pension is $\frac{40}{60}$ or two-thirds of final salary

● you can exchange part of this pension for a lump sum of $\frac{3}{80}$ of your final salary for each year of service, up to a maximum of forty years' service, that is, a maximum lump sum of $1\frac{1}{2}$ times your final salary (with an overall limit of £150,000 for people joining pension schemes from 17 March 1987 onwards)

● any payment for death in service (that is, life insurance cover) should not exceed four times yearly salary

● any widow's or widower's pension must not be more than two-thirds the pension the spouse would have got if still alive

● any pension paid to dependants following death in service must not be more than two-thirds of the amount a widow or widower would have got

● the total amount of pension which can be paid to your widow or widower and other dependants must not be more than the amount of pension you would have got if you had lived.

There are special rules for the maximum benefits payable to people who have less than forty years' service.

Usually, approved schemes allow pensions to be drawn from age sixty for a man, fifty-five for a woman. But earlier retirement dates are allowed where the job merits it, for example, jockeys and airline pilots can all draw pensions earlier (and qualify for full pensions with less than forty years' service). Early retirement on pension is also permitted in cases of ill-health and in certain other circumstances.

In fact, despite the maze of rules and precedents apparently restricting the options open to pension schemes, most employers' schemes fail to provide anything like as much as they could.

CONTRIBUTIONS

The amount you contribute to an employer's pension scheme is decided by your employer, but cannot exceed 15 per cent of your earnings. Provided the pension scheme is approved by the Inland Revenue, you can get tax relief at your highest rate of tax on these contributions. Your contributions will be deducted from your income before working out how much tax has to be paid under PAYE (though your National Insurance contributions are worked out on your full pay, that is, before deduction of pension contributions).

There are strict rules about the repayment of pension contributions to people who leave schemes before retirement: in general, repayment isn't possible unless you leave within five years of joining (to be reduced to two years from 6 April 1988 onwards).

ADDITIONAL VOLUNTARY CONTRIBUTIONS

Many pension schemes allow you to make extra pension contributions to improve the benefits you will get on retirement. You can get full tax relief on these Additional Voluntary Contributions (AVCs), provided that your total contributions to the pension scheme do not exceed 15 per cent of your earnings.

So if your pension contributions are 6 per cent of your salary, you can pay up to 9 per cent in AVCs (that is, 15 per cent – 6 per cent). Your AVCs will enjoy the same tax benefits as the rest of the pension fund, so should grow faster than if you invested the money yourself. But the money will normally be kept separate from the general fund of pension contributions; indeed, your employer may buy separate pension policies or open a deposit account to hold your AVCs (which still qualify for the tax benefits of the full pension fund).

You should be able to choose which of the retirement benefits is topped up by your AVCs (the lump sum, the pension itself or the widow's pension). But you cannot use AVCs to buy pension benefits greater than the maximums set by the Inland Revenue. So you can't increase your pension above two-thirds of final earnings.

Investing for your retirement through AVCs can be well worth doing if your employer's scheme doesn't pay the maximum benefits permitted by the Inland Revenue. And in the health service or local authorities, you can use AVCs to buy in past service (that is, make contributions for years of service in which you did not belong to the pension scheme). If you die before retirement, your AVCs will normally be repaid with interest.

From October 1987 onwards, you will be able to pay AVCs into a policy or account you choose yourself (you won't have to pay them into an employer's scheme). However, AVCs made after 7 April 1987 are now restricted to improving your pension benefits: you will no longer normally be able to make AVCs to increase your tax-free lump sum.

PERSONAL PENSION SCHEMES

Personal pension schemes (called *retirement annuities* by the taxman) offer tax benefits similar to those of an employer's pension scheme to two groups of people:

● the self-employed (including partners in a partnership)

● employees who do not belong to an employer's pension scheme, either because their employer doesn't have one, or, if there is one, they haven't joined it or can't join it (for example, if they don't work enough hours, or are too old to contribute).

Even if you do belong to an employer's pension scheme, you may still be able to contribute to a personal pension scheme if you have another source of earnings which is not pensionable. For example, if you have a spare-time job which has no pension, or you have some freelance earnings, you could take out a personal pension scheme even though you belong to a pension scheme at your main work.

HOW PERSONAL PENSION SCHEMES WORK

Personal pension schemes are sold by insurance companies (and will soon be available from banks, friendly societies, building societies and unit trust managers). When you take one out, you choose to pay either regular fixed contributions or one-off lump sums. The money is invested on your behalf by the company, and growth in the fund is free of income tax and capital tax (as with employers' pension funds). When you want to draw your pension, the fund which has been accumulated on your behalf is used to buy an annuity. This provides a regular income which is taxed as earnings rather than investment income (so a married woman can set wife's earned income allowance against it).

You do not have to decide the age at which you wish to draw benefits when you take out your personal pension scheme. However, the Inland Revenue specify that this must be some time between your sixtieth and seventy-fifth birthday (the lower limit will be reduced to fifty for new schemes from 4 January 1988 onwards). But you don't have to stop work to draw the income.

People in occupations where early retirement is the norm (such as sportsmen and entertainers) can draw their benefits earlier, as with employers' schemes. In practice, most companies allow you to vary the date at which you draw the pension as long as you stay within the age limits laid down by the Inland Revenue.

When you draw the benefits, the income you get depends on the amount of your contributions and the level of annuity rates at the time you draw the pension. Thus there is no guarantee that the pension you get will bear any relation to your income before retirement. Many companies guarantee to pay a fixed minimum pension when you take out the scheme, whatever the level of annuity rates, so that you can plan on getting at least that much. And with most personal pension schemes, you don't have to buy the annuity from the company you paid the premiums to: you have an *open market option* to shop around for the best annuity you can get.

As with employers' pension schemes, you can trade in some pension for a tax-free lump sum. You can take a tax-free lump sum of up to three times the pension the remainder of the fund will buy. But for schemes taken out after 17 March 1987, the maximum amount of the tax-free lump sum is one-quarter of the fund accumulated by your contributions with an upper limit of £150,000.

LIFE INSURANCE

If you die before drawing any benefits from a personal pension scheme, you'll normally get back the premiums you've paid, usually with interest. You can arrange with the company for this to be paid direct to your spouse, avoiding inheritance tax on the proceeds and reducing the delay before he or she gets the money (p. 307).

Return of premiums, with or without interest, is unlikely to be enough to provide for your dependants if you die before retirement. So if you are eligible to take out a personal pension scheme, you can also take out a special type of life insurance policy which pays out either a lump sum or an income for your dependants if you die before your planned retirement age. Full tax relief is available within limits on premiums paid on these Section 226A policies (named after the relevant section of the Taxes Act). Again, you should consider writing these policies in trust for your dependants so that there is no inheritance tax to pay on the proceeds.

CONTRIBUTIONS

The maximum personal pension contributions you can get tax relief on is a percentage of your *net relevant earnings*. A husband and wife each have their own net relevant earnings and their own allowance for tax relief. Net relevant earnings are defined as follows:

● if you're an employee, your earnings from non-pensionable jobs (including the taxable value of fringe benefits), less any allowable expenses (p. 135)

● if you're self-employed, your taxable profits (p. 179), less certain payments made by your business after deduction of tax (for example, patent royalties, covenant payments).

Until 5 April 1987, the percentage of your net relevant earnings which you could get tax relief on depended on your date of birth. If you were born in 1934 or later, the maximum you could pay into personal pension schemes was $17\frac{1}{2}$ per cent of your net relevant earnings. If you were born in 1933 or earlier, you could get tax relief on a higher percentage, as follows:

BORN	MAXIMUM PAYMENTS QUALIFYING FOR TAX RELIEF	
	1982–3 tax year onwards	*1980–81 and 1981–2 tax years*
1916–33	20%	$17\frac{1}{2}$%
1914 or 1915	21%	$20\frac{1}{2}$%
1912 or 1913	24%	$23\frac{1}{2}$%

From 6 April 1987 onwards, the percentage of net relevant earnings on which you can claim tax relief depends on your age, as follows:

50 or under	$17\frac{1}{2}$%
51–55	20 %
56–60	$22\frac{1}{2}$%
61–75	$27\frac{1}{2}$%

Payments for Section 226A life insurance policies also qualify for tax relief at your top rate of tax, provided they are 5 per cent of your net relevant earnings or less. But the amount you pay for such life insurance policies is deducted from your allowance for pension scheme payments. For example, if you are entitled to tax relief on personal pension scheme payments of up to £1,000 in a tax year, and you pay Section 226A life insurance policy premiums of £250, the maximum you can get tax relief on for personal pension payments is £1,000 − £250 = £750.

EXAMPLE

Lydia Naismith earns £28,000 a year from a job which has no pension scheme. She is thirty-five and entitled to tax relief at her top rate of tax on personal pension contributions of up to $17\frac{1}{2}$ per cent of her net pensionable earnings.

To work out her net relevant earnings, Lydia adds the £28,000 salary to the value of her fringe benefits (£1,100) and deducts any allowable expenses she can claim (£100). Thus her net relevant earnings are £28,000 + £1,100 − £100 = £29,000.

So Lydia can get tax relief on pension contributions of $17\frac{1}{2}$ per cent of £29,000, that is, on contributions of up to £5,075. If her top rate of tax is 45 per cent, her tax bill will be reduced by 45 per cent of £5,075, that is, £2,284. So £5,075 of contributions will cost Lydia only £2,791 after allowing for the tax relief.

BACKDATING PERSONAL PENSION CONTRIBUTIONS

If you make contributions to a personal pension scheme in one tax year and you paid less than the maximum you were entitled to get tax relief on in the previous year, you can opt to have some or all of the contributions treated as if they were made in that preceding year. If you had no net relevant earnings in the preceding tax year (because you made a loss in your business, or had no non-pensionable earnings), you can backdate the contributions a further tax year.

Suppose, for example, that you were entitled to make personal pension contributions of up to £4,000 in 1986/7, but made contributions of only £2,000. That leaves £2,000 of unused relief and you could backdate up to £2,000 of contributions made during the next tax year (1987/8) to the 1986/7 tax year. You might want to do this if you'd exceeded your allowance for 1987/8, or because your top rate of tax in 1986/7 was higher than in 1987/8.

To claim backdating, tell the taxman on or before 5 July following the end of the tax year in which you make the contributions. In the example above, the payments to be backdated are made in 1987/8, and the taxman would have to be notified by 5 July following the end of the 1987/8 tax year, that is 5 July 1988.

UNUSED RELIEF FROM THE LAST SIX YEARS

If you've used up all your tax relief for the tax year, you can still get tax relief on further contributions in that year if you've unused relief from the previous six tax years. This can be used in one of two ways:

● to make a one-off bigger-than-normal contribution in one tax year, drawing on previous years' unused allowances to make a contribution over the tax relief limit for that year

● to continue making regular contributions in years in which your non-pensionable income fluctuates below the level to permit such a contribution.

Unused relief from the earliest years is used first, as the following Example shows.

EXAMPLE

Linton Johnson's net relevant earnings over the past six complete tax years are as set out in the second column of the Table below. He is forty-five, so is entitled to tax relief on personal pension contributions of 17½ per cent of his net relevant earnings in each of those years (the figures are given in the third column of the Table).

TAX YEAR	NET RELEVANT EARNINGS	MAXIMUM PREMIUM	PREMIUM PAID	UNUSED RELIEF
	£	£	£	£
1981/2	10,000	1,750	1,200	550
1982/3	8,000	1,400	1,200	200
1983/4	10,000	1,750	1,200	550
1984/5	12,000	2,100	1,200	900
1985/6	14,000	2,450	1,800	650
1986/7	13,000	2,275	1,800	475

The fourth column of the table shows the pension contributions Linton made during those six years: for four of the years, he paid £100 a month (£1,200 a year); emboldened by improving results, he increased that to £150 a month in 1985/6 (£1,800 a year). In none of the six years have his premiums been greater than the amount on which he is entitled to tax relief, and so there is a total of £3,325 in unused tax relief for the past six complete tax years. This provides a useful cushion for 1987/8:

● if Linton's net relevant earnings fell below £10,000, he could continue to make personal pension contributions of £1,800 a year. Even though the maximum premium for that year should be less than £1,800, he could use some or all of the unused £550 from 1982/3 (and if that were insufficient, unused relief from 1983/4 and later years)

● even if Linton's net relevant earnings were over £10,000 (that is, more than enough to qualify for tax relief on £1,800 of premiums), he could draw on the unused relief from the previous six years to make a once-for-all lump sum contribution in 1987/8 of as much as £3,325, plus any unused relief for the 1987/8 tax year. However, the full current year's entitlement must be paid before any unused relief is taken up.

Note that unlike the backdating procedure outlined earlier, where the surplus premium is set off against tax at the top rate paid in the previous year, claiming unused relief for the past six years brings the allowance forward to the current tax year and gives tax relief at that year's top rate only. The maximum contributions limits for 1980/1 onwards are given on p. 211 to help you see whether you could claim any unused relief from earlier years.

CLAIMING THE TAX RELIEF

When you take out a personal pension scheme, the insurance company will send you a Self-Employed Premium Certificate (SEPC). Send this to your tax office to claim the tax relief.

If you make regular contributions, there'll be no further SEPC unless you alter the amount you pay. The details you enter on your Tax Return are all that the taxman needs. If you pay tax under PAYE, your PAYE code can be adjusted to give you the tax relief through lower tax deductions from your earnings (p. 138).

For personal pensions taken out from 4 January 1988 onwards employees will get tax relief on their contributions by paying them net of basic-rate tax – the pension company will claim the tax back from the Inland Revenue. So if the basic rate of tax is 27 per cent and you contribute £1,000 to a personal pension scheme, you would hand over £730 (£1,000 less 27 per cent of £1,000). The pension company would reclaim the £270 tax relief from the Inland Revenue. If you were entitled to higher-rate tax relief, you would have to claim it from your Tax Inspector.

If you are self-employed, you will continue to pay the full amount and get the tax relief when your tax bill is worked out.

THE NEW PENSION ARRANGEMENTS

From 4 January 1988, tax relief will be available on a new type of personal pension scheme for employees who contract out of the state earnings-related pension. The new personal pension schemes will also be open to employees who leave their employer's pension scheme or who belong to an employer's scheme which pays out pensions only for widows and dependants.

THE NEW PERSONAL PENSION SCHEMES

The new personal pension schemes will be offered by banks, building societies and unit trusts as well as insurance companies who currently offer personal pension plans (these newcomers will also be able to offer the existing personal pension schemes). If you take one out, you and your employer will have to make a minimum contribution towards it, equal to the extra National Insurance contributions payable if you do not belong to a contracted-out pension scheme. You'll get tax relief on this *NI rebate* (6.25 per cent of your earnings until 5 April 1988, then 5.8 per cent), and the government will add an extra 2 per cent until April 1993 (unless you have been in an employer's pension scheme for a reasonable period).

These minimum contributions will build up a fund which you use on retirement to buy an annuity providing a pension for you only. The income you get from the annuity must increase by 3 per cent a year or the rate of inflation if lower.

There will also be tax relief on contributions you and your employer make in addition to the NI rebate minimum. Any extra contributions can be made to the same company which provides the policy for the minimum contributions, or another company. These additional schemes can top up the minimum plan or provide extra benefits (for example, a pension for a spouse after you die). But the total contributions made by you and your employer must not exceed the following percentage of your net relevant earnings:

50 or under	$17\frac{1}{2}\%$
51–55	20%
56–60	$22\frac{1}{2}\%$
61–75	$27\frac{1}{2}\%$

The new personal pension contributions can be backdated against the previous tax year's earnings and unused relief can be carried forward for up to six tax years, as for the old personal pension contributions.

CLAIMING THE TAX RELIEF

Employees making contributions to the new personal pension schemes will get tax relief on their contributions by paying them net of basic-rate tax – the pension company will claim the tax back from the Inland Revenue.

So if the basic rate of tax is 27 per cent and you contribute £1,000 to a new personal pension scheme, you would hand over £730 (£1,000 less 27 per cent of £1,000). The pension company would reclaim the £270 tax relief from the Inland Revenue. If you are entitled to higher-rate tax relief, you will have to claim it from your Tax Inspector.

WHAT TO PUT IN YOUR TAX RETURN

There is normally no need to enter details of contributions made to an employer's pension scheme on your Tax Return. The figures you enter from your P60 for earnings from full-time employment are your before-tax earnings after deduction of pension contributions (unless the pension scheme is not approved by the Inland Revenue).

But you will have to give details of any contributions made to a personal pension scheme or Section 226A life insurance policy. With Forms 11 and 11P, enter details on the Tax Return under *Retirement annuity payments* in the ALLOWANCES section.

Form 11P

Fill in details of the source of the non-pensionable earnings: if self-employed, the nature of your business (the same as you entered when giving details of your taxable profits, see p. 197); if in a non-pensionable employment, give the name and address of the employer (again, as already entered when giving details of the earnings, see p. 149).

You'll also have to give details of the schemes themselves: if there's not enough room on the Form, draw up a list on a separate sheet of paper, attach it to the Return and enter 'See attached schedule' in the box asking for details of the company. Give the name of the company running the personal pension scheme and your contract or membership number (you'll find this in the policy document the insurance company gives you), the amount of contributions paid during the tax year just ended and the amount you expect to pay during the coming tax year. Give your year of birth; tick the box to get a Form 43 which you'll need if any of the following applies:

● your wife makes contributions to a personal pension scheme – there's no space to enter details of these on the Tax Return

● you want to backdate some or all of the contributions made in the tax year just completed

● you are claiming unused relief from the past six complete tax years.

With Form PI, there's no space to enter details about personal pension contributions, so attach a note to the Tax Return giving the details listed above.

If by any chance you haven't yet sent off the SEPC to the taxman, send it with the Tax Return.

28 · HOME

When it comes to spending money, buying a home is probably the biggest purchase you are likely to make. It is also likely to be a pretty good investment: over the past twenty years average house prices have risen at a yearly rate of 12 per cent. And there are two important tax incentives to encourage you to buy your own home:

● you can get tax relief (within limits) on interest you pay on a loan to buy your only or main home

● you won't have to pay capital gains tax on the proceeds of selling your only or main home.

This chapter looks at these two incentives and how to get the most out of them. For details of what happens if you let property, see the next chapter, 'Property', p. 230.

MORTGAGE INTEREST TAX RELIEF

You can get tax relief at your top rate of tax on interest you pay on loans of £30,000 or less to buy or improve your only or main home. So if you borrow money to buy a home at, say, 12 per cent, tax relief at the basic rate of 27 per cent can reduce the net rate of interest to 8.76 per cent. Higher-rate taxpayers do even better: tax relief at 60 per cent reduces a 12 per cent interest rate to 4.8 per cent net.

But to get the tax relief there are strict conditions to be met about what you spend the money on, the sorts of loans which qualify and what counts as your only or main home.

WHICH LOANS CAN YOU GET TAX RELIEF ON?

The relief is available on loans to buy a house or flat, leasehold or freehold, located in the UK or Republic of Ireland. Loans for a house-boat designed to be used as a home are also eligible. And loans for a caravan (or mobile home) can qualify for tax relief if any of the following conditions are met:

● the caravan is over 22ft long (excluding the drawbar)

● the caravan is over 7½ft wide

● you pay rates on it as occupier.

You can still get tax relief if part of the loan is used to pay the costs of buying the home. This would include stamp duty, valuation and survey fees, legal costs and insurance premiums (for example, for a mortgage indemnity policy). And if the loan is increased to cover buildings insurance premiums or unpaid interest, you can get tax relief on the extra interest paid on up to £1,000 added to the original loan (or twelve months' arrears, if greater).

The loan doesn't have to be a mortgage secured on your home for you to get tax relief on the interest. Interest on personal loans from banks and other lenders qualifies as long as the loans are used to buy or improve the home. But you won't get tax relief for interest on a bank overdraft or credit card debts – even if incurred on your home. And there's no tax relief if the loan has to be repaid within a year of being taken out (unless it's from a bank, stockbroker or discount house).

Note that the loan must be spent within a reasonable time of getting it. This is generally taken to be within six months on either side of the loan.

IMPROVEMENTS

Relief is also available on interest paid on loans for improvements to your only or main home. All permanent improvements to the building or land around it, including the adjoining roads, qualify. The following usually fall into this definition:

● extensions and loft conversions

● damp-proofing and treatment of dry rot, wet rot or woodworm

● insulation of walls or roof, or double-glazing

● installing or replacing central heating (but not portable radiators or night storage heaters), bathrooms, showers and mains drainage

● rewiring

- installing fitted furniture (for example, kitchen or bedroom units)

- building a garage, garden shed, greenhouse or fence

- making up, sewering or lighting adjoining roads

- building a swimming pool or sauna, or landscaping gardens

- laying driveways, patios and paths

- installing fire and burglar alarms.

Routine maintenance and repairs do not count as improvements, so while recovering a roof completely will probably qualify, replacing a few slipped slates or cracked tiles will not. Extensive repointing, comprehensive replacement of guttering, underpinning the walls and re-wiring can also qualify, but not minor work on these items. But if only a small part of the loan is spent on repairs and maintenance, in practice the taxman will give you tax relief on all the interest paid. And if you buy a home which has been neglected, you can get tax relief on work necessary to make it good.

MORE THAN ONE HOME?

Tax relief is restricted to interest on loans to buy or improve your only or main home. This is normally the one you live in for most of the time.

You can, however, get tax relief on loans for a home which you aren't living in as your main home if any of the following applies:

- you are temporarily absent from the home for a period of up to a year

- you are required to be away from home by your employer, provided the absence is expected to last no more than four years. If the absence lasts longer, you lose the tax relief from then on only (and if you move back for at least three months, additional such absence of up to four years is allowed)

- you live in *job-related accommodation* (that is, a home you must live in by the nature of your job, see p. 159). You can go on getting the tax relief indefinitely on your own home, provided you intend to live in it eventually

- you are self-employed and have to live in job-related accommodation (for example, over the shop or at the club). Again, you can go on getting the tax relief on your own home, provided you intend to live in it eventually.

You can also get tax relief on a second home in the year in which you get married (p. 98).

A HOME FOR AN EX-SPOUSE OR DEPENDENT RELATIVE

You can get tax relief on a loan to buy or improve a home which you own and is the only or main residence of your former husband or wife, or one from whom you are separated (whether by court order, deed of separation or in any other way which seems likely to be permanent).

And you can also get tax relief on a loan to buy a home which will be the only or main home of one of the following types of 'dependent relative':

● your mother or mother-in-law if widowed, separated or divorced

● any relative of yours or your husband or wife who is unable to look after him or herself because of permanent illness, disablement or old age (over sixty-four at the start of the tax year). The dependent relative must live in the home rent-free.

HOW MUCH RELIEF?

You can get tax relief on interest you pay for loans of £30,000 or less which qualify for tax relief. If you are married, the limit for both of you together remains £30,000. But two single people who share a home can each qualify for tax relief on loans of £30,000, that is, on £60,000 in all. Single in this case includes widowed, divorced and separated people.

If you borrow more than £30,000, you get the tax relief on the first £30,000. With a single loan over £30,000 you get tax relief on the following proportion of the interest you pay:

$$\frac{£30,000}{\text{Amount of loan}}$$

For example, if your loan is £40,000, the proportion of interest on which you get tax relief is:

$$\frac{£30,000}{£40,000} = \frac{3}{4}$$

If you miss some interest payments (or don't increase your payments when the mortgage rate goes up), your loan could creep up above £30,000. You will continue to get tax relief on all the interest you pay as long as no more than £1,000 of interest is added to the loan.

MORE THAN ONE LOAN

You can get tax relief on several different qualifying loans, provided they add up to £30,000 or less. If they add up to more than 30,000, you get the tax relief on the earliest loans first, up to the £30,000 limit. Thus, if you are getting two or more loans to buy a home (for example, a mortgage plus a top-up loan) and they take you over the £30,000 limit, make sure that you arrange to get the loan with the higher interest rate at least a day before the less expensive one.

Note that there is an exception to this general rule for interest-free loans which you get from your employer as a fringe benefit. Even if you get such a loan first, later loans for things which would entitle you to claim tax relief are counted first towards the £30,000 limit. There's an example of how this works in Chapter 20, 'Employees: Fringe Benefits', p. 159.

EXAMPLE

Fiona Quin bought a house three years ago with a £25,000 endowment mortgage (so that none of the loan has been repaid). This year she borrowed another £10,000 to build an extension.

Fiona gets tax relief on all the interest she pays on the first loan, because it is less than the £30,000 limit. But the second loan takes her total over £30,000, so she will get tax relief on only part of the interest on it. The proportion on which she will get tax relief is worked out as follows.

Since Fiona is already getting tax relief on the £25,000 first loan, that leaves £30,000 − £25,000 = £5,000 of the second loan which qualifies for tax relief on the interest paid. The proportion of interest paid on the second loan on which she gets tax relief is

$$\frac{£5,000}{£10,000} = \frac{1}{2}$$

So Fiona will get tax relief on only half the interest paid on the second loan.

MOVING HOME

If you take out a *bridging loan* to buy a new home before you have sold your old one, you can get tax relief on the interest for up to £30,000 of the bridging loan, as well as on £30,000 of loans on your old home. This second lot of tax relief is available for up to twelve months (longer if your Tax Inspector thinks that the delay is not unreasonable). It doesn't matter which of the homes you live in during the transitional period, but the second lot of relief will be taken back if you do not move into the new home at the end of the bridging period.

Newly-weds can get tax relief on *three* loans if they are moving into a joint home and selling the two homes they lived in when single (p. 98).

HOW YOU WILL GET THE TAX RELIEF

Most people get basic-rate tax relief on mortgage interest automatically by making reduced payments to the lender. This system is known as mortgage interest relief at source (MIRAS), and means that if £100 interest is due on your mortgage, you pay £100 less tax relief at the basic rate. So if the basic rate is 27 per cent, the tax relief on £100 is £27, and you pay a net amount of £100 − £27 = £73. The Inland Revenue pays the £27 of basic-rate tax relief direct to the lender – and if you pay tax at the basic rate only, you've had the tax relief you're entitled to.

If you pay tax at the higher rates, you will have to claim the extra tax relief you're due direct from the taxman. The tax relief will be given by a lower PAYE code if you are employed (p. 138) or by a lower tax bill if you are self-employed (p. 191). On the other hand, if you're not entitled to tax relief (because you pay little or no tax), you *won't* have to hand back the relief you've had through MIRAS.

Most building societies, banks, local authorities, insurance companies and other deposit-takers operate the MIRAS system, though it doesn't apply to interest on loans which are only partly for qualifying purposes. If the loans exceed £30,000 MIRAS gives you tax relief for interest on £30,000 of the loans. And if the loans over £30,000 were taken out before 6 April 1987, they come into the MIRAS scheme only if you ask the lender to operate the scheme on your loans *and* the lender agrees.

If you aren't getting basic-rate tax relief through the MIRAS scheme, you will have to claim it direct from the taxman. You'll need a certificate of interest from the lender if you want to claim tax relief from the taxman.

CAPITAL GAINS TAX ON HOMES

If you sell most types of investment (including property) for more than you paid for them, there may be capital gains tax to pay (see Chapter 33, 'Capital Gains Tax', p. 275). But if you sell your only or main home, or a home which a dependent relative lives in, there is normally no capital gains tax to pay.

However, there may be capital gains tax to pay on your home in certain circumstances, for example, if you use it for business or leave it for prolonged periods. And if you own more than one home, only one of them can be free of capital gains tax. If you do have to pay CGT on selling a home, it can mean a hefty tax bill, given the growth in house prices over recent years.

WHAT KIND OF HOME IS FREE OF CGT?

Your only or main home is free of capital gains tax. This applies whether it is a house or flat, freehold or leasehold, and wherever in the world it is situated.

If you live in a caravan or houseboat, there's normally no capital gains tax to pay on it, even if it is not your only or main home. Like other tangible movable property which is a wasting asset, a caravan or houseboat is already free from CGT (p. 277). But if you own the land on which a caravan stands, you might have to pay CGT if you sell it, unless the caravan was your only or main home.

You must occupy the home exclusively as your residence if it is to be free of capital gains tax. If part of the home is used for work or business, you may have to pay tax on part of the gain (p. 227). And letting out some or all of your home can mean a capital gains tax bill. For details, see the next chapter, 'Property', p. 239.

Note that if you regularly buy and sell houses for profit (for example, doing up unmodernized homes for resale), you might have to pay CGT on the gain, even though you live in the home while you own it. If you do it on such a scale that you are classified as a dealer in land, you will be liable to income tax on the profits.

IF YOU OWN MORE THAN ONE HOME

If you own more than one home, your main home will be free of capital gains tax and there'll be capital gains tax to pay on any other home you own when you come to sell it. But you can choose which of your homes is to be free of CGT as your main main home: it doesn't have to be the one you live in most of the time, or the one on which you get mortgage interest tax relief.

So you should work out which home is likely to make the largest gain and nominate it as your main home for CGT purposes. You must make your choice within two years of buying the second home: tell your Tax Inspector in writing. If you want to change your mind, you can do this at any time, backdating the change up to two years. Again, write and tell the taxman both that you wish to change your choice and when you want the change to operate from.

If you haven't nominated which is your main home, the Inspector of Taxes will decide probably on the basis of which home you spend the most time at. You can appeal against this decision in the normal way (p. 77), but you will have to prove that the Inspector's decision was wrong, that is, that the other home really was your main one.

So if you get married and keep the two homes you owned before the wedding, make sure that you nominate which is to be your main home within the two-year limit. And if you live in a home which you do not own because of your job, nominate the home that you own as your main one if you want to avoid paying CGT on it.

AWAY FROM HOME

If you don't live in your home for some or all of the time that you own it, you might have to pay CGT when you sell it, even though it is the only home you own or you have nominated it as your main home. Normally, you will have to pay tax on a proportion of the taxable gain, found by *time apportionment* as follows:

$$\frac{\text{Number of complete months of absence}}{\text{Number of complete months of ownership}}$$

But you won't have to pay capital gains tax for periods of absence if you are away for any of the following reasons (even if you let the home out while you are away):

● you or your spouse live in job-related accommodation (p. 159). Provided you intend to live in your home at some time in the future, you won't have to pay CGT, even if you never get round to living in the home (if you sell it while still living in the job-related accommodation, say). But you will have to pay CGT for periods living in job-related accommodation before 31 July 1978

● you or your spouse are required to work away from home by your employer. There is no CGT to pay for periods of absence, however long, working entirely abroad and absences totalling up to four years while working elsewhere in the UK. But you must have lived in the home before the job took you away and return to it afterwards (unless prevented by the job)

● you have just bought the home and haven't moved in because *either* it needs modernizing or rebuilding *or* you can't sell your old home.

There is no CGT to pay for the first year of ownership (longer if you can persuade the Tax Inspector that it is necessary), so long as you eventually move in

● you are about to sell the home and move out for whatever reason (including having a new home which you have nominated as your main one). Any gain over the last two years of ownership is free of CGT, provided you have lived in the home at some time before selling it

● any other absences totalling up to three years, provided you live in the home both before the first absence and after the last.

You can add together some or all of these reasons to make longer periods of absence which are free of capital gains tax.

EXAMPLE

Martin O'Grady bought a house in July 1970 and moved into it three months later after getting married. In February 1973 his employer sent him on an overseas posting lasting until February 1976. On Martin's return to the UK, his employer sent him to work away from home until February 1984. He lived in the home until October 1984, when he bought a new home near his next posting. Martin eventually sold his old home in February 1987.

There are four absences from the home totalling twelve years during the more than sixteen years Martin has owned the home. But much of these absences will not be taken into account in deciding whether CGT will be due on the gain made when the home was sold:

● July 1970 to October 1970 – these three months are free of CGT as part of the first year of ownership

● February 1973 to February 1976 – these three years are tax-free as a period of employment entirely abroad (however lengthy)

● February 1976 to February 1984 – four years of the eight years are tax-free as a period of employment elsewhere in the UK

● October 1984 to February 1987 – two years of the two years and four months are tax-free as part of the last two years of ownership.

Four of the years between February 1976 and February 1984 are not free of CGT under the working away from home in the UK rule. But because Martin returned to live in the home afterwards, three of these years of absence are tax-free under the 'any other absences' provision.

So only one of the four years during that period counts for CGT purposes.

To that one year must be added the four months between October 1984 and February 1987 which are also not free of capital gains tax. That means that just one year and four months (16 months) out of sixteen years and seven months (199 months) are taxable. So $\frac{16}{199}$ of the gain will be taxable.

HOMES OWNED BEFORE 1965

Capital gains tax was introduced with effect from 6 April 1965, so even where CGT is due on the sale of a home, only the gain since that date is taxable (see p. 282 for how this gain is is calculated).

If only part of the period since 1965 is taxable (because you lived in the home for part of the time, say), then the time apportionment calculation mentioned on p. 225 is amended as follows:

$$\frac{\text{Months of ownership since 6 April 1965 not free of CGT}}{\text{Total number of months of ownership since 6 April 1965}}$$

YOUR GARDEN

Freedom from capital gains tax applies to both your home and garden. But there are rules to stop people taking advantage of this to avoid capital gains tax on dealing in land.

For a start, if the area of your home and garden exceeds one acre in area, there may be tax to pay on the gain you make on the excess. The gain on the excess will be tax-free only if you can convince the Inspector of Taxes that a garden over one acre is appropriate for the home (for example, if it is a Capability Brown garden designed for the house).

If the area of the home and garden is less than an acre, you can sell part of the garden without having to pay capital gains tax. But if you divide the garden to build a second home which you sell off, there could be tax to pay on the gain. And if you sell the home and keep some of the land, there may be capital gains tax to pay when you eventually sell the land.

WORKING FROM HOME

If any part of your home is used exclusively for work, there may be a capital gains tax bill when you sell the home. This applies to both work for your own business (that is, if you are self-employed) and work for an employer.

So if you use one or more rooms entirely for business (as an office or workshop, for example), there will be tax to pay on a proportion of the gain when you come to sell the home. You will have to agree the proportion with the Tax Inspector, who may use one of the following yardsticks:

● the number of rooms used

● the floor area used

● the rateable value of the part used exclusively for business

● the market value of the part used exclusively.

If you claim a proportion of the rates and rent as business expenses (p. 182) or as expenses of employment (p. 136), the same proportion of the gain is likely to be taxable. But in modest cases you may be able to persuade your Inspector of Taxes to allow you the expenses without a CGT bill.

Even when tax has to be paid on a proportion of the gain from selling a home which has been partly used for work, the taxable gain will be reduced by indexation allowance (p. 280). No tax is due on gains under the tax-free limit (£6,600 for 1987/8, £6,300 for 1986/7). The tax can be deferred if you buy another home also partly used for business (see *roll-over relief* on p. 286). And if you are sixty or over when you sell the home, you may be able to claim *retirement relief* (p. 288).

WHAT TO PUT IN YOUR TAX RETURN

You have to give details of property loans in the OUTGOINGS section of the Tax Return. Information on loans to buy or improve your only or main home (including bridging loans) and on homes for dependent relatives should be given under *Interest on loans for the purchase or improvement of property, Loans for only or main residence* on Forms 11 and 11P.

With loans from building societies, you need give only the name of the society and the account number you'll find on mortgage statements. Tick the box if interest isn't paid under MIRAS. You must also enter details of any building society mortgage paid off during the last tax year.

With all other loans, enter the names of the lenders, the account numbers and the amounts paid in the tax year. If the loans were outside the MIRAS system (that is, not paid net of tax relief), you will have to send a certificate of interest paid, which the lender should give you.

Form 11P

Interest on loans for the purchase or improvement of property in the UK
Do not include bank overdrafts

Loans for only or main residence

Building society loan at 5/4/87 *Do not put amounts*

Name of society	Account number	Please tick box if you did not pay under the net interest arrangements (MIRAS) ▶

Building society loan paid off in year to 5/4/87 *Do not put amounts*

Name of society	Account number	Please tick box if you did not pay under the net interest arrangements (MIRAS) ▶

All other lenders *Include amounts*

Name(s) of lender(s)	Account number(s)	Self £	Wife £

If all interest is paid net, enclose an interest certificate **only** where you claim tax relief for rates higher than basic rate. Always enclose an interest certificate if you paid any interest outside the MIRAS arrangements.

You'll also need to send in such a certificate if the loan is under MIRAS but you are claiming higher-rate tax relief.

With Form P1, enter similar details in the OUTGOINGS section under *Interest on loans for buying or improving your home.*

You should also enter details of any purchases or sales of homes under *Capital gains*, see p. 289.

29 · PROPERTY

House prices have steadily out-performed many other types of investment in recent years so that investing in property has become increasingly attractive. And with a shortage of rented accommodation on the market, property owners can hope to earn a useful return in the form of rents, in addition to a profit when the property is eventually sold.

This chapter explains how income from property is taxed, whether it comes from letting out shops or offices, renting out your home while you are away from it, taking in lodgers or providing holiday accommodation. And it outlines the capital gains tax rules for let property.

TYPES OF LEASE

The tax rules in some cases depend on the type of lease which is involved. The following definitions should be borne in mind when reading the rest of this chapter:

● *full-rent lease* is one which brings in enough income to cover the expenses and interest over the years. You might make a loss in one year, but as long as over the longer term the income exceeds the outgoings, the lease can be a full-rent one

● *tenant's repairing lease* is one where the tenant is responsible for the repairs to the property (or at least most of the repairs).

INCOME FROM LAND AND PROPERTY

Most income from land or property is taxed as investment income under Schedule A. This includes rents from letting property or land, ground rent, feu duties and premiums on leases. But it excludes the following:

● income from furnished property, such as furnished flats and houses, and holiday accommodation is taxed under Schedule D Case VI

● income from a hotel or guest house is taxed as earned income under

Schedule D Case I (that is, as business income, see Chapter 24, 'The Self-Employed', p. 178).

● income from land and property abroad is taxed as investment income under Schedule D Case V.

Under Schedule A you are normally taxed on the income you are entitled to receive (whether or not you have actually received it), less certain allowable expenses. You may also be able to deduct interest paid on a loan to buy or improve the property from your rental income before working out your tax bill. And losses from letting out property may be deductible in certain circumstances.

ALLOWABLE EXPENSES

Allowable expenses can be deducted from rental income before calculating your tax bill. In general, you must deduct the expenses for a particular property from the rental income from that property only. But if you let out two or more properties at full rent which are not on tenant's repairing leases, you can set the expenses of one against the income from another.

The following expenses normally count as allowable:

● maintenance and repairs, including redecoration of the property while it is let. Repairs when the property is not let are allowable only if carried out while it is empty between lettings at full rent (unless it is a newly bought property)

● insurance premiums on policies which cover your liabilities as property owner and the buildings against perils like fire and flood (you can also claim the cost of valuations for insurance)

● management costs, including the costs of rent collection, legal and accountancy fees, stationery, phone bills and salaries

● costs of letting, including advertising, estate agents' fees or accommodation agency fees

● costs of maintaining common parts of let property, including heating, lighting, porterage, gardening and cleaning

● payments you make for rent (if sub-letting), ground rent, rates and water rates

● expenditure on the upkeep of an estate, if for the benefit of tenants (for example, on roads, drains and ditches)

● capital allowances on any equipment you buy for the upkeep of the property (for example, lawnmowers, cleaning equipment)

● any other payments you make as part of the agreement with the tenant, including gardening, gas and electricity (less any amounts you recharge to the tenant and money from slot meters).

If only part of a property is let out (one floor of your house, say), then only a proportion of the expenses incurred on the whole property will be allowable. For example, if you let out half your house, then only half the rates and water rates would normally be allowable expenses.

There are special rules for the expenses which you can claim on furnished lettings (p. 235).

EXPENSES WHICH ARE NOT ALLOWABLE

The following expenses cannot normally be deducted from rental income as allowable expenses:

● the cost of your own time, though you can claim the cost of wages and salaries paid to other people for managing the property (a husband could pay his wife to do this work, and the payments would be treated as her earnings)

● the cost of improvements, additions or alterations to the property

● depreciation for wear and tear on the property

● payments to tenants for moving out of the property.

INTEREST

If you take out a loan to buy or improve property in the UK or Republic of Ireland which you let out, you can get tax relief on the interest. The interest you pay can be set off against any income from letting property (but not against other sources of income). There is no limit on the size of the loan and it doesn't count towards the £30,000 limit for your only or main home (see Chapter 28, 'Home', p. 221). If the interest is more than your property income in any tax year, you can carry forward the excess to later years as long as you still own the property on which the loan was used.

To qualify, the loan must be for property which is let out at a commercial rent for at least twenty-six weeks in any fifty-two-week period. And when not let out, the property must either be available for letting or under repair or building work. But you won't get tax relief for interest on bank overdrafts or credit card debts. And there's no tax relief if the loan has to be repaid within a year of being taken out (unless it's from a bank, stockbroker or discount house).

If the property is your home (or that of your divorced or separated spouse or a dependent relative) and is let out during temporary absences, you can get tax relief on the interest as for any other loan on your only or main home. In this case, you can set the interest off against any other income (not just property income), but up to the £30,000 loan limit only (see Chapter 28 for more details).

HOW THE TAX IS CALCULATED

Under Schedule A all property income due to you in the tax year is taxable, even if you don't actually receive it. But you will not pay tax on unpaid rents if you have taken reasonable steps to enforce payment or the rent is unpaid because you waived it to avoid hardship.

Tax is payable on 1 January in the tax year in which the property income is due (that is, on 1 January 1988 for the 1987/8 tax year). This is before all the income is in, so the bill will normally be based on the property income you got in the previous tax year. After the end of the tax year, your Tax Inspector will revise the bill in the light of your actual income. If you know that your property income will be down on the previous year because you've lost a source of income (for example, sold off a house you let out), you can ask the Tax Inspector to reduce your provisional bill by a corresponding proportion.

If you prefer to be taxed on the income you have actually received, you can opt for the 'accounts basis' of assessment for Schedule A. This means putting your property income on a business footing, drawing up full accounts (including a balance sheet) at the same date each year. With the accounts basis, your tax bill is based on the income for the accounting period which ended in the previous tax year. Thus if you draw up your property income accounts to 30 June every year, your Schedule A tax bill for the 1987/8 tax year would be based on your income for the accounting year ending in the 1986/7 tax year (that is, on 30 June 1986). Once you have switched to the accounts basis, you can't change back.

LOSSES

If your allowable expenses plus loan interest come to more than your property income, you have made a loss. If the loss is from loan interest, it can be carried forward and set off against property income in future years, as long as you still own the property on which the loan was spent.

If you're unable to use all your allowable expenses, the loss may be carried forward as follows:

● with a full-rent lease which is *not* a tenant's repairing lease, any unused expenses which cannot be set off against income from other properties of the same type in the same tax year can be carried forward and set off against income from the same property only

● with a full-rent lease which is not a tenant's repairing lease, you can set off the unused expenses against either income in the same tax year from full-rent leases which are tenant's repairing leases or any future income of the same type (that is, from that property or any other let on full rent which is not a tenant's repairing lease)

● with a lease which is not full rent, the loss can be set only against future income from the same lease (that is, the same property and the same tenant).

PREMIUMS ON LEASES

If you receive a premium from a tenant in return for granting a lease, this will be taxable if the lease lasts less than fifty years. So, too, will be the value of any work the tenant agrees to do for you on being granted a lease.

Part of the premium will be taxable under Schedule A, and the rest will be subject to capital gains tax. The proportion on which you will have to pay income tax is calculated as follows:

$$\frac{51 - \text{number of years of the lease}}{50.}$$

So if the lease is a ten-year one, the proportion of the premium which is taxable is

$$\frac{51 - 10}{50} = \frac{41}{50}$$

Capital gains tax is payable on the remainder of the premium, that is 9/50.

Paying tax on the premium in one tax year could mean a greatly increased tax bill, especially if it increases your taxable income so much that you end up paying tax at the higher rates. Individuals can claim *top-slicing relief* to spread the premium equally over the period of the lease: this works in much the same way as for the gain on a life insurance policy (p. 263).

If you are paid the premium in instalments, the total premium is still taxable in the year in which the lease is granted. But you can ask your Tax Inspector to allow you to pay by yearly instalments if paying in one go would cause you hardship. The maximum number of instalments is eight (or the number of instalments you are getting the premium over, if less).

There are complicated rules to stop the granting of leases being used to avoid tax.

FURNISHED PROPERTY

With furnished property, the income is normally taxed as investment income under Schedule D Case VI, unless you provide sufficient services to the tenants for the income to count as earnings from a trade. With a hotel or guest house, for example, all the income will normally be taxed as earnings from a business (see Chapter 24, 'The Self-Employed', p. 178). If you provide services such as laundry and cleaning to tenants, then at least part of the rent may be taxed as earnings, the rest as investment income from letting the property. Furnished holiday accommodation has a special treatment (see p. 237).

In calculating the tax due on income from furnished accommodation, you can deduct allowable expenses, interest and losses from the rents in the same way as for unfurnished accommodation. But only rents actually received will be included (not rents due as with Schedule A).

If you prefer, you can opt to have the income from the property taxed under Schedule A, with only the income from the furnishings taxed under Schedule D Case VI. This might be worth doing if you have losses which you can't set off against other income in the current tax year. Tell the taxman if you wish to make the switch within two years of the end of the tax year.

ALLOWABLE EXPENSES

You can claim much the same expenses for furnished lettings as for property in general, plus the cost of drawing up an inventory of contents. But you can't claim capital allowances on either furnishings or equipment you need to service the lettings (for example, vacuum cleaners). Instead you can claim an allowance for *wear and tear* on the furnishings, in one of the following ways:

● what you actually spend on replacing fixtures and fittings during the tax year (a *renewals basis*)

● 10 per cent of the rents less rates and service charges if you pay them (a *notional basis*).

Once you have chosen a method, you can't switch. If you agreed an alternative method of allowing for wear and tear with your Tax Inspector before the 1975/6 tax year, you can carry on using this.

If you clean the rooms or provide meals, you can claim the cost of materials as allowable expenses. You can't claim the cost of your time, but you can claim the cost of paying someone else to do this work (your wife, for example). The payments are taxable as earnings on the person you pay; with a wife not in paid employment, she can earn up to the wife's earned income allowance without paying tax on it.

EXAMPLE

Eddie Carlisle has divided his house, converting half his rooms to furnished flats which he lets out, providing cleaning. The total income per year from the lodging is £3,640 but the following expenses can be deducted from this rental income before tax is assessed:

● a proportion of the outgoings on the house (rates, water rates, gas and electricity) which add up to £1,800 a year; since Eddie is letting out half his house, he could claim half this amount

● the cost of cleaning (cleaner's wages plus materials), say £15 a week or £780 a year

● an allowance for wear and tear of the furniture and furnishings in the flats; Eddie could claim the actual costs of replacement (£100 for this year, say).

Thus Eddie's tax bill would be calculated as follows:

	£	£
Total rent received		3,640
Less		
½ of the outgoings (£1,800)	900	
Cost of cleaning	780	
Cost of replacing furniture and furnishings	100	
Total allowable expenses		1,780
Taxable rental income		1,860

Note that if Eddie does the cleaning, then no allowance can be made for his time. But if, as the above example assumes, he pays someone else to do the work (his wife, say), he could claim this cost as an allowable expense. The wages would be taxable income for whoever Eddie paid, but if he or she had no other income, there would be no tax to pay on this income since it is less than the amount of all the various tax allowances.

LOSSES

Losses from furnished lettings can be set off against any other Schedule D Case VI income in the same tax year or future years (this includes freelance earnings and the Enterprise Allowance, see p. 199). If the loss is created by interest payments, it can be set off only against other income from property.

LODGERS

If you take in lodgers in your own home, providing meals and other services, the income is likely to be taxed under Schedule D Case I (that is, as business income). You can claim as allowable expenses a proportion of your household bills such as rates, water rates and (unless separately metered) gas and electricity, plus similar allowable expenses to those for furnished lettings (p. 235).

You will have to negotiate with your Tax Inspector to agree the proportion of household bills which can be claimed. The number of rooms let as a proportion of the total number of rooms is often used. If the lodging covers only certain weeks of the year (university terms, for example), then the amount which can be claimed is further reduced in proportion to the number of weeks of letting.

FURNISHED HOLIDAY LETTINGS

Income from furnished holiday lettings is taxed under Schedule D Case VI. But it can be treated as if it were income from a trade, provided certain conditions are met. This means that you can enjoy the following benefits normally reserved for the self-employed business:

● the income is treated as earnings, not investment income

● tax is payable in two instalments on 1 January and 1 July

● you can claim capital allowances on purchases of plant and equipment

● losses can be set off against any other income in the same tax year or from the previous three tax years (but not any tax year less than three years after the property was let as normal furnished accommodation)

● the income counts as 'relevant earnings' for getting tax relief on self-employed pension payments (p. 211)

● you can claim roll-over relief and retirement relief for capital gains tax purposes (pp. 286, 288).

To enjoy these benefits, the furnished holiday accommodation must be available for letting to the general public on a commercial basis (that is, with a view to a profit) for at least 140 days in any twelve-month period *and* actually let for at least seventy of those days. No letting should normally exceed thirty-one days in a row for at least seven months of the twelve-month period (which should include any days when the property is let commercially).

If you own more than one furnished holiday letting, you can average out the letting and occupancy periods between all of them.

OVERSEAS PROPERTY

Income from property overseas is normally taxed under Schedule D Case V in much the same way as other overseas investment income (p. 255) for details). Thus you are liable for tax on the income even if you do not bring it back to the UK and tax is assessed on a *preceding-year basis*. You can deduct expenses incurred in letting the property broadly similar to those allowed for UK property income, including the cost of managing and collecting the income (for example, paying an agent).

If tax is deducted from the income in the country where the property is, this tax can normally be deducted from your UK tax bill (though you won't be able to claim it back if it is more than your UK tax bill). The Inland Revenue has signed *Double Tax Agreements* with more than eighty countries to try to ensure that income isn't taxed twice when earned in one country by a taxpayer in another country. Under these agreements, tax is deducted from investment income by the foreign country at a reduced rate to reduce the likelihood that you will pay tax abroad that can't be reclaimed in the UK.

CAPITAL GAINS TAX ON PROPERTY

If you sell a property which you have let out, the gain will normally be subject to capital gains tax, unless the property is your only or main home and you let it while absent for one of the reasons set out on p. 225.

Similarly, if you let part of your home, then you may have to pay capital gains tax on the part that is not occupied by you. If you let two of your six rooms, for example, one-third of the gain on selling the home is taxable (less if you haven't let the two rooms for all the time that you've owned the home). But there is no CGT to pay on let property if either of the following applies:

● you take in a lodger who shares your living rooms and eats with you (that is, is treated as a member of the family)

● the gain is £20,000 or less *and* the gain from the letting is no more than the gain on the part you've lived in. If either limit is exceeded, CGT is due only on the excess (the higher excess if both limits are exceeded).

If your property letting counts as a business (you run a hotel or guest house, or furnished holiday lettings, for example), you will be able to put off the tax bill on selling a property if you buy another for the same business by claiming roll-over relief (p. 286). And you may be able to benefit from retirement relief if you sell after the age of sixty (p. 288).

WHAT TO PUT IN YOUR TAX RETURN

Details of your UK property income should be entered on your Tax Return under *Property in the UK* in the INCOME section of the 11P and 11 forms. You are asked for information on the type of property income (delete those listed which do not apply), the address of the property, the gross rental income including premiums and profit on gas or electricity supply, allowable expenses and the net amount (that is, gross amount less allowable expenses). The space is limited and you should attach schedules setting out details, especially of expenses.

Form 11P

Property in the UK *delete as appropriate	Address	Gross income including premiums £	Expenses (enclose statement) £	Self £	Wife £
*Unfurnished lettings *Furnished lettings *Furnished holiday lettings *Ground rents or Feu duties *Land					

With Form P1, these details should be entered under *Rents from land or property in the UK* in the INVESTMENTS section.

Enter details of loan interest on let property in the OUTGOINGS section of the Tax Return under *Let property* (*other than furnished holiday lets*) on Forms 11 and 11P. With Form P1, give details under *Interest payments on UK property for letting*. Give the address of the property, the number of weeks in the tax year in which it was let and the amount of interest. Enclose a certificate of interest paid which the lender should supply.

Form 11P

Interest on loans for the purchase or improvement of property in the UK continued Do not include bank overdrafts				
Let property (other than furnished holiday lets) Address *enclose certificate*		Number of weeks let	Self £	Wife £

Interest paid on furnished holiday lettings should be claimed as an allowable expense when you give details of income from such lettings.

Details of income from overseas property should be entered under *Untaxed income from abroad* on Forms 11P and 11 and under *Income from abroad* on Form P1. Enter the full amount due to you during the tax year, less any expenses. If any foreign tax has been deducted from the income, give details of this.

Enter details of property you have bought or sold during the tax year in the CAPITAL GAINS section of the Tax Return (see Chapter 33, 'Capital Gains Tax', p. 289).

30 · INVESTMENTS

The investment climate has greatly improved in recent years with interest rates well above the rate of inflation. Many more people are dabbling in share ownership with new share issues aimed at the small investor, the Business Expansion Scheme offering tax relief on investments in growing enterprises and tax relief available to people who invest modest amounts through Personal Equity Plans (PEPs).

With more and more organizations competing to look after your savings, the choice of investments can seem bewildering. The different tax treatment of the various types of investment means that going for the highest pre-tax return is not always the best thing to do. You must consider what the return will be after two different taxes have been deducted from the proceeds:

● *income tax* – payable on interest or dividends, even if not paid out to you but added to your investment. Income from investments is added to the rest of your income for the tax year before working out your tax bill, and taxed at the basic and higher rates

● *capital gains tax* – payable on increases in the value of the investments themselves (for example, if the value of the shares or the property rises). There's no tax to pay if your total net capital gains in the tax year are below a set limit (£6,600 for 1987/8, £6,300 for 1986/7). If capital gains tax is due, it is payable at a flat rate of 30 per cent.

This chapter looks at how income tax applies to most investments (for how capital gains tax applies, see Chapter 33, 'Capital Gains Tax', p. 275). There are details of the Business Expansion Scheme and Personal Equity Plans, two types of investment with special tax incentives for savers. The taxation of life insurance is a particularly complicated subject so it is dealt with in more detail in the next chapter. For details of the taxation of property investments, see the previous chapter.

INCOME TAX ON INVESTMENTS

Income from some investments is tax-free (that is, there is no income tax to pay). For a list of these, see below.

All other investment income is taxable. And with more and more investments, tax is deducted from the income before it is paid to you. There is no further tax to pay on such income unless you pay tax at the higher rates. Non-taxpayers may be able to reclaim the tax deducted from some of these investments, but not others. The tax treatment of investment income paid after deduction of tax is covered on the opposite page.

A diminishing number of investments still pay a taxable income without deducting any tax from it. A list of these and how they are taxed is on p. 249.

TAX-FREE INVESTMENT INCOME

The proceeds of the following investments are free of income tax:

● National Savings Certificates including index-linked certificates and Yearly Plan

● Save-As-You-Earn (SAYE) schemes

● the first £70 of interest in any tax year from National Savings Ordinary Account (a married couple can have up to £70 each or a total of £140 of such interest tax-free from a joint account)

● Premium Bond prizes

● loan interest paid to members of credit unions

● Personal Equity Plans, provided the income is reinvested and the plan is held for at least one calendar year (p. 251)

● interest paid on damages for personal injury or death

● interest paid by the Inland Revenue on overdue tax rebates.

The proceeds of qualifying life insurance policies and some policies issued by friendly societies are also free of tax (see Chapter 31, 'Life Insurance', p. 260 for details).

INVESTMENT INCOME PAID AFTER DEDUCTION OF TAX

Income on most investments is now paid after deduction of tax. Among the investments to which this applies are building society accounts, bank deposit accounts, shares and unit trusts, government stock (gilts), local authority loans and bonds and annuities.

There is no further tax bill if you pay tax at the basic rate only on your income. And with some of these investments, you may be able to reclaim the tax which has been deducted if your income is too low to pay tax. The taxation rules for each of these types of investment income is examined below, starting with details of how any higher-rate tax bill is worked out.

HIGHER-RATE TAX ON INCOME PAID AFTER DEDUCTION OF TAX

If you get investment income after tax has been deducted and pay tax at the higher rates, there will be a further tax bill to pay on the investment income.

To calculate the amount of higher-rate tax payable, you must work out the *grossed-up* amount of the investment income. This is the amount which after deduction of tax at the basic rate would leave you with the net income you actually got. So if the basic rate of tax is 27 per cent, and you get £73 after deduction of tax, the grossed-up amount of the interest is £100 (because you'd have £73 after deducting tax at 27 per cent from £100).

You can work out the grossed-up amount using the following formula:

$$\text{Amount paid to you} \times \frac{100}{100 - \text{basic rate of tax}}$$

The higher-rate tax on these types of investment income is normally due on 1 December following the end of the tax year in which you get the income. So if you got investment income taxed at source during the 1986/7 tax year, any higher-rate tax due on it will be payable on 1 December 1987. But if the assessment is issued after 1 November, the tax is due thirty days after the date the assessment was issued.

EXAMPLE

Avis Garbutt gets £50 interest on her building society account in the 1987/8 tax year. Tax has already been deducted from the interest before it is credited to her account, so this £50 is the net (that is, after deduction of tax) amount.

To work out the before deduction of tax amount of interest, Avis must gross-up the net amount. The basic rate of tax for 1987/8 is 27 per cent, so the grossed-up amount of interest is:

$$£50 \times \frac{100}{100 - 27} = £50 \times \frac{100}{73} = £68.49$$

In other words, Avis is assumed to have paid £68.49 − £50 = £18.49 in basic-rate tax on the interest received. If Avis should pay tax at 40 per cent on this interest, her overall tax liability is 40 per cent of £68.49 = £27.40. But she is treated as having already paid the basic-rate tax (that is, £18·49), so only has to pay £27.40 − £18.49 = £8.91 in higher-rate tax.

BANK, BUILDING SOCIETY AND OTHER DEPOSIT ACCOUNTS

UK banks, building societies, finance houses, organizations offering high-interest cheque accounts and other licensed deposit-takers all deduct tax from interest they pay UK-resident taxpayers Tax is also deducted from interest on local authority loans before it is paid to you. Tax is deducted at what is known as the *composite rate*, fixed at 24.75 per cent for the 1987/8 tax year (25.25 per cent for the 1986/7 tax year). This tax cannot be claimed back if you are not a taxpayer.

The composite rate is meant to collect the same amount of tax as the basic-rate tax that would be due if customers were individually assessed. Many customers would not have to pay tax on the interest (because their income is too low), which is why the composite rate is less than the basic rate of tax. This works in favour of taxpayers, since tax is deducted at the composite rate (24.75 per cent for 1987/8) rather than the basic rate (27 per cent for 1987/8). But it works against people whose income is too low to pay tax: they can't reclaim the composite-rate tax which has been deducted, even though they are non-taxpayers.

COMPANY SHARES

Dividends paid to shareholders by UK companies are treated as having been paid after deduction of basic-rate tax. When the net dividend is paid, it comes with a tax voucher which sets out the amount paid and a *tax credit*, the amount of basic-rate tax that is taken to have been paid on the dividend. This tax voucher is normally attached to the dividend warrant and looks something like this (different companies lay out the information differently):

Tax Voucher

TAX VOUCHER

TAX VOUCHER

244   **Lloyds Bank Plc**

SECURITY CODE
0–521–103

3rd April, 1987

I enclose a warrant for a final dividend for the year ended 31st December, 1986, at 11·75p per share, on the ordinary shares of £1 each, fully paid up, registered in your name on 12th March, 1987. I certify that Advance Corporation Tax of an amount equal to that shown below as a Tax Credit will be accounted for to the Collector of Taxes.

A. J. MICHIE, *Secretary.*

SPECIMEN

This voucher should be kept. It will be accepted by the Inland Revenue as evidence of Tax Credit in respect of which you may be entitled to claim payment or relief.

REGISTRAR:–
LLOYDS BANK PLC.
REGISTRAR'S DEPARTMENT.
GORING-BY-SEA.
WORTHING, WEST SUSSEX,
BN12 6DA

REFERENCE	SHAREHOLDING	TAX CREDIT	DIVIDEND PAYABLE
· 014/			

Lloyds Bank Plc
HEAD OFFICE, LONDON

30·00·00T

3rd April, 1987

PAY   ## SPECIMEN   *or Order*

This warrant should be presented for payment through a banker within six months, and if not, returned to the Registrar for verification.

Smith & Ouman Ltd
3-44530 12/86

NOT NEGOTIABLE

244

⑈040657⑈ 30⑈0002⑈ 1134219⑈

The grossed-up dividend for tax purposes is normally the net dividend plus the tax credit. But some dividends paid in the early part of the 1987/8 tax year will be paid with a tax credit which is worked out using the 1986/7 basic rate of tax (29 per cent) rather than the 1987/8 rate (27 per cent). If you get a dividend to which this applies, you will need to work out the tax credit using the formula above, ignoring the tax credit figure on the tax voucher.

If you are a non-taxpayer, or should have paid less tax overall than the amount of the tax credit, you can claim back the amount overpaid. For how to do this, see p. 62.

Note that similar rules apply if you receive a stock dividend, that is, new shares instead of a cash dividend. The value of the stock dividend is known as the 'cash equivalent' (the amount of cash dividend foregone) and you are treated as having received the grossed-up amount of the cash equivalent. If you pay tax at the basic rate only, there is no further tax to pay. But unlike with a cash dividend, non-taxpayers cannot claim back any tax credit. And if you pay tax at the higher rates, there will be extra tax to pay, based on the grossed-up amount of the cash equivalent.

UNIT TRUSTS

Income from most authorized unit trusts (known as distributions) is treated as having been paid after deduction of basic-rate tax in the same way as dividends from shares. Distributions will be paid with tax credits which can be claimed back by non-taxpayers. The tax voucher you get from the company running the unit trust will set out the amount of the distribution and the tax credit:

Unit Trust Tax Voucher

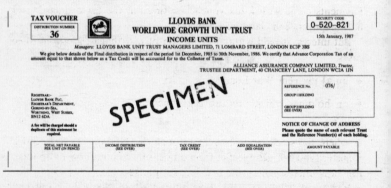

The income from certain authorized unit trusts does not come with a tax credit: this includes unit trusts which invest in government stocks and other fixed-interest investments. But tax is deducted from the income at the basic rate before you get it, and you will get a tax voucher specifying the amount paid (non-taxpayers can claim the tax back).

With accumulation unit trusts, income is automatically reinvested to increase the amount of your investment. But this income is taxable in the year in which it is reinvested, so you will still get a tax voucher with tax credit after each distribution. Non-taxpayers can reclaim this tax credit, even though they haven't received the income.

Note that when you get your first distribution from a unit trust, this sometimes includes an *equalization* payment. This is a return of part of the amount you originally invested and isn't taxable as income.

BRITISH GOVERNMENT STOCKS

Interest on most British Government stocks (commonly known as gilt-edged securities or gilts) is paid after deduction of basic-rate tax. Payments come with a tax voucher setting out the tax deducted, and non-taxpayers can claim back this tax.

But interest is paid without deduction of tax (that is, gross) in three cases:

● on $3\frac{1}{2}$ per cent War Loan

● on holdings which produce gross income of less than £2.50 half-yearly

● where the stocks were bought through the National Savings Stock Register (you can get a leaflet from a post office about how to do this). For how interest paid gross is taxed, see p. 250.

If you sell gilts (or other fixed-interest securities) bought since 28 February 1985, there may be an income tax bill to pay on part of the proceeds. This is because the sale price will reflect the next interest payment due (accrued income), so this part of the proceeds is taxed as income. If you buy such securities, the income tax due on the first interest payment you receive is reduced because the seller will have paid tax on part of the proceeds to reflect the value of this interest payment.

These provisions, designed to stop tax avoidance by turning income into capital gains ('bond-washing'), apply only if you own fixed-interest securities with a nominal value in excess of £5,000 at any time during the current or preceding tax year. If you think they may apply to you, ask your Tax Inspector to send you Inland Revenue leaflet IR68 (*Accrued Income Scheme*).

LOCAL AUTHORITY INVESTMENTS

The interest on local authority stocks and yearling bonds is paid after deduction of tax at the basic rate. As with British Government stocks, you can reclaim the tax if it is more than you should have paid.

The same applied to the interest on local authority loans until 6 April 1986. But tax is now deducted at the composite rate (p. 244) from interest on local authority loans and cannot be reclaimed by non-tax-payers.

ANNUITIES

If you buy an annuity, you pay a lump sum to an insurance company and it pays you an income for an agreed period (ten years, say, or until you die). Part of the income will be treated as interest, part as return of your capital: only the part which is treated as interest is taxed as income. The insurance company will deduct tax at the basic rate from the interest part before handing over the payment. You will get a tax voucher with each payment which tells you how much tax has been deducted. You can claim the tax back if you are a non-taxpayer.

Note that this treatment applies only to annuities you buy voluntarily with your own money. If you buy the annuity for another reason, basic-rate tax will be deducted from all the income before it is paid to you.

INCOME AND GROWTH BONDS

These are lump sum investments sold by insurance companies, which provide either a guaranteed income or a guaranteed growth for a fixed number of years. Companies achieve this in different ways and some bonds can be complicated packages of insurance policies and annuities.

You will have to ask the insurance company for details of what income is due under the bond each year, whether it is taxable and whether tax has been deducted. In some cases, the income is provided by cashing in part of a life insurance policy: only higher-rate tax will be due (p. 262). With growth bonds, there may even be a tax liability before the bond matures even though no income has been paid out to you.

TRUSTS AND ESTATES

Income from a trust or settlement is paid after tax has been paid on it by the trustees. With discretionary trusts (including accumulation and maintenance trusts), the rate of tax paid is 45 per cent; for other trusts, tax is paid at the basic rate (that is, 27 per cent for 1987/8).

If the income is paid out to you, you will get a tax credit for the tax deducted (you should also get a certificate R185 from the trustees, setting out the amount of income and tax credit). If this is more tax than you should pay on the grossed-up income, you can claim a rebate. Non-taxpayers will be able to claim back all the tax paid with trust income. But basic-rate taxpayers will also be able to claim back some of the tax deducted from income paid out by a discretionary trust. You can claim back the difference between the 45 per cent deducted before the income is paid to you and the basic rate of tax: so for the 1987/8 tax year, when the basic rate is 27 per cent, you could claim back 45 − 27 = 18 per cent tax.

Income paid to you from the estate of someone who has died by the executors is also paid after deduction of basic-rate tax. This can be claimed back by non-taxpayers.

TAXABLE INVESTMENT INCOME PAID WITHOUT DEDUCTION OF TAX

Interest on the following types of investment is taxable, but paid without deduction of tax (that is, gross):

● National Savings Ordinary Account and Investment Account (but the first £70 a year of interest on Ordinary Account is free of tax – see p. 242)

● National Savings Income and Deposit Bonds

● $3\frac{1}{2}$ per cent War Loan

● British Government stocks bought through the National Savings Stock Register (you can get a leaflet from a post office about how to do this)

● interest of less than £2.50 gross overall per half year on other British Government stocks

● shares with a cooperative society or credit union.

Interest paid to you by someone to whom you personally make a loan is also taxable in this way.

The interest is taxable even if it is not paid to you (for example, if it is credited to your account). As far as the taxman is concerned, you get the interest when it is paid or credited to you, even if it relates to an earlier period. For example, if you get interest half-yearly, and it is credited to your account on 6 April 1987, it is treated as if all of it was earned in the 1987/8 tax year (even though almost all of it was earned in the 1986/7 tax year).

HOW THE TAX IS COLLECTED

This type of interest is normally taxed on a *preceding-year basis*. This means that your tax bill for one tax year depends on the interest you got in the previous tax year. The tax is collected on 1 January in the tax year or within thirty days of the date the Notice of Assessment is issued, if this is later. So on 1 January 1988, you would have to pay the tax on this type of income for the 1987/8 tax year, which would be based on what you got in the 1986/7 tax year.

But if you are just starting to get interest of this type from a particular source, there will be no previous tax year to base your tax bill on. The tax due in each of the first two tax years will therefore depend on the interest you actually get in that year (that is, a *current-year basis*). In the third tax year, *you* can choose between paying tax on what you got in either the second tax year (preceding-year basis) or the third tax year (current-year basis). If you do nothing, tax will be charged on a preceding-year basis for the third tax year, so check whether you would pay less if you opted for current-year basis – you have up to six years after the end of the third tax year to tell the taxman that this is what you want.

There are also special rules to cover the last two tax years before you stop getting interest of this type from a particular source. When you close the account, the tax bill for that tax year will be based on the interest you actually got in that tax year (current-year basis). And the taxman can also increase your tax bill for the last-but-one tax year to collect the tax due on what you actually got in that tax year (that is current-year basis) if that would be more than you would have paid on the preceding-year basis.

Note that each source of this type of investment income can be treated separately by the taxman to the extent that a large deposit in, or withdrawal from, an account can be treated as opening or closing a source. In practice, all interest from banks is usually treated as a single source by the taxman, unless you ask for each to be treated separately. And the tax on smaller regular amounts of interest may be collected under PAYE. But if the taxman thinks that you're manipulating accounts to avoid tax, he may treat each account as a separate source.

EXAMPLE

Marcus Campbell opened a National Savings Investment Account in the 1982/3 tax year. The following table shows the interest he got and the amount he paid tax on up until the 1987/8 tax year:

Tax year	Interest	Amount he pays tax on
1982/3	£100	£100 – interest he actually got
1983/4	£200	£200 – interest he actually got
1984/5	£150	£200 – interest he got in the preceding year, but Marcus can choose £150 (the interest he actually got)
1985/6	£200	£150 – interest he got in preceding year
1986/7	£250	£200 – interest he got in preceding year
1987/8	£100	£250 – interest he got in preceding year

If Marcus closed the account during the 1987/8 tax year, his tax bill for that year would be based on the interest he actually got (that is, £100, not £250). But the taxman would be able to change the basis of assessment for 1986-7 to make the tax bill depend on the interest Marcus actually got in that tax year (£250) if this is more than the interest he got in the preceding year (£200). Since it is more, the taxman would make the change.

PERSONAL EQUITY PLANS

The proceeds from shares and unit trusts owned through a Personal Equity Plan (PEP) are free of tax provided certain conditions are met. PEPs have been available only since 1 January 1987 and there are strict limits on the investment you can make in PEPs. The most important restrictions are as follows:

● you can invest no more than £2,400 (either by lump sum or monthly instalments) in any calendar year and you can invest in only one plan per year

● the plan must be held for one complete calendar year after the year in which the investment is made and any income made on the investments during that period must be reinvested – there will be no tax on that income if this condition is met

● after the plan has been held for a complete calendar year, the income will continue to be free of tax as long as it is reinvested – if it is paid out, you will have to pay tax on it

● if any shares are sold during the first complete calendar year, the proceeds must be reinvested otherwise the plan comes to an end. After the first year, you can sell the shares without being liable to capital gains tax, whether the proceeds are reinvested or not.

Thus, if you invest in a PEP between 1 January and 31 December 1987, there will be no tax to pay on the income if you hold the investment for the whole of 1988. From 1 January 1989 onwards you would be able to cash in some or all of the investments without any tax bill. If you keep the investments after that date, there will be no tax to pay on the proceeds unless you draw the dividends on the investments (when income tax only will be due on the income you draw).

HOW PEPS WORK

PEPs are marketed by investment managers – many insurance companies, banks and building societies offer them. They must invest your money in ordinary shares of UK companies listed on the Stock Exchange or quoted on the Unlisted Securities Market (USM). But up to 25 per cent of your investment (or £420 a year if this is more) can be invested in UK investment trusts or unit trusts.

There are two sorts of PEPs on offer:

● *non-discretionary plans*, where the managers decide what to invest in, when to sell existing investments and buy new ones, and the like

● *discretionary plans*, where the managers follow your instructions about what to invest in, when to sell and so on.

With both types, the managers make charges for the work of buying and selling, collecting dividends, reclaiming the tax credits, looking after the share certificates and so on. The charges come on top of the maximum investment – that is, you can invest the maximum of £2,400 paying the charges on top of this amount.

Even though the PEP manager handles the administration of the plan, you are the legal owner of the shares or unit trusts. The annual reports and accounts will be forwarded to you by the manager.

IS IT WORTH INVESTING IN PEPS?

The limits on the amount you can invest may seem low, especially if the sort of capital gains you make each year fall within the tax-free limit (p. 276). And if your income is too low to pay income tax, then PEPs will not offer much benefit in the short term. But the benefits of tax exemption will build up over the years, especially if all income is reinvested. If you invest the maximum in PEPs each year, leaving all the income to be reinvested, and the value of the shares and unit trusts rose by 10 per cent a year, your tax-free investment would be worth £42,075 after ten years.

BUSINESS EXPANSION SCHEME

Although there are quite a few investments which pay a tax-free income, the Business Expansion Scheme (BES) gives you tax relief on the money you invest. And there is no capital gains tax to pay when you sell BES investments bought after 18 March 1986, provided they have been owned for a minimum period. But there are strict and complicated rules to qualify for the reliefs and the scheme is designed to encourage investment in growing unquoted companies. These are naturally riskier propositions than many other sorts of investment, so the Business Expansion Scheme is not for the faint-hearted. And you should not invest money in the BES which you cannot afford to lose.

WHICH INVESTMENTS QUALIFY?

Two types of investment qualify for BES tax relief:

● new ordinary shares in unquoted UK companies carrying out qualifying trades (which excludes banking, insurance, share-dealing, dealing in land, leasing and providing legal or accountancy services). Unquoted companies exclude those listed on the Stock Exchange or traded on the Unlisted Securities Market but includes those traded on the Third Market or the Over the Counter (OTC) markets

● approved funds, organized by investment managers, which invest in such companies.

The rules about which companies qualify are complex and in general the company or fund seeking investment will make sure that it meets the requirements. Take professional advice if you are uncertain about whether a venture qualifies.

WHO CAN GET THE RELIEF?

You must be resident and ordinarily resident in the UK (p. 174) when the shares are issued. And you can't use the scheme to put money into your own business, since only outside investors can qualify for the tax relief.

Thus you can't get the BES reliefs on investments in a business in which you work whether as an employee, partner or paid director. And you can't get relief on investments in a company if you own more than 30 per cent of it. In deciding how much of the company you own, you must include the holdings of *connected persons* – your spouse and you and your spouse's children, parents and grandparents (but not brothers or sisters) – and *associates* such as business partners.

HOW MUCH TAX RELIEF?

You can get tax relief at your highest rate of tax on BES investments of up to £40,000 in total in any tax year. To qualify, the investment must be at least £500 unless it is made through an investment fund. If you are married, the £40,000 limit applies to you and your spouse jointly.

You get the tax relief in the tax year in which the shares are issued, but for investments made after 5 April 1987 you can claim the tax relief for the previous tax year. If you make a BES investment between 6 April and 5 October (inclusive), half the investment up to a maximum of £5,000 can be set off against your income for the previous tax year.

You can't claim the tax relief until the company has carried out its qualifying trade for at least four months. If the company ceases to qualify as under the Business Expansion Scheme within three years, you will lose the relief. And if you sell the shares within five years, you lose relief on the amount you sell them for (that is, if you sell them for more than they cost you, you lose all the relief).

The investment reduces your taxable income but not your *total income* (p. 20). So investing in the BES won't help reduce your income for age allowance purposes (p. 124) or in calculating top-slicing relief (p. 263).

Claim the tax relief on the back of Form BES 3 (for an investment in an individual company) or BES 5 (for an investment fund). These forms will be given to you by the company or fund once they have been authorized as BES investments by the Inland Revenue.

CAPITAL GAINS TAX

If you sell BES investments which you bought after 18 March 1986, any gain is free of capital gains tax, provided the tax relief has not been lost (that is, this exemption applies only if you hold the shares for at least five years). Any losses made on selling BES investments cannot be set off against taxable gains to reduce your capital gains tax bill.

OVERSEAS INVESTMENTS

Income from overseas investments is taxable if you are domiciled and resident in the UK, even if you do not bring it back into the UK. This applies to sterling and non-sterling investments, including those made in the 'offshore' islands such as the Channel Islands and the Isle of Man.

Most overseas investment income is taxed in a similar way to UK investment income paid without deduction of tax. Thus it is taxed on a preceding-year basis except in the opening and closing years. The collecting agent (probably your bank) will deduct UK income tax from the dividends at the basic rate. If tax is deducted from the income in the country where the investment is held, this tax can normally be deducted from your UK tax liability (though if the overseas tax is more than your UK bill, you cannot claim back the excess).

The Inland Revenue has signed *Double Tax Agreements* with more than eighty countries to try to ensure that income isn't taxed twice when earned in one country by a taxpayer in another country. Under these agreements, tax is deducted from investment income by the foreign country at a reduced rate: this reduces the likelihood that you will pay tax abroad that can't be reclaimed in the UK.

The taxation of overseas investment income is complex and more detail is available in Inland Revenue leaflet IR6, *Double Taxation Relief*. Your Tax Inspector may be able to offer help, but, if not, contact the Inspector of Foreign Dividends at Lynwood Road, Thames Ditton, Surrey.

OFFSHORE FUNDS

Until 1 January 1984 investors in offshore funds based in tax havens were able to reinvest (or 'roll up') income, adding to the value of their investment. When the investment was sold, the increase in value was taxed under capital gains tax (maximum 30 per cent, with the first slice of gains tax-free, see p. 276) rather than income tax (maximum tax rate 60 per cent). But since 1 January 1984 gains on selling offshore fund investments have been taxed as income unless the fund qualifies as a *distributor fund* – one which distributes most of its income as dividends.

WHAT TO PUT IN YOUR TAX RETURN

Considerable space is made available in the INCOME section of the Tax Return for entering details of investment income under various headings. If there isn't enough room in any section, make a separate list, attach it to the Return and write 'See attached schedule' in the space.

With Forms 11 and 11P, the first major heading is *Interest not taxed before receipt:*

Form 11P

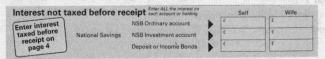

The first items under this heading are taxable National Savings investments, split into *NSB Ordinary account, NSB Investment account* and *Deposit or Income Bonds.* Enter the amounts of interest paid or credited to you and your spouse for the tax year, including any Ordinary account interest which may be tax-free (p. 242). With Form P1, enter this under *National Savings Bank.*

Under *Other banks* on Forms 11 and 11P, enter only interest paid (or credited) without deduction of tax – this is likely to be from a non-UK bank.

Form 11P

Give the name of the bank. On Form P1, enter this under *Interest from banks not already taxed.*

Any other interest paid or credited without deduction of tax should be entered on Form 11P under *Other sources (including War Loan, British Savings Bonds and loans to private individuals).* This will include interest from gilts bought through the National Savings Stock Register, and from private loans.

Form 11P

Other sources (including War Loan, British Savings Bonds and loans to private individuals)

On Form PI enter these details under *Interest not already taxed from any other source*.

Give details of investment income received from abroad without deduction of UK tax (such as overseas bank interest) under *Untaxed income from abroad* on Forms 11 and 11P.

Form 11P

Untaxed income from abroad	Self	Wife
Details	£	£

Enter the full amount due to you for the tax year (whether remitted to the UK or not), less any expenses. If you have paid any foreign tax on the income, give details. This information should be entered on Form PI under *Income from abroad*.

The next major heading on Forms 11 and 11P is *Income treated as taxed before receipt* (*Composite Rate Tax*), with separate spaces for banks and other deposit-takers and building societies.

Form 11P

Interest treated as taxed before receipt (Composite Rate Tax)		
Interest from UK banks and deposit takers taxed before receipt	Self	Wife
Name of bank or deposit taker	£	£
Interest from UK building societies		
Name of Society	£	£

Again list the name of each organization and the amount of interest paid or credited during the tax year to you and your spouse. Enter this information on Form PI under *Interest from any other banks and building societies*. Note that the interest from building society SAYE schemes is tax-free and should not be included.

Income from shares and unit trusts which comes with a tax credit must be entered under *Dividends from UK companies and tax credits* on Forms 11 and 11P.

Form 11P

Dividends from UK companies and tax credits	Amount of dividend	Amount of tax credit
Name of UK company		
Self	£	£
Wife	£	£

For each share or unit trust, enter the exact amounts of dividends or distributions and the tax credits (as set out on the tax vouchers). Do enter details of accumulation trusts, but don't enter equalization payments. With Form P1, enter the details under *Company dividends and unit trusts*, giving the gross income (dividend or distribution plus tax credit) from each.

Under *Other dividends, trust income, etc, already taxed* on Forms 11 and 11P, give details of interest from government stocks paid after deduction of tax, dividends from overseas shares, unit trust distributions which don't come with tax credits (those investing in gilts, for example), income from trusts, annuities and the like.

Form 11P

Other dividends, trust income, etc, already taxed	Gross amount of income
Name of source (show each separately)	
Self	£
Wife	£

Enter the gross (before-tax) amount of the income. With overseas income, the gross amount is the amount before deduction of both UK and foreign tax but give details of how much has been deducted in each country. With Form P1, enter these details under *Other dividends, interest, etc, including income from trusts*.

Under *Payments from estates* on Forms 11 and 11P, give details of income paid to you by the personal representatives (or executors) of an estate.

Form 11P

For payments by estates, enter the name of the person who has died, the date of death and the name and address of the personal representative. Say what type of interest you have in the estate and give the gross amount of income received – this should be on any tax certificate given to you by the personal representative.

Under *Settlements* on Forms 11 and 11P, give details of any income from trusts and other settlements which you have set up yourself which is treated as yours for tax purposes. This should include income from a trust you have set up which benefits you or your spouse and income payable by you under a deed of covenant which does not meet the conditions for tax relief (p. 120). Give the name of each settlement.

Form 11P

Settlements Include income and capital from settlements, parental gifts, etc. and transfers to be treated as your income	Self	Wife
	£	£

These details should be entered under *Payments from settlements and estates (gross amount)* on Form P1.

If you have received stock dividends, enter details under *Any other profits or income* on Forms 11 and 11P (*Any other income or gains* on Form P1). Give the cash equivalent which the company will give on the voucher. Also enter here details of accrued income you received when buying or selling stock (p. 247). If you're due to pay tax on less than the full amount of interest on such stock (because the person you bought them from has already paid it), enter details in the OUTGOINGS section under *Other outgoings*.

Form 11P

Other outgoings enter gross amounts before deduction of tax Covenants, bonds of annuity, settlements, covenanted payments to charities, accrued income purchased etc.		Self	Wife
Details		£	£

31 · LIFE INSURANCE

Gone are the days when you could get extra tax relief by taking out life insurance policies (though if you've got a qualifying policy taken out before 14 March 1984, you can continue to get tax relief on the premiums). But the proceeds of many types of life insurance policy can be tax-free and you can use life insurance to build up valuable investments, as well as to provide for your dependants should you die. This chapter looks at the taxation of life insurance policies.

It also examines the rules behind life insurance premium tax relief which millions of taxpayers continue to benefit from on policies taken out before 14 March 1984. But the chapter begins by defining the types of life insurance and the crucial difference between qualifying and non-qualifying policies.

TYPES OF LIFE INSURANCE

Life insurance comes in two basic forms:

● *protection-only life insurance* pays out only if you (or whoever is insured) die within a period you choose when you take out the policy. Also known as term insurance, the policy will pay out either a lump sum or an income to your dependants

● *investment-type life insurance* pays out if you die within the period the policy covers or, if you don't die, when the policy comes to an end. These policies are normally known as endowment policies and, since you are guaranteed to get something no matter when you die, they combine life insurance and investment. Whole of life policies, which pay out when you die (whenever this is), are also investment-type policies, since a return on your premiums is guaranteed (albeit when you die)

Two groups of organizations are allowed to offer life insurance in the UK. Insurance companies have the lion's share of the market and most of what follows applies to their policies. But friendly societies (a sort of mutual self-help organization surviving from pre-welfare state days) offer policies which enjoy special tax privileges and can be well worth investigating: their policies are covered in a special section at the end of the chapter.

QUALIFYING POLICIES

The key distinction for tax purposes is between *qualifying* and *non-qualifying* life insurance policies. If a policy is a qualifying one, there is no income tax or capital gains tax to pay on the proceeds unless you do something which stops it being a qualifying policy (for example, cash it in inside certain time limits). With a non-qualifying policy, there is never any basic-rate tax to pay on the proceeds but there will be a tax bill if the proceeds of the policy (added to your other taxable income) are taxable at the higher rates.

A life insurance policy is almost certain to be a qualifying one if it involves paying regular premiums. So, most term insurance policies, including family income benefit and mortgage protection policies, will be qualifying. The insurance company will make sure that their policies meet the other requirements to qualify so as to be attractive to customers.

With investment-type life insurance policies, the most important of these other requirements is that the policy should be designed to last for ten years or more. And if you stop paying the premiums within ten years (or within the first three-quarters of the term of the policy, if shorter), the policy ceases to be a qualifying one. So the minimum period you have to keep up the premiums on an endowment policy to avoid it becoming non-qualifying is seven and a half years (on a ten-year policy).

If a life insurance policy involves only a single premium or irregular premiums, it will almost certainly be a non-qualifying policy (that is, the proceeds will be taxable at the higher rates). But you can still benefit from such policies if, for example, you pay higher-rate tax now but do not expect to at some time in the future (when you can draw the proceeds of the policy without a tax bill). And you can cash in up to 5 per cent of the premiums paid each year without immediately having to pay a higher-rate tax bill. So you can use this to draw a 'tax-free' income and, if you are not a higher-rate taxpayer when the policy ends, there will be no further tax to pay.

HOW THE PROCEEDS ARE TAXED

How the proceeds of a life insurance policy are taxed depends on both the type of policy it is and when you collect the proceeds.

QUALIFYING POLICIES

There is no income tax or capital gains tax to pay on the proceeds of a qualifying life insurance policy when it pays out on maturity or because the person whose life is insured dies. This applies to protection-only policies and to investment-type policies.

You may collect a pay-out if you cash in an investment-type policy before the end of the term (though this is not usually recommended, especially in the early years of a policy). These proceeds will also be free of income tax and capital gains tax if you have paid the premiums for at least ten years or three-quarters of the term, if this is shorter. If you cash in a qualifying policy within these time-limits, it becomes a non-qualifying policy (see below for how the proceeds are taxed).

NON-QUALIFYING POLICIES

The proceeds of a non-qualifying policy are taxable at the higher rates of income tax as a *chargeable gain*, even if the policy is paying out because of the death of the person whose life is insured. The gain is normally the amount you get back less the total premiums paid. But if the pay-out occurs because of the death of the person whose life is insured, the gain is calculated using the cash-in value of the policy at the time of death if this is less than the amount paid out. For how the tax is calculated on this chargeable gain, see below.

If you draw an income from the policy by cashing in part of it each year, this too counts as a chargeable gain. But as long as the amount withdrawn each year does not exceed 5 per cent of the premiums paid so far, the withdrawals aren't taxed until the policy comes to an end (when they're added to the gain made at the final pay-out). If you use less than 5 per cent in any year, you can carry the unused allowance forward to later years. If you draw more than the 5 per cent allowance, the excess is taxed as a chargeable gain in the year in which you get it. With a policy which lasts more than twenty years, the allowance for each year after the twentieth is 5 per cent of the premiums paid in that year plus the premiums paid in the previous nineteen years.

Note that if you sell a non-qualifying policy, there will also be a chargeable gain if you sell it for more than the premiums paid.

HOW CHARGEABLE GAINS ARE TAXED

The gain is added to your investment income for the tax year in which it is chargeable, but no basic-rate tax is due on the gain. Only if the gain, added to the rest of your taxable income, is taxable at the higher rates will there be any tax to pay. So for the 1987/8 tax year, there will be tax to pay on a gain only if your taxable income including the gain exceeds £17,900 (£17,200 for 1986/7).

Even if the gain is taxable at the higher rates, the tax charged on the gain is not the full rate of tax, but the difference between the higher rate and the basic rate. So, if the rate of tax applicable to the gain is 60 per cent, and the basic rate is 27 per cent, tax is charged on the gain at 60 − 27 = 33 per cent.

This could mean a very large tax bill in the year in which you cash in a non-qualifying policy. But you may be able to benefit from *top-slicing relief* which spreads the gain you make over the years of the policy. Your Tax Inspector should automatically apply top-slicing relief if it means a smaller tax bill but you can check the calculations as follows:

STEP 1 Work out the average gain made in each year on the policy, that is, the total gain divided by the number of complete years you held the policy.

STEP 2 Calculate the higher-rate tax which would be due if the average gain was added to the rest of your taxable income (you can do this by working out how much tax would be due on the gain if it was your top slice of income and then subtracting the amount of basic-rate tax which would be due on the gain).

STEP 3 Multiply the higher-rate tax due on this average gain by the number of complete years you held the policy to find the total tax due on the gain.

STEP 4 The answer will be the tax due on the gain if it is less than the amount worked out by adding the whole gain to your income for the tax year in which the policy comes to an end.

EXAMPLE

Deirdre Moss buys a single premium bond (that is, life insurance policy) for £20,000 at the age of fifty, when she pays higher-rate income tax on her earnings. Each year, she can draw an income of 5 per cent of the premiums paid without paying tax in that year: thus Deirdre can draw 5 per cent of £20,000 = £1,000 a year without increasing her tax bill for the year.

When Deirdre retires at sixty-five, she cashes in the bond for £40,000. The chargeable gain is the proceeds she has drawn from the bond (£40,000 + 15 × £1,000 = £55,000) less the premiums paid (£20,000): £55,000 − £20,000 = £35,000.

If her taxable income from her pension and other investments is £17,000 (that is, taxable at the basic rate only), this gain of £35,000 will increase Deirdre's total taxable income to £52,000. A taxable income of £52,000 would be taxable at the higher rates up to 60 per cent. Indeed, the higher-rate tax due on the gain of £35,000 would be £8,818. But she will be able to benefit from top-slicing relief as follows:

STEP 1 Calculate the average yearly gain over the fifteen years; this is £35,000/15 = £2,333.

STEP 2 Calculate the higher-rate tax due on this average gain of £2,333 when added to the rest of Deirdre's taxable income for the year of £17,000, that is, a total taxable income of £19,333. Remember that tax is due only at the difference between the higher rate of tax and the basic rate:

Taxable income without gain = £17,000
Tax due (at the basic rate only, see p. 21)   = 27% of £17,000
        = £4,590
Taxable income with gain = £17,000 + £2,333 = £19,333
Tax due on £19,333:
   27% of £17,900   £4,833
   40% of £1,433   £573
         —————
Total   £5,406
Tax due on gain of £2,333 = £5,406 − £4,590
         = £816
Basic-rate tax due on gain of £2,333 = 27% of £2,333
         = £630
Higher-rate tax due on gain of £2,333 = £816 − £630
         = £186

STEP 3 Multiply the higher-rate tax due on the average gain (£186) by the number of years the bond was held (fifteen) to find the higher-rate tax due on cashing in the bond:

$$15 × £186 = £2,790.$$

STEP 4 Since the amount of tax due with top-slicing relief (£2,790) is less than if the whole gain was added to Deirdre's taxable income for the year (£8,818), the tax bill on the gain will be £2,790.

LIFE INSURANCE GAINS AND AGE ALLOWANCE

The gain made on ending a non-qualifying life insurance policy counts as part of your total income for working out whether you are entitled to age allowance. If a chargeable gain reduces the amount of your age allowance, there will be extra tax to pay on your income (p. 124). This is particularly important if you buy a single-premium bond with the intention of cashing it in after retirement when you expect your top tax rate to be lower than when at work.

INHERITANCE TAX

If a life insurance policy, qualifying or otherwise, pays out on the death of the person who took it out, the proceeds will be paid into his or her estate and be liable to inheritance tax (see Chapter 34, p. 291). This inheritance tax bill (and the delay in getting the money while probate is sought) can be avoided if the policy is written in trust for someone else: your spouse, say. With policies written in trust, the proceeds go straight to the person or people for whom they are written in trust without passing through the dead person's estate. The premiums count as gifts but are likely to be exempt from inheritance tax as regular gifts made out of normal income (p. 294).

Note that if a non-qualifying policy is written in trust, you will be liable for any income tax due on the gain, whether this becomes due during your lifetime or because of your death (the income tax is charged on your estate in this case). But the tax can be reclaimed from the trustees (that is, from the proceeds of the policy).

TAX RELIEF ON LIFE INSURANCE PREMIUMS

If you took out a qualifying life insurance policy before 14 March 1984, you got tax relief on the premiums (within limits). Provided you haven't substantially changed the policy, you can still get the tax relief on premiums for policies taken out before midnight on 13 March 1984. The rate of tax relief is 15 per cent and you get it by paying reduced premiums to the insurance company. So you pay 85 per cent of the gross premium and the insurance company reclaims the 15 per cent tax relief direct from the Inland Revenue.

Even if you continue to pay premiums on policies taken out before 14 March 1984, there are limits on the amount of tax relief. You can get tax relief on no more than £1,500 of gross premiums in any tax year (that is, on £1,275 of net premiums) or one-sixth of your total income, if this is greater. If you pay more than the limit, the taxman will reclaim the tax relief you have automatically been given on the excess.

And if you change the policy so as to get more benefits, you will lose the tax relief: for example, you will lose the tax relief if you extend the term of the policy, increase the amount of cover or convert the policy into a different type of policy (for example, from term to endowment). But you won't lose the tax relief if the benefits increase automatically as part of the policy (for example, if the sum insured increases by 5 per cent every year). Check with the insurance company before making any changes.

CLAWBACK

If you stop paying the premiums for an investment-type life insurance policy within four years of taking it out, and you got tax relief on the premiums, some or all of the tax relief will be taken back. This *clawback* will be made by the insurance company, which will make a deduction from what you get back. There may also be clawback if you cash in a policy or make it paid up within the first four years.

SELF-EMPLOYED LIFE INSURANCE

If you are self-employed or work for an employer but don't belong to a pension scheme, you can still get tax relief on life insurance premiums and at your top rate of tax (within limits). Full tax relief is available on premiums for a special sort of term insurance known as Section 226A policies, which pays out if you die before reaching retirement age. You can get the tax relief on premiums of up to 5 per cent of your *net relevant income*. For more details, see p. 210.

FRIENDLY SOCIETIES

Friendly societies supported their members before the arrival of the welfare state by paying sickness benefit, unemployment benefit and widow's pensions. Some continue in existence and you can get tax relief on premiums you pay on certain combined sickness and life insurance policies they offer. The tax relief is at half your top rate of tax on the life part of the premium; you can also get the same tax relief on part of your trade union subscription if it includes superannuation, funeral or life insurance benefits.

Friendly societies also offer investment-type life insurance policies which can offer a tax-free return in the same way as normal life insurance policies. But there are strict limits on the size of the policies which qualify for this tax relief: for policies taken out before 1 September 1987, the sum assured (excluding bonuses) must be £750 or less; for policies taken out on 1 September 1987 onwards, the premiums must not exceed £100 a year (£9 a month or £2 a week). If these limits are stuck to, the policy is a qualifying one and the friendly society pays no income tax or capital gains tax on the business. But if you cash the policy in early and it becomes a non-qualifying policy, you will have to pay tax on the chargeable gain at both the basic rate and the higher rates (not just the higher rates, as with life insurance policies).

Some of these 'tax-exempt' policies offer highly competitive returns because the society doesn't have to pay tax on the investment returns. But you can't take out several policies with different societies each below the limits for tax relief to take advantage of these returns. If you take out a policy which takes all your tax-exempt policies over the limits, the policy automatically ceases to be a qualifying one and loses its tax-exempt status. However, these limits don't apply to policies taken out before 14 March 1984, so if you've already got several of these, you can enjoy the benefits on all of them.

WHAT TO PUT IN YOUR TAX RETURN

Most people don't need to enter any details of their life insurance policies on their Tax Return but you will have to enter details if any of the following applies:

● you pay more than £1,275 a year in net life insurance premiums which qualify for tax relief (that is, on policies taken out before 14 March 1984). Enter the total amount under *Life assurance–limits to relief* in the ALLOWANCES section of Forms 11P and 11. With Form P1, give details in an accompanying letter.

Form 11P

Life assurance-limits to relief
If in the year ended 5 April 1987 you and/or your wife paid more than –

| £1275 in life assurance premiums (including deferred annuity premiums) *enter the total paid* | £ | £85 in deferred annuity premiums and compulsory payments to provide annuities for widows and orphans *enter the total paid* | £ |

● you pay more than £85 a year in net premiums for deferred annuities or other premiums you have to pay to provide annuities for widows and orphans. Enter the details in the same place as for life insurance premiums on Form 11P, under *Death, sickness and superannuation benefits* in the ALLOWANCES section of Form 11 and under *Death and superannuation benefits* in the ALLOWANCES section of Form P1

● you have made a chargeable gain on a non-qualifying life insurance policy. Enter the details under *All other profits or income* in the INCOME section of Forms 11P and 11; with Form P1, enter details under *Any other income or gains* under INVESTMENT, SAVINGS, ETC.

Form 11P

Any other income not entered elsewhere *eg: accrued income charges and taxable gains on life assurance policies*		
	£	£

● you are paying premiums on a Section 226A life insurance policy. Enter details with information about your personal pension contributions (p. 216)

● you pay premiums to a friendly society on a combined life and sickness insurance policy which qualifies for tax relief. Tick the box in the ALLOWANCES section of Form 11P to get a claim form; with Form 11, give details under *Death, sickness and superannuation benefits*; with Form P1, give details under *Death and superannuation benefits*.

Form 11P

To claim any of the following allowances, tick the box that applies and I will send you the appropriate claim form.

☐ Son or daughter whose services you depend on	☐ Housekeeper allowance	☐ Friendly Society and Trade Union Death and Superannuation benefits

32 · GIVING TO CHARITY

If you want to give money to charity, there are some highly useful tax concessions to search out. Whether it's a regular donation to your local church, a response to a disaster appeal or a legacy in your will, you can maximize the amount the charity gets from your money by taking advantage of these concessions.

This chapter looks at the income tax relief you can get on regular gifts under covenant or through employers' payroll-giving schemes. And there are details of the tax-free gifts you can make for various good works.

COVENANTS TO CHARITY

You can get tax relief at your highest rate of tax on payments you make to registered charities if you make them under deed of covenant. A deed of covenant is a legally binding agreement to make a series of payments and to get the tax relief on payments to charity they should continue for more than three years. You won't get the tax relief if you get any benefit from the payments, so you can't use a covenant to pay school fees to a private school which is a charitable foundation.

HOW A COVENANT WORKS

Suppose you draw up a covenant to give your favourite charity a *gross* amount of £100 a year (the gross amount is what you give before deduction of the tax relief). When you make the payment, you deduct tax at the basic rate from the gross amount and hand over the *net* amount. So if the basic rate of tax is 27 per cent, you deduct £27 from the gross amount of £100 and hand over the net amount of £73 (that is, £100 − £27).

You can keep the tax you deduct from the gross amount of your gift provided you pay at least that much basic-rate tax on your income, so the £100 gift has cost you just £73. And the charity can reclaim the £27 you have deducted, so it ends up with the gross amount of your gift of £100.

This process automatically gives you the basic-rate tax relief on the gift. If you are entitled to higher-rate tax relief on the payment, you will have to claim it from your Tax Inspector (you'll get it either through PAYE or in a reduced tax bill).

If the basic rate of tax changes, you will have to change the amount you hand over: for example, if the basic rate fell to 25 per cent, you would deduct £25 from the gross amount of £100 and hand over £75. To avoid having to recalculate the amount to hand over every time the basic rate changes (and having to alter your banker's order), you can instead agree to hand over a fixed net amount.

For example, if you agree to hand over a net amount of £73 a year, this would be equivalent to a gross amount of £100 if the basic rate of tax was 27 per cent. If the basic rate fell to 25 per cent, the gross amount would become £97.33 to leave £73 after deduction of basic-rate tax. So, agreeing to pay a net amount means that you know exactly how much you have to hand over each year but the charity doesn't know exactly how much it is going to get from year to year.

DRAWING UP A COVENANT

Most charities will have printed covenant forms for you to complete if you wish to make regular donations. These usually specify payments for four years to meet the over-three-years rule. They will also probably be expressed as a net amount rather than a gross amount, so that you don't have to keep changing your banker's order every time the basic rate of tax changes. You will have to fill in your name, address, the date of the first payment and the amount you wish to give.

The deed of covenant will contain the words 'signed, sealed and delivered'. It must be signed and dated before the first payment is due (you can't backdate the covenant to cover payments already made). And the signing must be done in the presence of a witness who must also sign the deed (the witness should not be a relation). The deed should technically be sealed by sticking on a disc of paper but the Inland Revenue has said that it won't insist on this. You 'deliver' the deed, once you've completed these steps, by sending it to the charity (keeping a photocopy for reference).

If you're drawing up a covenant in Scotland, you don't need to seal or deliver the deed, nor is a witness required. But you must write the words 'Adopted as holograph' in your own handwriting above your signature and at the bottom of previous pages if the deed covers more than one.

MAKING THE PAYMENTS

It is important to fulfil the promises in the deed of covenant to the letter, handing over the net amount on the stated date. Filling out a banker's order form should ensure that the payments are made on the correct dates.

Form R185AP

Certificate of deduction of Income Tax - Annual payment under Deed of Covenant

Person making the payment
Only complete this form if you have made the payment and deducted tax from it. If you are deducting the tax on behalf of your employer as a secretary, cashier, etc, you should say so after your signature. Send the completed form to the person who receives the payment.

Your name and address

Postcode

Your employer's name and address or, if a company or business, the business address

Postcode

District (and reference) to which you make your tax returns

For official use
District stamp

'Duty assessed 'stamp

National Insurance number

I certify that
- I have made the payment, details of which are given below, and deducted the income tax shown
- this tax has been or will be paid by me either directly or by deduction from other income when I receive it.

Name and address of person receiving the payment

Postcode

Payment made under Deed of Covenant executed on	Consecutive number of the annual payment	Date payment made

Gross payment

£

Income tax I have deducted

£

Net payment

£

Signature ....

Date ....

Person receiving the payment
Keep this form until you claim repayment. Then send it with your claim as evidence of the tax deducted.

R185(AP)New

Printed for Her Majesty's Stationery Office by Harvest Printers Ltd. 6/86 Dd. 8975754

After the first payment has been made, the charity will send you Inland Revenue Form R185AP to sign. This sets out the amount you have handed over and the tax you have deducted, so that the charity can reclaim the tax. Fill it in and return it to the charity when you have signed it. With small amounts, you'll have to fill in Form R185AP only after the first year's payment: but if the amount you hand over after deduction of tax is over £175 a year, you'll have to complete Form R185AP every year.

USING COVENANTS FOR ONE-OFF PAYMENTS

The tax relief on covenant payments is designed to encourage regular payments lasting over three years. But it is possible to get tax relief on single donations if you make regular donations to a charity which acts as a clearing house for payments to other charities.

It works like this: you sign a covenant to make regular payments to the intermediary charity. You can deduct tax at the basic rate from the payments before handing them over. The intermediary reclaims the basic-rate tax you deduct and probably makes a yearly charge to cover expenses. When you wish to give a donation to a particular charity (in response to an appeal, perhaps), you instruct the intermediary to forward the amount you wish to give.

The largest organization acting as an intermediary in this way is the Charities Aid Foundation (CAF), 48 Pembury Road, Tonbridge, Kent TN9 2JD. They give you a book of cheques which you can sign and send direct to the charities of your choice who claim the money from the CAF. Other bodies, such as local voluntary service councils, provide a similar service.

PAYROLL-GIVING SCHEMES

If your employer has an approved payroll-giving scheme, you can get tax relief at your highest rate of tax on donations to charity (within limits). The money goes to the charities of your choice and there's no need to draw up a covenant or agree to make donations for several years.

Payroll-giving schemes have been in operation only since 6 April 1987 and allow employees to get tax relief on donations to charity of up to £120 a year. To get the tax relief, your employer must have set up a payroll-giving scheme: this means signing up with an Inland-Revenue-approved agency which collects the money employees wish to give and passes it on to the charities of their choice.

Once a scheme has been set up, you tell your employer how much you want to give and the charities you want to give it to. The money is deducted from your pay before working out how much tax is due on it, as with contributions to an employer's pension scheme. This automatically gives you the tax relief: a £100 gift out of your before-tax pay costs you £73 of your after-tax pay if you pay tax at the basic rate of 27 per cent only. Your employer hands over all the money deducted from employees' pay under the payroll-giving scheme to the agency which then acts as a clearing house, passing on the money to the charities nominated by the employees.

Although the £120 limit may be less than you want to give, the simplicity of the scheme and the absence of the sort of paperwork needed with covenants makes payroll-giving schemes most attractive.

CAPITAL TAXES

Inheritance tax may be payable on gifts of money made on your death or within seven years of your death (for more details, see Chapter 34, p. 291). Gifts of things such as paintings, historic homes, *objets d'art* and other heirlooms are also taxable in the same way but, if made during your lifetime, you may have to pay capital gains tax on them as well (p. 275).

But gifts and legacies to UK charities are free of inheritance tax, no matter how large they are. And if you give an asset which is showing a chargeable gain to a charity, there is no capital gains tax to pay.

Note, however, that if you give an asset which is showing a chargeable loss, this cannot be set off against other taxable gains. So if you wish to combine the greatest tax-saving in giving some property to charity, you should give things which are showing a taxable gain. If an item is showing a taxable loss, you would do better to sell it and give the proceeds to charity: this would create a loss which could be used to reduce your CGT bill on other disposals.

Other gifts which fall in the 'good works' category are also free of inheritance tax and capital gains tax, and include:

● gifts to certain national institutions, such as the National Trust, the National Gallery, the British Museum (and their Scottish, Welsh and Northern Irish equivalents)

● gifts for the public benefit to non-profit-making concerns like local museums

● gifts of certain types of heritage property (for example, paintings, archives or historic buildings).

WHAT TO PUT IN YOUR TAX RETURN

You should give details of covenant payments made during the last complete tax year on your Tax Return. With Forms 11P and 11 enter the details under *Covenants, bonds of annuity, settlements, etc.* in the OUTGOINGS section of the Tax Return.

Form 11P

Give the date you signed the covenant, the name of the charity and the gross amount (that is, before deduction of tax amount) paid in the tax year. If you're not sure what the gross amount is, use the ready reckoner on p. 318. With Form P1, enter the details under *Covenants*, also under OUTGOINGS.

There is no need to report gifts which are exempt from inheritance tax (p. 293). But if you give something to charity which would normally be liable to capital gains tax on disposal, you should enter the details under CAPITAL GAINS on the income tax return (see p. 289 for what to enter).

33 · CAPITAL GAINS TAX

If you own items which increase in value, you may find yourself paying capital gains tax at some time. For example, shares and unit trusts, land, property and antiques can increase in price, giving you a capital gain. If you sell them or give them away, for example, you may be faced with a capital gains tax bill.

The teeth of this tax have been getting blunter over the last few years. You are now less likely to have to pay tax on increases which are simply the result of inflation. And because of the ways you are allowed to reduce the bill by claiming various allowances, it means that the average taxpayer is unlikely to be faced with a CGT bill.

If you are a higher-rate income taxpayer, it can make sense for you to invest your money to give yourself a capital gain rather than extra income. If you do have to pay tax on your capital gains, the rate is a flat 30 per cent on the net taxable gains over and above the yearly tax-free limit. This 30 per cent tax rate compares very favourably with higher-rate income tax bands starting at 40 per cent and rising to 60 per cent. The higher the rate of income tax you pay, the more attractive it becomes for you to choose to invest for capital gains.

WHEN DO YOU HAVE TO PAY CAPITAL GAINS TAX?

You may have to pay capital gains tax when you dispose of an asset. What is meant by 'dispose' is not defined by law. But, for example, if you sell an asset, swap one asset for another, give something away, lose an asset, or it is destroyed or becomes valueless, you might find yourself caught up with CGT. If you are insured and make a claim you will not be treated as having disposed of the asset as long as you spend all the insurance money you receive replacing whatever it is you lost or was damaged.

There are some occasions when there is no capital gains tax to pay, regardless of what is being disposed of or how much it is worth. These occasions are when:

- you die

- you give something to your husband or wife, unless separated (p. 111)

- you donate an asset to a charity.

There are also a number of assets on which the gains are tax-free. There is a list of these starting on p. 277. If you owned any assets before 6 April 1965, the gain made before that date is also tax-free; there are complicated rules for working this out, see p. 282.

It is important to give information about any possible capital gains to your Tax Inspector by the end of October at the latest, otherwise interest could be charged. If you find that you owe CGT, the tax is due on 1 December after the end of the tax year in which you make the gains, or thirty days after the issue of a Notice of Assessment, if this is later. If you do not agree with the Notice of Assessment, appeal against it in writing within thirty days of the date on it, p. 52.

HOW MUCH TAX DO YOU HAVE TO PAY?

The basic rule is that you pay tax at the rate of 30 per cent on the net chargeable gains (that is, taxable gains) you make in each tax year. While that seems fairly straightforward, there are a number of additional rules which mean that you could end up paying less tax than would seem at first sight. What you must do, to keep your CGT bill as low as possible, is to know and take advantage of all the ways you can to reduce your bill.

First, there is a certain amount of gains you can make each year free of tax. For 1987/8, you can make net taxable gains of £6,600 free of tax; for 1986/7, the tax-free band was £6,300. Husband and wife have only one tax-free band between them.

Second, the tax is paid on *net* taxable gains. If you have made any losses during the tax year, these can be set off against the gains (p. 285).

Third, the way in which the gain is worked out can mean a lower tax bill than you might initially think. You do not simply deduct the purchase price from the selling price in all cases, for example. You may find that there are some other expenses you can allow for. And if you do not buy and sell the asset, you need to know how to work out the value for CGT when you acquire and dispose of it. Even after all this, you can now get a tax deduction to allow for the effect inflation had on pushing up the price or the value of the asset. The rules for working out the size of the gain are on the next page.

As well as these general rules which reduce the size of the CGT bill, there are a number of special rules which allow you to get more tax relief in particular circumstances, for example, when you retire, or to pass the bill to someone else, for example, when you make a gift. These are explained in more detail on p. 285.

WHO HAS TO PAY CAPITAL GAINS TAX?

Anyone may have to pay tax on capital gains. This includes you as an individual in your private life or in your business, if you are self-employed or in partnership. There are some organizations which do not pay tax on all the gains they make, for example, a charity, certain friendly societies, housing associations, pension funds and unit and investment trusts (although you may have to pay CGT on a gain from a unit or investment trust).

HOW TO WORK OUT THE GAIN

To find out how much your gain is, follow these steps:

STEP 1 Have you disposed of an asset? (see p. 275 for what is a disposal)

STEP 2 Is the gain tax-free? (see below)

STEP 3 What is the final value of the asset? (p. 279)

STEP 4 What is the original value of the asset? (p. 279) Deduct this from final value

STEP 5 Are there any allowable expenses? (p. 279) Deduct from the final value. You now have the unindexed gain or loss

STEP 6 What is the indexation allowance you can claim? (p. 280) Reduce the unindexed gain or increase the unindexed loss by the amount of the indexation allowance

STEP 7 If you owned the asset before 6 April 1965, work out what time apportionment you can apply, if you choose to do so (p. 280)

There are special rules for working out the gain on shares (p. 284) and personal belongings (p. 284).

TAX-FREE GAINS

There is no CGT to pay on a gain you make on any of the following assets; however, if you make a loss on one of these, you cannot use it to set off against other gains, reducing your tax bill that way:

● your home, but if you own a second property, CGT is payable on a gain on a second property. Chapter 28, p. 218, explains in more detail how capital gains on a home are taxed

● various National Savings investments, for example, National Savings Certificates, Save-As-You-Earn

● a decoration for bravery, unless you bought it

● foreign currency for your personal spending abroad (including what you pay to maintain a home abroad), but not foreign currency accounts

● British Government stock and any options on these to buy or sell. Before 2 July 1986, the gain was only tax-free if you held the stock for a year or more

● proceeds of an insurance policy (unless you bought the policy and were not the original holder)

● certain corporate bonds, such as company loan stock and debentures which you acquired after 13 March 1984 and any options on these to buy or sell. Before 2 July 1986, the gain was tax-free only if you held the stock for a year or more

● interest in a settlement, unless you bought it

● betting or lottery winnings

● as long as they qualify for income tax relief, shares you bought in a Business Expansion Scheme after 18 March 1986

● damages or compensation for a personal injury or wrong to yourself or in your professional capacity, for example, libel

● certain gifts for the public benefit

● Personal Equity Plans from 1 January 1987, as long as the conditions are met

● personal belongings (chattels) sold for £3,000 or less. If you dispose of them for more than £3,000, any gain is partly tax-free, see p. 284

● a wasting asset with a useful life of fifty years or less, for example, a boat, but not if you could have claimed a capital allowance on it. But gains on leases are not tax-free

● British money, including sovereigns dated after 1837.

THE FINAL VALUE OF THE ASSET

If you sell the asset, the final value taken to work out the gain will be what you received for the sale; if you give it away, the market value is the important figure.

There are special rules for establishing the value if you dispose of an asset to a *connected person*. The value will be taken as market value, whatever you sold it for (but see p. 287 for how you can delay the tax bill).

A connected person includes your wife or husband, your relatives and your spouse's relatives. A relative is a brother or sister, grandparent or grandchild and their wives or husbands, but not (as far as the taxman is concerned) a cousin, aunt or uncle, nephew or niece.

THE ORIGINAL VALUE OF THE ASSET

What is the starting point for a gain? If you bought the asset, it will be what you paid for it; if you were given it, the market value at that time is the original value; and if you inherited it, the market value (probate value) at the time the person died will be taken. There are special rules for assets acquired before 6 April 1965, see p. 282.

Remember to note down somewhere and keep a record of the assets you have acquired and their acquisition cost; file away any receipts.

ALLOWABLE EXPENSES

You can deduct allowable expenses in computing the gain for capital gains tax. These include:

● acquisition costs, such as payments to a professional adviser (for example, surveyor, accountant, solicitor), conveyancing costs and stamp duty, and advertising to find a seller

● what you spend improving the asset (but not your own time)

● what you spend establishing or defending your rights or title to the asset

● disposal costs, similar to acquisition costs, but including the cost of valuing for CGT.

Remember to note down somewhere the expenses which will be allowable and keep any receipts or invoices, as you will have to satisfy your Tax Inspector of the amounts you are claiming when you come to disposing of the asset.

EXAMPLE

Benny Barber buys a painting for £25,000 in April 1982. He pays an additional fee to the auction house of £2,500. Subsequently in July 1982, he spends £1,000 having the painting cleaned. He sells the painting for £55,000 in June 1986, paying £5,000 to the auction house.

The gains before indexation allowance (see below) will be:

Final value		£55,000
less allowable expenses:		
original cost	£25,000	
cleaning	1,000	
buying cost	2,500	
selling cost	5,000	33,500
Unindexed gain		£21,500

INDEXATION ALLOWANCE

Once you have deducted the original value and the allowable expenditure from the final value, you have your unindexed gain or loss. Because many gains will include increases which are simply the result of inflation, you can set off an allowance against the unindexed gain or loss. As long as prices in general are rising, the allowance will decrease the size of the gain, increase the size of the loss or even turn a gain into a loss (see Example 3, p. 282). Losses which occur because of the indexation allowance can be set against gains in the normal way to arrive at a figure for the year of net taxable gains, see p. 285.

You have to do a different calculation for the initial value and each item of allowable expenditure if they are made at different dates. Adding these together gives you the amount of the indexation allowance.

For assets which you disposed of on or after 6 April 1985:

Multiply the initial value and each item of allowable expenditure made on or after 31 March 1982 by

$$\frac{\text{RPI for month of disposal} - \text{RPI for month of expenditure}}{\text{RPI for month of expenditure}}$$

Note that RPI stands for Retail Prices Index. For any expenditure you made before 31 March 1982 always use the Retail Price Index for March 1982, instead of RPI for month of expenditure. You should work out the sum to three decimal places. The month of expenditure is the month it becomes due. For the values of the Retail Prices Index, see Tax Facts on p. 318.

EXAMPLE I

Benny Barber (see left) works out what indexation allowance he can claim. First, he works it out for the original cost and the buying fee, a total of £27,500.

$$\text{This comes to } £27,500 \times \frac{\text{RPI June 1986} - \text{RPI April 1982}}{\text{RPI April 1982}}$$

$$= £27,500 \times \frac{385.8 - 319.7}{319.7} = £27,500 \times 0.207 = £5,692$$

Now he works out the indexation allowance for the cost of cleaning. This comes to:

$$£1,000 \times \frac{\text{RPI June 1986} - \text{RPI July 1982}}{\text{RPI July 1982}}$$

$$= £1,000 \times \frac{385.8 - 323.0}{323.0} = £1,000 \times 0.194$$

$$= £194$$

Benny's total indexation allowance comes to £5,692 plus £194 = £5,886. His taxable gain is £21,500 − £5,886 = £15,614

There is a further complication for assets you acquired on or before 31 March 1982. You can choose to work out the indexation allowance (but not the unindexed gain or loss) on its market value on 31 March 1982 instead of its original cost. It would pay you to do this if the market value is higher than the original cost.

EXAMPLE 2

Harold White bought a country cottage as a second home in June 1965; its cost was £1,600. Its value on 31 March 1982 was £50,000 and he sold it for £85,000 in May 1986. The indexation allowance based on cost would be:

$$£1,600 \times \frac{\text{RPI May 1986} - \text{RPI March 1982}}{\text{RPI March 1982}}$$

$$= £1,600 \times \frac{386.0 - 313.4}{313.4} = £1,600 \times 0.232$$

$$= £371$$

The taxable gain would be:

Proceeds		£85,000
less cost	£1,600	
indexation allowance	371	1,971
		£83,029

But if Harold works it out on its market value on 31 March 1982, it becomes:

$$£50,000 \times \frac{386.0 - 313.4}{313.4} = £50,000 \times 0.232$$

$$= £11,600$$

The taxable gain would be £85,000 − £1,600 − £11,600 = £71,800

Harold should choose to work out the indexation allowance on the basis of market value on 31 March 1982, not cost.

EXAMPLE 3

Jayne Bennett acquires a piece of antique silver in January 1984 for £8,000. But when she sells it in January 1986 she receives only £8,200, making a small unindexed gain of £200. She works out the indexation allowance she can claim.

$$= £8,000 \times \frac{\text{RPI January 1986} - \text{RPI January 1984}}{\text{RPI January 1984}}$$

$$£8,000 \times \frac{379.7 - 342.6}{342.6} = £8,000 \times 0.108$$

$$= £864$$

Jayne's unindexed gain of £200 turns into a loss after indexation allowance of £8,200 − £8,000 − £864 = £664 loss

If you disposed of an asset before 6 April 1985, there were different rules about calculating an indexation allowance.

In the case of shares, there are special difficulties in identifying which have been disposed of and which you still hold. Brief guidelines are given on p. 284.

ASSETS YOU OWNED BEFORE 6 APRIL 1965

Capital gains tax was a new tax introduced on 6 April 1965 and gains or losses before that date should be left out of the calculations. This can be done in one of two ways. Your Tax Inspector will automatically apply the first method, unless you choose the second. You must make the choice within a time limit – not more than two years after the end of the tax year in which you dispose of the asset. With stocks and shares, you must make your choice for all shares or for all your fixed interest investments at one time.

In the first method, you apportion the gain on a time basis over the period you have owned it. The method assumes that the gain rose evenly over the period. You calculate your gain following the steps 1 to 6 on p. 277. Once you have arrived at a figure for the gain after indexation allowance from step 6, you find the number of whole months you have owned the asset, but not counting back further than 6 April 1945. The next step is to divide the gain by the number of months you have owned it. Finally, you multiply by the number of months between 6 April 1965 and the month you dispose of the asset. This gives you the taxable gain on that asset (see Example below).

If you have made allowable expenses after you acquired the asset, the calculation becomes a little tricky and you may find it helpful to get professional advice.

The second method allows you to use the market value of the asset on 6 April 1965 as the initial value of the asset. You should choose this method if more of the gain occurred before that date than after. Once you have opted for this second method, you cannot change your mind and revert to the first method. So, before you tell your Tax Inspector what choice you want to make, do the sums carefully.

You cannot choose this second method if it gives a bigger loss than you would have by deducting cost, allowable expenses and indexation allowance from the disposal proceeds, ignoring time apportionment. If you have stocks and shares you cannot choose the second method if it would mean you could claim a loss instead of a gain. If this is the case, your Tax Inspector will assume that you have neither a gain nor a loss from the asset.

EXAMPLE

Harold White has worked out the taxable gain on the cottage he bought in June 1965 as £71,800 (see previous page). Suppose that he had bought the cottage in June 1963 instead of June 1965, what effect would choosing the first method of time apportionment have on the taxable gain? He finds the number of whole months since June 1963. He bought it on 6 June and sold it on 12 May 1986. He has owned it 275 complete months. He divides the gain of £71,800 by 275, which comes to £261.09

per month. The number of complete months between 6 April 1965 and when he disposes of it is 253, so Harold's taxable gain after time apportionment is 253 times £261.09 = £66,056.

SPECIAL RULES FOR SHARES

To work out the indexation allowance, you need to be able to identify which shares you have sold. Easy enough if you only buy one lot of shares in a company or you sell all your shares in a company at the same time. But if you buy shares at different times in the same company, deciding which are the ones you have sold and which you still hold can be difficult. The tax laws do it for you; according to these, you have sold the shares in the following order:

● if you buy shares in a company on the same day as you sell shares in that company, it is assumed that these are the shares you have sold first of all

● the second lot of shares you are assumed to sell are any you have acquired within ten days of the disposal. Note that you cannot claim any indexation allowance on shares owned for ten days or less

● third,.shares you acquired after April 1982 and which are not included in the two categories above. These are all put together in one pool

● fourth, shares in that same company which you acquired between 6 April 1965 and 5 April 1982 are in one pool. You would also include with this lot any shares you acquired before 6 April 1965, if you have told your Tax Inspector you want to have them valued for CGT on the basis of their market value on 6 April 1965

● finally, any shares which you acquired before 6 April 1965, excluding any included above. The shares in this lot are treated on the assumption that the last shares you acquired are the first to go.

There are several complications about how gains on shares are handled for CGT, for example, scrip and rights issues and takeovers, so it would be wise to take professional advice.

SPECIAL RULES FOR PERSONAL BELONGINGS

These are known as chattels by the taxman and are tangible movable property, such as a piece of furniture, silver, paintings and so on. A set of something counts as one chattel. If the chattel is sold for £3,000 or less, any gain is tax-free. If it is sold for more than £3,000, the gain will be partly tax-free.

This relief is given by setting a maximum on the size of the gain used for working out the amount of CGT to pay. The gain will be no more than 5/3 of the amount of the disposal over £3,000.

EXAMPLE

Caroline Burns bought a piece of furniture for £1,500 and sold it for £4,500. Although sale proceeds less original cost comes to £3,000, for CGT purposes the gain can be no more than 5/3 times £4,500 less £3,000. This equals $5/3 \times £1,500 = £2,500$.

If your capital gains tax bill would be less, using the normal way of working out a gain, use that instead of this relief.

Note that with the relief, the amount of any allowable loss you could claim is also restricted to the excess of the cost less £3,000.

HOW TO REDUCE OR DELAY YOUR CAPITAL GAINS TAX BILL

There are a number of ways in which you may be able to reduce or delay your bill. These include:

● making sure you claim all the allowable expenses you can and your indexation allowance (pp. 279, 280)

● setting off any losses you have made (see below)

● taking advantage of the band of tax-free gains you can make each year (p. 286)

● claiming roll-over relief when you dispose of business assets (p. 286)

● claiming hold-over relief when you give something away (p. 287)

● claiming retirement relief when you retire from your business (p. 288).

SETTING OFF LOSSES

You pay capital gains tax at the rate of 30 per cent on the net taxable gains you make. You find the net amount by deducting losses, as well as any allowances you can claim, from the amount of your taxable gains. You have to set off the losses in the year in which they occur, but if your losses are more than your gains for the year, the excess can be carried forward to the next tax year and as far forward as you like. You can use the carried forward losses to reduce your net taxable gains in the next tax year, but you do not have to bring them lower than the tax-free band (£6,600 for 1987/8; £6,300 for 1986/7).

EXAMPLE

Hattie Wilson has made taxable gains of £4,500 in the tax year 1986/7 and allowable losses of £7,000 in the same year. She has to set off losses of £4,500 against her gains even though she would not have to pay tax on them as they are within her tax-free band for the year. She can carry forward losses of £7,000 − £4,500 = £2,500 to the next tax year 1987/8.

In 1987/8 Hattie makes taxable gains of £7,200. She can use part of her losses carried forward from the previous year to reduce her net taxable gains to the tax-free limit. So she sets off £600 of her losses to bring her net taxable gains for 1987/8 to £7,200 − £600 = £6,600 and hence reduce her CGT bill to zero. The remaining £2,500 − £600 = £1,900 losses she carries forward to 1988/9.

You cannot carry back losses, except losses made in the tax year you die. Your executors will be able to carry back these losses to set against gains you made in the three previous tax years.

Married couples do not necessarily have to set off the losses made by one against the gains made by the other during the same tax year. You can choose to carry forward allowable losses to another tax year to set against your own future gains in another year, but not against your spouse's. You should do this if your spouse has made gains of the tax-free amount or less. If you want to do this, you must tell your Tax Inspector by 5 July in the tax year of assessment.

A loss made when you dispose of an asset to a connected person (p. 287) can only be set off against a gain made to a connected person. This applies even if the loss was made when you disposed of your asset for a genuine commercial value.

TAKING ADVANTAGE OF THE TAX-FREE BAND

If you do not use up all the tax-free band in a tax year, that is, because your net taxable gains are too small, the unused portion cannot be carried forward to another year. If you know you are going to dispose of a number of items, try to space it out over the years to take advantage of the tax-free amount, rather than dispose of them all in one year and find yourself paying capital gains tax unnecessarily.

REPLACING BUSINESS ASSETS

If you sell, or otherwise dispose of, assets from your business, and make a gain, you could pay capital gains tax on the gain. But if you replace the assets in the three years after the sale or one year before the sale of the old ones, you can claim *roll-over relief* and defer paying CGT. You can also claim the relief if you do not replace the exact asset but you use the proceeds to buy another qualifying business asset.

You usually get the relief by deducting the gain for the old asset from the acquisition cost for the new one. So, when you sell the new one, the gain on it has been increased by the size of the gain on the old one. However, if you replace again, you can claim further roll-over relief. And so on. Capital gains tax will not have to be paid (under current legislation) until you fail to replace the business asset.

The gain from the asset is worked out following steps 1 to 7 from pp. 277–83, so, for example, it is the gain after deducting indexation allowance.

Not every business asset qualifies for the relief. But if it is land or a building used by the business, goodwill, fixed plant or machinery, for example, it will qualify for roll-over relief.

GIFTS

You can claim hold-over relief if you give an asset away and do not receive the full commercial payment for it. Both you, the giver, and the person who receives the gift have to claim the relief. If you give it away without receiving anything for it, the relief works by reducing to nil the gain you have made on the asset between acquisition and giving it away. However, the original value of the gift, as far as the person who receives the gift is concerned, is not its market value at the time of the gift. It is reduced by the amount of the gain *you* made between acquisition and disposal. The amount of the gain is worked out in the normal way following steps 1 to 7 on pp. 277–83.

When the recipient comes to dispose of the asset, the gain made on it as far as the taxman is concerned will be much larger than the actual increase in value during that person's ownership. In this way, the payment of CGT for that particular asset is passed on from you to the person who gets the asset.

EXAMPLE

Lucy Warden gives a brooch valued at £8,500 to her favourite niece, Rebecca. Lucy had bought the brooch herself five years before at a cost of £4,000. Together they apply for hold-over relief. Rebecca some years later sells the brooch for £12,000. Her gain, ignoring indexation allowance, is not £12,000 − £8,500. Instead, Lucy's original purchase price is taken as the original value, so Rebecca's gain is £12,000 − £4,000 = £8,000.

There is no point in making a hold-over election, if your net taxable gains for the year, including the gift, will be within the tax-free band for the year (£6,600 in 1987/8).

To make the election, you jointly have to tell your Tax Inspector within six years of the tax year you made the present. Hold-over relief is available only if the person receiving the gift is resident or ordinarily resident in the UK. If that person subsequently becomes non-resident, you may find that *you* have to pay a CGT bill. Take professional advice.

If you give something to a trust, you can still get hold-over relief. In this case, you alone can make the election.

DISPOSING OF YOUR BUSINESS (RETIREMENT RELIEF)

You can dispose of your business (or of shares in a family company, see below) at the age of sixty, or earlier if you are retiring due to ill-health, and claim relief on any gain you make. If you are disposing of the business or businesses on or after 6 April 1987, the maximum relief is £125,000; before that date, the maximum relief was £100,000. What this means is that you do not have to pay capital gains tax on the first £125,000 of the gains you make.

But this maximum amount applies only if you have owned the business or shares for at least ten years. The amount is reduced by 10 per cent to £112,500 if your ownership is nine years. It carries on decreasing by this percentage for every year's reduction until it is only 10 per cent of the maximum (that is, £12,500) if you have owned the business for only one year.

EXAMPLE

Rupert Foot sells his business in June 1987 when he is sixty-two. He started the business five years before and he sells it for £500,000. He claims retirement relief. As the business has been going for less than ten years, he cannot claim the maximum relief. He can claim £12,500 for each year so, for the five years the business has run he gets relief of $5 \times £12,500 = £62,500$. The amount of his taxable gain after working through steps 1 to 7 on pp. 277–83 is reduced by £62,500.

You can also claim the relief if you dispose of shares in a family company if you have been a full-time director of the company for the last ten years. A family company is one in which you have 25 per cent of the voting rights, or you and your immediate family have more than 50 per cent and you yourself at least 5 per cent.

Note that although this relief is called retirement relief, you do not have to retire to claim it, unless you are selling or disposing of your business because of your ill-health (which can be strictly defined). If you wish to claim this relief because of ill-health, you must do so within two years of the end of the tax year in which you dispose of the business.

Before 6 April 1985, the rules were different. For example, the relief was tapered if you were aged between sixty and sixty-five, and you couldn't get relief for an earlier retirement due to ill-health.

WHAT TO PUT IN YOUR TAX RETURN

You are asked to give details about capital gains in your Tax Return. For the Tax Return 1987/8, for example, this refers to gains made in the year ending 5 April 1987.

For the Tax Return 1987/8 (Forms 11P and 11), under the heading *Chargeable assets disposed of*, the details of the assets and the amount of the taxable gains and allowable losses should have been entered. Write 'gain' or 'loss', whichever is appropriate. Include details of how the losses and gains were worked out; for example, you could staple a separate sheet to the form showing the calculation.

Form 11P

Chargeable assets disposed of			Amount of gain for year	
Date of disposal	Description		Self	Wife
			£	£

However, if all the following were correct:

● the gains on taxable assets were within the tax-free limit (£6,600 for 1987/8, £6,300 for 1986/7), *and*

● the total value of the chargeable assets disposed of was within another limit (£13,200 for 1987/8; £12,600 for 1986/7),

and

● you and your husband or wife have not chosen to have your capital gains assessed separately and neither of you want your own losses to be set against only your own individual future gains *write*

'Gains not exceeding £6,600 and disposal proceeds not exceeding £13,200' for the 1987/8 tax year and 'Gains not exceeding £6,300 and disposal proceeds not exceeding £12,600' for the 1986/7 year.

If you have been sent Form P1, the information goes under CAPITAL GAINS on the last page. If the above applies to you, you do not need to enter anything.

For Tax Returns before the 1987/8 one, in the section headed *Chargeable assets acquired*, describe and give the value of the new chargeable assets you acquired in the tax year and the date you acquired them. In your figure for value, remember to itemize all allowable expenses. Do not write in details of any assets on which gains are tax-free (although strictly you should enter your home), nor gifts of money.

34 · INHERITANCE TAX

Inheritance tax is the latest in a line of three taxes designed to tax wealth passed on at death (or shortly before). The first, estate duty, ran from 1909 until 1974; it was succeeded by capital transfer tax (CTT), which also covered wealth passed on during your lifetime. Since 18 March 1986 CTT has been replaced by inheritance tax which largely eliminates tax on lifetime gifts unless made in the seven years before death.

Nonetheless there is much that you can do in your lifetime to reduce the inheritance tax bill that will be due on your death. Tax is payable on quite modest estates: if you leave just £150,000 (not improbable for anyone owning a home in London or the south-east), there could be £19,000 to pay in inheritance tax or more if you've made taxable gifts in the seven years before your death.

A little planning now can ensure that as much as possible of your worldly wealth goes to your heirs and as little as possible to the taxman.

WHAT YOU PAY TAX ON

Inheritance tax is payable on the value of what you leave on death and anything you have given away in the previous seven years (these are called *transfers of value* by the taxman). It may also be due on gifts made outside this seven-year zone to certain types of trust or to a company. But many gifts and bequests are free of inheritance tax: for example, gifts to your husband or wife are always tax-free, whether made in your lifetime or on death (for a full list of tax-free gifts, see p. 293).

Because a gift made during your lifetime will be taxable if you die within seven years of making it, lifetime gifts are often described as *Potentially Exempt Transfers* (*PETs*): they are potentially tax-free but you must survive for seven years after they are made for the tax to be avoided.

THE TAX RATES

Tax is payable on a progressive scale, that is, the rate of tax increases the higher the total. The following is the scale for deaths on or after 17 March 1987:

TAXABLE GIFTS	RATE OF TAX	TOTAL TAX PAID TO TOP OF BAND
£	%	£
0–90,000	nil	nil
90,001–140,000	30	15,000
140,001–220,000	40	47,000
220,001–330,000	50	102,000
Over 330,000	60	

For deaths after 17 March 1986 but before 17 March 1987 the rates are as follows:

TAXABLE GIFTS	RATE OF TAX	TOTAL TAX PAID TO TOP OF BAND
£	%	£
0–71,000	nil	nil
71,001–95,000	30	7,200
95,001–129,000	35	19,100
129,001–164,000	40	33,100
164,001–206,000	45	52,000
206,001–257,000	50	77,500
257,001–317,000	55	110,500
Over 317,000	60	

TAPERING RELIEF

The tax payable on gifts made between three and seven years before your death is reduced on the following scale (this is known as *tapering relief*):

YEARS BETWEEN GIFT AND DEATH	% OF TAX PAYABLE
0–3	100%
3–4	80%
4–5	60%
5–6	40%
6–7	20%

TAX-FREE GIFTS

There are three different types of tax-free gift:

● gifts that are always tax-free, whether made in life or on death

● gifts that are tax-free on death only

● gifts that are tax-free only if made during your lifetime.

GIFTS THAT ARE ALWAYS TAX-FREE

There is no inheritance tax to pay on *gifts between husband and wife*, whether made on death or during their lifetime. This applies however large the gift and even if the couple are legally separated. But gifts totalling more than £55,000 from one partner domiciled in the UK (p. 310) to a partner who is not domiciled in the UK are taxable.

This is by far the most important category of tax-free gift, and the one most likely to be available to readers of this Guide. But the following gifts which can be loosely classed as 'good works' are also free of inheritance tax:

● gifts to UK charities

● gifts to certain national institutions such as the National Trust, the National Gallery, the British Museum (and their Scottish, Welsh and Northern Irish equivalents)

● gifts for the public benefit to non-profit-making concerns like local museums

● gifts of certain types of heritage property such as paintings, archives or historic buildings

● gifts of shares in a company into a trust for the benefit of most or all of the employees which will control the company.

Quaintly, the politicians who drew up the rules for inheritance tax believed that their own parties were also worthy of charity. Thus gifts to political parties (or at least established ones) are also tax-free if made in lifetime. Gifts made on death or within a year of death are tax-free only up to £100,000.

GIFTS THAT ARE TAX-FREE ON DEATH ONLY

There is no inheritance tax to pay on lump sums paid out on your death by a pension scheme provided that the trustees of the scheme have discretion about who gets the money. Also free of inheritance tax is the estate of anyone killed on active military service in war or whose death was hastened by such service.

GIFTS THAT ARE TAX-FREE IN LIFETIME ONLY

Anything given away more than seven years before your death is free of inheritance tax (unless to certain types of trust, see p. 302). And many routine gifts made in your lifetime are free of tax even if you die within seven years of making them. Although there are limits on the size of these tax-free gifts, they can add up over the years and allow you to give away tens of thousands of pounds free of inheritance tax during the seven-year period before death.

For example, gifts of up to £250 to any number of people in any one tax year are free of inheritance tax. This *small gifts exemption* applies to the total that you give each person in the year. So if you give someone £500, you can't claim the exemption on the first £250 – the whole £500 will be taxable.

Regular *gifts made out of your normal income* are also free of inheritance tax. The gifts must come out of your usual after-tax income and not from your capital: after paying for the gifts, you should have enough income left to maintain your normal standard of living. Even if you have made only one payment, it can be tax-free provided that there is evidence that there will be further payments (for example, a covenant or letter of intent). Paying the premiums on a life insurance policy which will pay out to someone else on your death is usually a tax-free gift under this heading (it can also provide some cash to pay any tax which is due on any taxable bequests you leave on death).

Gifts on marriage to a bride or groom can also be exempt from inheritance tax, within limits:

● £5,000 if you are a parent of the bride or groom (that is, £10,000 in all if both parents make such gifts)

● £2,500 if you are a grandparent or remoter relative of the bride or groom

● £2,500 if you are either the bride or groom yourself (once you're married, of course, all such gifts are free of inheritance tax)

● £1,000 for anyone else.

The gift must be made 'in consideration of marriage', so it can be made before the great day but if the marriage is called off, the gift becomes taxable.

There are other gifts which aren't really gifts at all and which are therefore free of inheritance tax. For example, if you hand money over to your divorced ex-spouse under a court order, there will be no tax to pay on the gift. Similarly money used for the *maintenance of your family* in the manner to which they've become accustomed is not taxable: this exemption covers spending on your spouse, certain dependent relatives and children under eighteen or still in full-time education. The children can be yours, step-children, adopted children or any other children in your care.

After all these tax-free gifts have been made, you can make further tax-free gifts each year of up £3,000 in total. If you don't use the whole £3,000 *annual exemption* in one year, you can carry forward the unused part to the next tax year only. But note that you can't use the annual exemption to top up the small gifts exemption: if you give someone more than £250 in a year, all of it must come off the annual exemption if it is to be free of inheritance tax.

NIL-RATE BAND

Even if a gift or bequest is taxable, the rate of tax on the first £90,000 of taxable transfers in 1987/8 is 0 per cent. So transfers within this nil-rate band are effectively free of tax.

If you give away £90,000 in taxable gifts, and survive for seven years, you can then give away another £90,000 without incurring tax since the first £90,000 drops out of the reckoning.

EXAMPLE

Hugh James wants to give away as much as possible free of tax before he dies. He is married and he and his wife Queenie have more than enough income to live on for the foreseeable future.

Anything Hugh gives to Queenie is free of inheritance tax. And both Hugh and Queenie are entitled to make the tax-free gifts outlined above. So Hugh gives half his spare wealth to Queenie so that they can each make the maximum of tax-free gifts.

First, Hugh and Queenie make £250 gifts every year to each of their ten grandchildren – a total of £5,000 a year free of inheritance tax as small gifts. Both also hand over £1,000 to each of their three children under the annual exemption – another £6,000 a year free of tax.

Hugh and Queenie can also afford to pay the premiums on insurance policies on their own lives out of their normal income. So they take out three policies each, one in favour of each of their three children. The premiums come to £120 a month each and will be tax-free as gifts made out of their normal income (when they die, the money from the insurance policies will be paid straight to the children without being taxable).

Overall, Hugh and Queenie manage to give away almost £15,000 a year free of inheritance tax. This is over £100,000 in a seven-year period, and even if they die within seven years of starting this programme of gifts there will be no inheritance tax to pay on them. If they want to give away more than this, they could also make gifts of £90,000 each to take advantage of the nil-rate band, repeating this every seven years when the last £90,000 gift drops out of the reckoning.

HOW THE TAX BILL IS WORKED OUT

In working out the amount of tax due on your estate and taxable lifetime gifts, the taxman starts with the earliest taxable gifts first, which are therefore taxed at the lowest rates. The tax on a lifetime gift is charged on its value at the time of the gift. But the tax rates to be used are those which apply at the date of your death, not when the gifts were made.

Use the following steps to calculate an inheritance tax bill:

STEP 1 Work out the tax due on the first taxable gift.

STEP 2 Then add the second gift to the first gift and work out the tax due on the cumulative total. Subtract the tax due on the first gift from the tax due on the cumulative total to find the tax due on the second gift.

STEP 3 Add the third gift to the cumulative total so far and work out the tax due on this new cumulative total. Subtract the tax due on the previous gifts from the tax due on the new cumulative total to find the inheritance tax due on the third gift.

STEP 4 Repeat step 3 for all taxable gifts made before death to find the tax due on each.

STEP 5 Finally, add the taxable value of your estate to the cumulative total of your taxable lifetime gifts and work out the inheritance tax due on what you leave on death.

STEP 6 If any of the tax due is on a lifetime gift made between three and seven years before your death, the amount payable will be reduced by tapering relief (see the scale on p. 292).

EXAMPLE

Eileen Dover gave her son Ben a taxable gift of £50,000 in September 1986, having given no other taxable gifts before then. In April 1988 she gives her daughter Angela the same amount (£50,000). And in December 1990 she gives her daughter Ruth another taxable gift of £50,000. Eileen dies in June 1991, leaving an estate valued at £120,000.

The inheritance tax bill due on Eileen's death is worked out as follows (using the tax rates in force in 1987/8):

STEP 1 All the taxable gifts were made in the seven years before Eileen's death and are therefore subject to inheritance tax. The first £50,000 gift to Ben is taxed at the nil rate, that is, no tax to pay.

STEP 2 The second taxable gift of £50,000 to Angela is added to the £50,000 gift to Ben to produce a cumulative total of £100,000. The tax due on this £100,000 is worked out using the rates in the Table on p. 292 as follows:

The cumulative tax on £90,000 is	£0
The remaining £10,000 is taxed at 30%	£3,000
TOTAL TAX	£3,000

Since no tax was due on the first gift, all £3,000 of this total is due on the gift to Angela.

STEP 3 The gift of £50,000 to Ruth is added to the cumulative total of £100,000 to produce a new total of £150,000. The tax due on this new cumulative total is calculated using the rates in the Table on p. 292 as follows:

The cumulative tax on £140,000 is	£15,000
The remaining £10,000 is taxed at 40%	£4,000
TOTAL TAX	£19,000

£3,000 of this total tax was due on the gift to Angela, so the tax due on Ruth's gift is £19,000 − £3,000 = £16,000.

STEP 4 There are no other taxable gifts made before Eileen's death, so we can move straight to the next step.

STEP 5 The taxable value of Eileen's estate of £120,000 is added to the cumulative total of £150,000 to produce a total of £270,000. The inheritance tax due on this is worked out as follows:

The cumulative tax on £220,000 is	£47,000
The remaining £50,000 is taxed at 50%	£25,000
TOTAL TAX	£72,000

£19,000 of this total tax was due on the lifetime gifts, so the tax due on Eileen's estate would be £72,000 − £19,000 = £53,000.

STEP 6 The tax bills due on gifts between three and seven years before death are reduced, using the scale on p. 292. The gift to Ben was made five years before Eileen's death but as no tax is due on it no reduction is necessary. But the gift to Angela was made between three and four years before death and only 80 per cent of the £3,000 tax bill is payable – £2,400 in all. The gift to Ruth was made within three years of Eileen's death and so all the £16,000 tax bill is payable (as is the £53,000 on Eileen's estate).

The tax bills on the lifetime gifts must be paid by the children who got them. So, although Eileen gave £50,000 to each of her three children, they end up with different amounts once the tax is paid. Ben would have got and kept £50,000; Angela would have £47,600 after paying the £2,400 inheritance tax bill; Ruth would have just £34,000 after paying inheritance tax of £16,000.

If Eileen had lived for at least seven years after making the last gift to Ruth, none of her gifts would have been taxable. If she wanted them to get and keep all £50,000 each, she could have taken out special life insurance policies designed to cover the tax bills on her death within seven years of making the gifts.

SPECIAL INHERITANCE TAX RULES

Applying the rules above to gifts and legacies of money is fairly straightforward but special rules are needed to value non-cash goods. And there are special reliefs to help those who own farms and small businesses, designed to ensure that inheritance tax does not threaten the survival of the business when you die.

VALUABLES

Bequests of valuables such as antiques, jewellery, cars, boats, heirlooms and the like – and gifts within seven years of your death – will all be taxable. The rule for valuing such gifts is that their value is the amount by which your wealth (or estate) is reduced by the gift: in most cases, this will be the market value of the item in question.

But the value may be somewhat higher if the item is part of a set or group whose collective value is greater than the sum of its parts. For example, a set of antique silver cutlery may be worth more than the value of the individual pieces. If a single piece worth, say, £500 is given away, the value of the remaining pieces may fall by more than £500. It is the fall in value of the remainder which is the value of the gift for inheritance tax purposes, not the £500 the single piece would fetch at auction.

HOUSES AND LAND

The value of your home and any other real estate that you own is the market value at the date of your death or the gift. This value must be agreed with the District Valuer (an employee of the Inland Revenue).

INVESTMENTS

For stocks and shares listed on the Stock Exchange, the value is found from the prices recorded in the Official Daily List (which can be supplied by a stockbroker or bank) on the date of the gift or bequest. If the Stock Exchange was closed, you can choose between the prices on the first working day before and the first working day after the transfer. The value for inheritance tax purposes is the lower selling price, plus a quarter of the difference between the selling price and the (higher) buying price: this is known as the 'quarter-up rule'.

Shares quoted on the Unlisted Securities Market (USM) are valued in the same way as listed shares for transfers on or after 17 March 1987. USM shares transferred before 17 March 1987 and shares quoted on the Third Market or the Over the Counter (OTC) markets are treated as 'unquoted securities' (see overleaf). Authorized unit trusts are valued at the price you could sell them for (that is, the bid price) on the day of transfer or the most recent date such prices were quoted before then.

If quoted shares or unit trusts left on death are sold within twelve months at a lower price than that established under the quarter-up rule at the time of the death, the sale price may be used to value them instead.

UNQUOTED SHARES

The value of a gift or bequest of unquoted shares depends on the size and importance of the holding. If the holding is a controlling interest (for example, 55 per cent of the voting shares), they might be valued as a proportion of the value of the assets the company owns. A minority holding (30 per cent, say) might be valued using the price/earnings ratio (or even, if the shares are quoted on the Third Market or OTC, related to their market prices). Whatever the solution, it must be agreed with the Share Valuation Division of the Inland Revenue: this cannot be negotiated in advance and reaching agreement can be a lengthy business.

The valuation becomes more complicated still if the gift or bequest turns a majority shareholding into a minority one. Since the value of a transfer is measured by the loss to the giver rather than the gain of the receiver, the value of such a share transfer is more than the value of the shares alone: the giver loses not only the shares but also control of the company. Professional advice from an accountant or solicitor is essential in these circumstances.

Note that you may not have to pay the full inheritance tax bill due on the value of the unquoted shares if you can claim business property relief (see below).

YOUR OWN BUSINESS

If you are self-employed or involved in a small business, *business property relief* reduces the inheritance tax you have to pay if you leave business property on death or give it away within seven years of death. The value of assets used in the business such as goodwill, land, buildings, plant, stock, patents and the like (reduced by any debts incurred in the business) is reduced by 50 per cent under the relief. This will more than halve the inheritance tax due since the tax is on a progressive scale.

If the business is a company, you can get business property relief on transfers of the shares. The rate until 17 March 1987 was 50 per cent if you had a controlling interest in the company, 30 per cent if you owned less than 50 per cent of the shares. From 17 March 1987 onwards, holdings of more than 25 per cent are eligible for relief at 50 per cent, provided you have owned at least 25 per cent for two years or more. The value of the shares transferred must be reduced by the amount of any loans you have taken out to acquire the shares before the relief is applied.

You can't normally get business property relief for businesses which consist mainly of dealing in stocks and shares, land and buildings or investments.

AGRICULTURAL PROPERTY

Agricultural property relief reduces the inheritance tax payable on agricultural land or pasture (including ancillary woodland), cottages, farm buildings and on farm houses and buildings used to rear animals for human consumption. You must either have owned the property for agriculture for at least seven years or have owned and farmed it (alone or in partnership) for at least two years.

The value of agricultural property left on death or given away within seven years of death is reduced by 50 per cent if you farm the land or let it out under an agreement which gives vacant possession within twelve months. If you let it out and haven't the right to vacant possession within twelve months, the rate of relief is 30 per cent.

As with business property relief, the value of agricultural property must be reduced by any loans secured on it. Transfers of shares in agricultural companies may also qualify for relief under certain conditions. But the relief does not apply to farm plant, machinery, livestock or deadstock: these may, however, qualify for business property relief.

ASSOCIATED OPERATIONS

You might think that there are some rather obvious wheezes to get round the inheritance tax rules and avoid tax. For example, you might give tax-free gifts of £250 to several friends, taking advantage of the small gifts exemption, on condition that they pass the money on to someone else (your adult child, say). But there are provisions for the taxman to 'see through' such associated operations and treat them as direct gifts.

RELATED PROPERTY

In working out the value of a bequest or gift, the taxman treats as yours property which he reckons is related to yours. Suppose, for example, you own 30 per cent of the shares in a company and your spouse owns another 30 per cent. The taxman will value your 30 per cent as worth half the value of a 60 per cent controlling interest, which is generally higher than the value of a 30 per cent minority interest. Property will be treated as related if it belongs to your spouse or if it has been owned at any time in the previous five years by a charity, political party or national institution to which you or your spouse gave it.

TRUSTS

Trusts (sometimes called settlements) are independent legal bodies set up to look after money or other property such as shares or a home. They do so on behalf of *beneficiaries*, who may be a single individual (such as your daughter) or a class of individuals (such as your children, or unmarried women over eighteen in the parish of Deptford). The person or people who put the goodies into trust are called *settlors*: once in the trust, the property is administered on behalf of the beneficiaries by *trustees*.

There are several types of trust, including:

● *trusts with an interest in possession:* with this type of trust someone has the right to the income from it or to use property it owns (for example, to live in a house belonging to it)

● *discretionary trusts:* the trustees have discretion about what to pay out, the amount to pay out and which of the possible beneficiaries should receive the pay-out

● *accumulation and maintenance trusts:* a special type of discretionary trust designed to provide for children and grandchildren under twenty-five. The beneficiaries must be entitled to the capital in the trust or to the income from it (that is, to an interest in possession) on or before their twenty-fifth birthday.

The advantages of setting up a trust can be purely administrative. It is a way of providing for someone after your death or while you are unable to look after them yourself. Trustees control the property in the trust but they must do so in accordance with the wishes of the settlor, which are usually set out in the document setting up the trust known as a *trust deed*. But they are also governed by Acts of Parliament which aim to protect the interests of beneficiaries from unscrupulous trustees. For example, trustees must invest in specified low-risk investments like National Savings and building societies unless the trust deed gives them wider powers (most modern trust deeds give trustees these powers).

But there are also tax advantages in using trusts to hold family property. The property can be used for the benefit of the family but, since no one ever owns it, it is never passed on by gift or bequest. This doesn't mean that inheritance tax is never paid: there are special rules to tax trusts because of this very fact. But the amount of inheritance tax due is likely to be much less with trusts than with individual ownership. There are also added tax advantages gifts for three sorts of trust (see below).

However, trusts are one of the most complex areas of the law and professional advice should always be sought from a solicitor or accountant if you think that trusts might suit your needs. What follows is no more than a summary of the tax position to show the advantages of using trusts and help you understand the professional advice you might get.

GIFTS TO TRUSTS

If you make a gift to a trust, you may have to pay inheritance tax on the gift at the time you make it, even if it is more than seven years before you die. But no inheritance tax is payable at the time of gifts to the following types of trust:

- an accumulation and maintenance trust

- a trust for disabled people.

Gifts made to a trust with an interest in possession on or after 17 March 1987 are also free of inheritance tax.

If the gift is to one of these types of trust, there will be an inheritance tax bill only if you die within seven years of making the gift (worked out in the same way as for any other gift).

If you make a gift to any other sort of trust, there is an immediate inheritance tax bill. The gift is added to the value of other such gifts made within the previous seven years and tax is charged on the cumulative total at half the rates in the Tables on p. 292. If you survive for another seven years, then no further inheritance tax is due but if you die within seven years or leave property to a trust on your death, then the gifts to trusts are included in the reckoning for inheritance tax on your death. The full rate of tax is payable (reduced by tapering relief if made between three and seven years of death): any tax already paid on the gift (including any capital transfer tax paid before inheritance tax was introduced) is deducted from the tax due on death. But if the tax paid when the gift was made is greater than that due on death there is no refund of the excess.

PROPERTY HELD BY TRUSTS

The inheritance tax treatment of property held by trusts depends on the type of trust:

- *trusts with an interest in possession:* the property owned by the trust is treated as the property of the person who has the interest in possession. If he or she dies or gives away the right within seven years of death, inheritance tax is due as if it was their property (but the trustees pay the bill, not the beneficiary's estate)

● *discretionary trusts:* there are complicated rules designed to collect inheritance tax from the trustees as if the property belonged to a single individual and was passed on at death once every thirty-three years

● *accumulation and maintenance trusts:* no inheritance tax is payable on the property until it is disposed of by the beneficiary.

PAYMENT OF INHERITANCE TAX

In most cases inheritance tax will have to be paid because of the death of someone whose taxable estate and taxable gifts during the previous seven years exceed the nil-rate band. This could create two sets of tax bills: on the executors or personal representatives of the dead person for the tax due on the estate; and on people who got taxable gifts from the dead person during the seven years before their death on which tax is now due.

Inheritance tax is due six months after the end of the month in which the death happened. In practice, it can often take longer for the executors to sort out the will and tidy up the dead person's affairs. As part of the process of seeking probate, they must submit an Inland Revenue account, listing the value of the dead person's property (including property owned jointly with anybody else) and the amounts of any debts. Probate will not be granted until the tax has been paid. Interest must be paid if the tax is paid after the six-month deadline (see below).

INTEREST ON UNPAID TAX

Interest is charged on inheritance tax which is paid late, from the time that the tax was due. Likewise, if you pay too much inheritance tax, you will get interest on the over-payment from the taxman. The rate is currently 6 per cent per annum.

PAYMENT BY INSTALMENTS

With certain gifts and bequests, inheritance tax can be paid in ten equal yearly instalments rather than as a lump sum. This option is allowed only with bequests on death and lifetime gifts where the recipient still owns the property when the death occurs. Interest may be due on the instalments in some cases but this may be preferable to having to find the tax in one go (if it would mean selling the family home, for example).

Two groups of assets qualify for payment of tax by instalments:

● *land and property* – but interest from the date the tax was due is payable except with business property and agricultural land

● *a business, including certain holdings of unquoted shares* – with shares, no interest is payable on the deferred tax unless the instalments are paid late.

If you want to pay in instalments, tell the taxman before the normal payment date for the tax. The first instalment is due on the date the whole tax would have been payable.

If you take out a loan to pay inheritance tax before probate is granted, you can get tax relief on the interest on it for up to twelve months.

QUICK SUCCESSION RELIEF

Inheritance tax is largely designed to tax wealth when it changes hands on death. Normally this would happen once a generation but family fortunes could be cruelly hit if two deaths in quick succession meant two inheritance tax bills in a short space of time. Quick succession relief helps reduce the tax impact of deaths within five years of each other.

If you die within a year of receiving a gift on which inheritance tax or capital transfer tax has been paid, the inheritance tax due on your estate is reduced by a fraction of the tax previously paid. The fraction is calculated as follows:

$$\frac{\text{Value of gift at time of first transfer}}{\text{Value of gift at transfer} + \text{tax paid on first transfer}}$$

If you die between one and five years after receiving the gift, the fraction is reduced by 20 per cent for each complete year since the first transfer.

EXAMPLE

Larry Morris inherited £40,000 from his parents, a legacy on which inheritance tax of £10,000 had been paid. Three and a half years later Larry dies leaving an estate on which £20,000 inheritance tax is payable.

Because his death is within five years of receiving the legacy from his parents, quick succession relief reduces the inheritance tax bill on

Larry's estate. The fraction of the previous tax bill which can be taken into account is worked out as follows:

$$\frac{£40,000}{£40,000 + £10,000} = \frac{£40,000}{£50,000} = 0.8$$

The fraction of 0.8 is reduced by 20 per cent for each complete year that Larry received the legacy before his death. Since he received the legacy three and a half years before his death, the fraction is reduced by $3 \times 20\% = 60\%$. Sixty per cent of 0.8 is 0.48. Thus the tax on Larry's estate is reduced by 0.48 of the tax due on the legacy when he got it (£10,000), that is, £4,800. That means a tax bill of £20,000 − £4,800 = £15,200.

PLANNING FOR INHERITANCE TAX

There is much that you can do to reduce the inheritance tax bill on your estate by making gifts which are free of tax or making taxable gifts more than seven years before your death. But it's worth bearing in mind that your heirs will be better off as a result of the bequests and legacies you make, even if inheritance tax is due on them. Don't give away so much that you or your spouse are left impoverished in old age, merely to cheat the taxman of every last penny of tax. Allow a good margin in deciding how much to keep for yourself – inflation can make generous provision look very inadequate after a few years. And remember that many people enjoy considerably more than three score years and ten: it is not unusual for retirement to last twenty-five years or more.

If you do have some resources to spare, make as full use as possible of the tax-free small gifts, gifts on marriage and the like. For regular gifts to grandchildren or other non-taxpayers, consider using a covenant to get income tax relief on the payments (p. 119). And make sure that your spouse has enough to make similar tax-free gifts.

If you want to make larger gifts, the earlier you make them the better. If you live for seven years after making the gifts, they are not taxable. Even if you die within seven years of making a gift, the tax will be reduced if the gift is made more than three years before your death.

Again, a married couple can share their wealth and each make gifts; the inheritance tax on each partner's estate depends only on what they own or have given away. And if each partner has a share of the family wealth on death, each is entitled to £90,000 taxable at the nil rate, £50,000 at 30 per cent and so on. If all the family wealth is owned and left by one partner, more will be taxed at the higher rates of inheritance tax.

In practice, it may not be easy to split your worldly goods and give them away during your lifetime: it may make more sense to pass all or most of them on to the survivor of the two of you, so that he or she has enough to live on. But the principle of 'estate-splitting' is a basic strategy to be followed where possible.

'Estate-freezing' is another technique for reducing inheritance tax by freezing the value of some of your wealth now and allowing any increase in value to go to someone else. Trusts offer one way of doing this, as assets are taken out of your possession and used for the benefit of someone else. But the tax treatment of trusts is complex (p. 302), so don't attempt this without professional advice.

YOUR HOME

If your home is jointly owned with your spouse under a *joint tenancy*, it automatically goes to the survivor when one of you dies. There will be no inheritance tax to pay in this case, since bequests to a husband or wife are tax-free. With a joint tenancy between two people who are not married to each other (a mother and daughter, say), the half of the tenancy which is transferred to the other person is a taxable gift.

If your home is jointly owned with someone else as a *tenancy in common*, you can bequeath your share to anyone you please. For example, you could bequeath a half of your half-share to your spouse and the other half to the next generation. This would reduce the size of your spouse's estate but leave him or her in control of the home.

One thing which won't save tax is to bequeath your home to your children on condition that your spouse can continue to live in it. This counts as an interest in possession and the home will be treated as your spouse's.

There are other ways of reducing the inheritance tax due on a home. But unless you've got a particular reason to want it to pass intact to the next generation (it's the family seat, say), it may be best to avoid doing anything which could jeopardize your future life in it and leave your heirs to pay the tax.

LIFE INSURANCE

If you want to make sure that there is enough money to pay an inheritance tax bill on a large gift (for example, a home or business), you can take out a term life insurance policy which pays out if you die within seven years of giving it away. And if you plan to leave a large asset on death, whole life insurance policies pay out whenever you die, again providing cash to pay the taxman.

When the insurance policy pays out, the money will be added to your estate and inheritance tax charged on it (there will also be a delay before your heirs can get their hands on it when probate is granted). But if the policy is written in trust to the person you want to have the money, the proceeds will be paid directly to that person on your death and be free of inheritance tax. The premiums for a policy written in trust count as gifts, but will be tax-free if the policy is for your spouse. And if you pay the premiums out of your normal spending, they will be tax-free whoever is to benefit (p. 294).

WHAT TO PUT IN YOUR TAX RETURN

There's no space on your Tax Return for details of transfers which are liable to inheritance tax. But you are expected to tell the Inland Revenue if you make lifetime gifts which are liable to inheritance tax (broadly, gifts to certain trusts).

And if someone dies within seven years of making taxable gifts to you, you may have to tell the taxman. However, there is no need to send details if the gifts do not add up to more than £10,000 in any tax year or £40,000 over seven tax years.

Inheritance tax is dealt with by the three Capital Taxes Offices:

England and Wales:	Minford House Rockley Road London W14 0DF
Scotland:	16 Picardy Place Edinburgh EH1 3NB
N. Ireland:	Law Courts Building Chichester Street Belfast BT1 3NU

If you want to claim tax relief on interest for a loan to pay inheritance tax until probate is granted, enter details in the OUTGOINGS section of the Tax Return under *Interest on other loans* on Forms 11P and 11 and under *Other loan interest paid* on Form P1.

Form 11P

Interest on other loans *enclose certificates*		Self	Wife
Name of lender		£	£

GLOSSARY

Your Tax Inspector, tax advisers and others offering advice (objective or otherwise) will all tend to slip into jargon, if given half a chance. Many of the terms they use can be found in the Index to this Guide. But you may find that words in common usage, which you think you understand, are being used in a particular sense when applied to your tax affairs. This brief Glossary explains the meaning of some everyday words used in a tax context.

ALLOWABLE

Anything which a Tax Inspector is likely to agree is acceptable. For example, if you spend money in the course of your business, you will be able to deduct it from the takings in working out your taxable profit if the expenses are allowable.

ASSESSMENT

An assessment is a calculation of your tax bill. Your Tax Inspector may send you a copy of the calculation, a Notice of Assessment (p. 63).

BASIC RATE

The basic rate of income tax is the rate paid on the first slice of your taxable income: for the 1987/8 tax year, the basic rate is 27 per cent, payable on the first £17,900 of taxable income. About nineteen out of twenty taxpayers pay tax at the basic rate only, that is, have a taxable income below the upper limit.

BENEFITS

May be used in two ways: to refer to social security benefits and to group together fringe benefits such as a company car, low interest loans and free travel.

CAPITAL ALLOWANCE

A tax allowance against the cost of buying plant and equipment like business vehicles, computers and machinery (p. 184).

CASE

Schedule D income tax is divided into six Cases, each with somewhat different tax rules (p. 33).

CONSIDERATION

Anything you get in return for a service or a possession. For example, if you exchange your house for a luxury yacht, the taxman will say that you have sold it for the consideration of the yacht (the price being the value of the yacht).

DEDUCTION AT SOURCE

Some types of income are paid after tax has been deducted from them: for example, earnings under PAYE and building society interest. The tax deducted 'at source' is paid directly to the Inland Revenue; if further tax is due on the income, it will normally be collected direct from you.

DISPOSAL

If you sell, give away or otherwise part with a possession, this counts as a disposal for capital gains tax purposes (p. 275).

DOMICILE

The country you regard as your natural home. For most people, their domicile is the place of their birth, and while it is possible to change your domicile, it can be a lengthy process.

DUE DATE

The date by which you must do something: for example, pay tax, send in a Return.

EARNED INCOME

Income from a job or business, earned by your own work. Some pensions are also taxed as earned income; they can be seen as deferred earnings.

EMOLUMENTS

The rewards of working which are taxable, including salary, fees, wages, fringe benefits, expense allowances, bonuses, etc.

EMPLOYMENT

A job working for someone else or a company.

EXEMPTION

Another word for tax relief or tax allowance: an exemption is an amount of income, a gain or a gift on which tax is not payable.

FISCAL YEAR

See *Tax Year*.

GROSS

Before deduction of tax.

GROSSED-UP

The amount before deduction of tax. For example, if you get income after tax has been deducted, adding back the tax which has been deducted gives you the grossed-up amount.

HIGHER-PAID

People earning at more than a set rate (currently £8,500 a year) face tougher rules on the taxation of their fringe benefits and expense allowances (p. 152). People in this bracket are described as 'higher-paid employees'.

HIGHER RATES

People earning more than the top limit for the basic rate of tax (£17,900 for the 1987/8 tax year) pay tax at higher rates from 40 to 60 per cent.

INVESTMENT INCOME

Income which is not earned from a job or a business, such as income from shares, property and deposits in a bank or building society.

LIABILITY

Tax bill.

LIABLE

Taxable. Something which is liable to tax must be taken into consideration when working out your tax bill. But you may not have to pay tax on it: for example, you may be liable to income tax on bank interest you receive but there will be no tax to pay if your income is too low to pay tax.

LOSS

If you lose money in a business, or on selling something you own, you may have made a loss for tax purposes and this can usually be used to reduce your overall tax bill. There are special rules for working out whether you have made a loss (see Index) and you may make a tax loss without having made a loss in a business sense (or vice versa).

NET

After deduction of tax. If you get £100 after £27 tax has been deducted from it, you receive a net amount of £100 − £27 = £73.

NET RELEVANT EARNINGS

You can get tax relief on personal pension payments provided they do not exceed a certain proportion of your net relevant earnings (see p. 211 for how these are defined).

OUTGOINGS

Certain payments you make which can be deducted from your income before working out how much tax you have to pay (see Chapter 5, p. 36).

PENSION AGE

Pension age is normally the age at which you can draw the state pension: sixty-five for men, sixty for women. But in some cases, it may have a different meaning: for example, the age at which you can draw a personal pension or a pension from your employer.

PENSIONABLE

Earnings are pensionable if they come from a job where the employer has a pension scheme *and* you are a member of the scheme.

RELIEF

Anything which reduces your tax bill may be described as a relief: for example, a tax allowance or a payment which counts as an outgoing reduces your taxable income. If some or all of a particular type of income can be left out of your reckoning for tax, this is also a relief.

RESIDENCE

Where you are treated as living for tax purposes (p. 174).

RETURNS

The Inland Revenue forms on which you are asked to give information on your income, capital gains and gifts on which inheritance tax may be due are known as Returns.

SCHEDULES

Income tax is divided into six different types (A–F), each with its own rules and with restrictions on how they may be related to each other (p. 33).

SEPARATE ASSESSMENT

A husband and wife can choose to fill in their own Tax Returns, receive their own tax bills and account for their own tax. But with separate assessment, their tax bill remains the same: it is merely shared out between them (p. 98).

SEPARATE TAXATION

If a husband and wife opt for separate taxation (technically, the *wife's earned income election*), their earnings are taxed as if they were single: each is entitled to the single person's allowance and can have up to

£17,900 of income taxed at the basic rate. But the couple's investment income is still added together and taxed as the husband's (p. 93).

TAX CREDIT

If you receive income with a tax credit, you are taken to have paid tax equal to the amount of the tax credit. Your total before-tax income is the amount of income you get plus the amount of the tax credit.

TAX-FREE

Income which is described as tax-free should be free of all income tax and capital gains tax, that is, no further tax is due on it whatever your rate of tax. Sometimes erroneously used to describe income which is *tax-paid* (see below). Also misleadingly used to describe income drawn from a single-premium life insurance bond by cashing in up to 5 per cent of it each year; although no tax is due when the income is drawn, there may be a tax bill later (p. 262).

TAX-PAID

Tax-paid income comes after deduction of tax at the basic rate. Further tax may be due if you pay tax at the higher rates. If your income is so low that you should pay no tax at all, in many cases you can claim back the tax deducted.

TAX YEAR

Tax years run from 6 April to 5 April of the following calendar year. So the 1987/8 tax year runs from 6 April 1987 to 5 April 1988.

TOTAL INCOME

All your income for a tax year, less certain deductions (p. 20).

UNEARNED INCOME

See *Investment income*.

THIRTY WAYS TO SAVE TAX

Here are thirty tips to help you cut your tax bill. They are all relatively straightforward and do not involve reorganizing your life in search of tax savings.

1 Investigate the past. It may not be too late to claim an allowance or outgoing you have forgotten about. Some of the more important deadlines for claims are given on p. 23.

2 Always check your tax forms. As soon as you receive a Notice of Coding or a Notice of Assessment make sure your Tax Inspector has got the sums right. And you only have thirty days to do it for a Notice of Assessment. Chapter 8, p. 48, gives the details.

3 If you can choose which allowance to claim, go for the bigger one. Chapter 6, pp. 41–2, outlines five choices to make.

4 Keep your records well-organized. Take copies of your Tax Return. Note down all the expenses you could claim, for example, if you are self-employed.

5 Do not pay tax before you have to. If your Tax Inspector wants to collect tax on some income through the PAYE system, and this is earlier than you have to pay it by law, ask to pay it at the later due date. Chapter 3, pp. 22–3, tells you when income tax is due.

6 Highly-paid married couples may be able to save tax by having the wife's earnings taxed separately. Chapter 13, pp. 93–8, tells you how to work out whether separate taxation is right for you.

7 An unmarried couple with two children could each claim the additional personal allowance, thus giving themselves £7,590 of personal allowances between them for the 1987/8 tax year. The details are on p. 102.

8 A couple who are thinking of marrying might think twice if the woman has a lot of investment income. After marriage, investment income cannot be taxed separately and you could end up being much worse off. Chapter 13, pp. 90–100, explains. The other tax advantages of

staying single are greater tax relief for mortgages and twice the tax-free limit for capital gains.

9 If you are an unmarried couple and only one of you has an income, it means that the other has personal allowances which cannot be claimed. You can use these by transferring income from one to the other. This can be done by either of you making a covenant to the other or, if you have a child, the woman can ask for an affiliation order against the man. Read Chapter 14, p. 102.

10 If you are a married couple and only one of you can work, for tax reasons only, it should be the wife. She can claim both the wife's earned income allowance and the married man's allowance. The husband can claim only the married man's (p. 92 for more details).

11 Separated and divorced people should consider paying maintenance direct to a child under a court order. In this way, you can get the benefit of a child's personal allowances which would otherwise be unused. Chapter 15, p. 109, gives more information.

12 If you want to give money to a non-taxpayer, for example, your grandchild or an elderly relative, doing so by using a covenant makes sense (but not if it is to your child who is under eighteen). Chapter 17, pp. 119–22, tells you how to do it.

13 If you are elderly, watch out for the income trap, that is, the region of income where, because of the withdrawal of age allowance, you are effectively taxed at a very high rate. Chapter 18, p. 127, explains why. Consider tax-free investments if that is the case.

14 Fringe benefits can be a tax-efficient way of being paid. The taxable value put on them may be much lower than the value to you, for example, a company car. There is a rundown of how they are taxed in Chapter 20, p. 151.

15 If you leave a job to become self-employed, ask your Tax Inspector for a rebate. It will help your finances, although not cut your actual tax bill, see p. 166.

16 If you are unemployed and not claiming social security benefits, ask your Tax Inspector for a rebate, see p. 164.

17 Try to get your freelance earnings classified as self-employment. If the earnings are likely to rise, it means paying tax on lower income earned earlier. Chapter 25, p. 199, explains why.

18 If you are self-employed, do not miss out on claiming any expenses. Look at the checklist on p. 181.

19 You can still claim as an expense for your business something you use partly for business and partly in your private life, for example, using your home for work, sharing the car (p. 181).

20 When you first start your business, claim capital allowances on any equipment you already own but take into the business, for example, a car, desk, etc.

21 You do not have to claim all the capital allowances you are entitled to. It may save you more tax to claim less and carry forward a higher value to the next year when your profits may be higher or your personal allowances lower.

22 The self-employed should choose their accounting year-end carefully to maximize the delay between earning the profits and paying tax on them – an advantage if earnings are rising. Chapter 24, p. 192, shows you how.

23 If you are starting in business, read the rules on p. 193 about how you are taxed. You can choose in the second and third years to be taxed one way rather than another and it could save you lots of money.

24 If the husband has his own business, it could save money if he employs the wife and pays her just under the bottom limit for National Insurance contributions (p. 196).

25 The government offers lots of tax incentives to persuade you to save for a pension. Take advantage of them. Chapter 27, p. 206, tells you how to do this.

26 Borrowing money to buy a home can be very cheap because you get tax relief on loans of £30,000 or less at your highest rate of tax. A home can be one of the best (and safest) investments. Chapter 28, p. 218, tells you the rules so you can ensure you get the maximum relief.

27 Higher-rate taxpayers should consider investments which give a capital gain rather than income. Apart from the tax-free slice of net taxable gains which you can make each tax year, the tax paid on capital gains is relatively low, 30 per cent. Tax-free investments could also be attractive, see p. 275.

28 Non-taxpayers should be careful about investing in banks, building societies and other investments where the interest is paid with no more basic-rate tax to pay but where the tax deducted cannot be claimed back. Instead, they should look carefully at investments paid without tax deducted or where the tax can be claimed back from the taxman, see p. 244.

29 Take advantage of the tax-free gains you can make each year when you dispose of assets, such as antiques, shares, etc. If possible, spread your disposals over a number of years. Chapter 33 on capital gains tax (p. 275) gives you many more hints about saving capital gains tax.

30 Draw up a will: it should help you start thinking about inheritance tax. There are simple steps you can take to minimize the tax payable on your estate when you die and to reduce the complications for those you leave behind (p. 291).

TAX FACTS

This section gives you bits and pieces of information which could be useful in sorting out your tax bill.

TAX SUMS

Here is a ready reckoner to help you work out your tax calculations quickly.

Table: How to gross-up income and outgoings

Net amount	1986/7 Gross amount	1987/8 Gross amount
£	£	£
1	1.41	1.37
2	2.82	2.74
3	4.22	4.11
4	5.63	5.48
5	7.04	6.85
6	8.45	8.22
7	9.86	9.59
8	11.26	10.96
9	12.67	12.33
10	14.08	13.70
20	28.16	27.40
30	42.24	41.10
40	56.32	54.79
50	70.42	68.50
60	84.51	82.19
70	98.59	95.89
80	112.68	109.60
90	126.76	123.29
100	140.85	137.00

200	281.00	273.97
300	422.54	410.96
400	563.38	547.95
500	704.23	684.93
600	845.07	821.92
700	985.92	958.90
800	1,126.76	1,095.89
900	1,267.61	1,232.88
1,000	1,408.45	1,369.86

EXAMPLE

Pete Elliott has received net income of £1,469 in 1987/8. He finds the gross income from the ready reckoner:

	net	gross
	1,000	1,369.86
	400	547.95
	60	82.19
	9	12.33
TOTAL	£1,469	£2,012.33

RETAIL PRICES INDEX

	1982	*1983*	*1984*	*1985*	*1986*	*1987*
January		325.9	342.6	359.8	379.7	394.5
February		327.3	344.0	362.7	381.1	396.1
March	313.4	327.9	345.1	366.1	381.6	396.9
April	319.7	332.5	349.7	373.9	385.3	401.6
May	322.0	333.9	351.0	375.6	386.0	
June	322.9	334.7	351.9	376.4	385.8	
July	323.0	336.5	351.5	375.7	384.7	
August	323.1	338.0	354.8	376.7	385.9	
September	322.9	339.5	355.5	376.5	387.8	
October	324.5	340.7	357.7	377.1	388.4	
November	326.1	341.9	358.8	378.4	391.7	
December	325.5	342.8	358.5	378.9	393.0	

Note that from January 1987 the RPI was reorganized and became 100 again. These figures in the Table are recalculated for you.

USEFUL LEAFLETS

You can get these leaflets free from your tax office.

IR4	Income tax and pensioners
IR4A	Income tax – age allowance
IR6	Double taxation relief
IR11	Tax treatment of interest paid
IR13	Income tax – wife's earnings election
IR23	Income tax and widows
IR24	Class 4 National Insurance contributions
IR26	Income tax assessments on business profits – changes of accounting date
IR27	Notes on the taxation of income from real property
IR28	Starting in business
IR29	Income tax and one-parent families
IR30	Income tax – separation and divorce
IR31	Income tax and married couples
IR32	Income tax – separate assessment
IR33	Income tax and school-leavers
IR34	Income tax – PAYE
IR35	Income tax – profit-sharing
IR36	Approved profit-sharing schemes
IR37	Income tax and capital gains tax: appeals
IR38	Income tax: SAYE share options
IR39	Approved savings-related share option schemes
IR41	Income tax and the unemployed
IR42	Income tax: lay-offs and short-time work
IR43	Income tax and strikes
IR45	Income tax, capital gains tax and capital transfer tax: what happens when someone dies.
IR47	Income tax: deed of covenant by parent to adult student
IR51	The Business Expansion Scheme
IR52	Your tax office: why it is where it is
IR53	PAYE for employers: thinking of taking someone on?
IR55	Bank interest: paying tax
IR56	Employed or self-employed?
IR57	Thinking of working for yourself?
IR59	Students tax information pack
IR60	Income tax and students
IR61	Student deeds of covenant
IR65	Giving to charity: how individuals can get tax relief

IR68	Accrued income scheme
IR74	Deeds of covenant (getting it right for tax)
IR75	Tax reliefs for charity
CGT4	Capital gains tax – owner-occupied houses
CGT8	Capital gains tax
CGT11	Capital gains tax and the small businessman
CGT12	Capital gains tax – indexation
MIRAS6	Mortgage interest and your tax relief
480	Notes on expenses payments and benefits for directors and certain employees
P7	Employer's guide to PAYE

INDEX

Bold numerals indicate main entry

330

FOR THE BEST IN PAPERBACKS, LOOK FOR THE

In every corner of the world, on every subject under the sun, Penguin represents quality and variety – the very best in publishing today.

For complete information about books available from Penguin – including Pelicans, Puffins, Peregrines and Penguin Classics – and how to order them, write to us at the appropriate address below. Please note that for copyright reasons the selection of books varies from country to country.

In the United Kingdom: For a complete list of books available from Penguin in the U.K., please write to *Dept E.P., Penguin Books Ltd, Harmondsworth, Middlesex, UB7 0DA*

In the United States: For a complete list of books available from Penguin in the U.S., please write to *Dept BA, Penguin, 299 Murray Hill Parkway, East Rutherford, New Jersey 07073*

In Canada: For a complete list of books available from Penguin in Canada, please write to *Penguin Books Canada Ltd, 2801 John Street, Markham, Ontario L3R 1B4*

In Australia: For a complete list of books available from Penguin in Australia, please write to the *Marketing Department, Penguin Books Australia Ltd, P.O. Box 257, Ringwood, Victoria 3134*

In New Zealand: For a complete list of books available from Penguin in New Zealand, please write to the *Marketing Department, Penguin Books (NZ) Ltd, Private Bag, Takapuna, Auckland 9*

In India: For a complete list of books available from Penguin, please write to *Penguin Overseas Ltd, 706 Eros Apartments, 56 Nehru Place, New Delhi, 110019*

In Holland: For a complete list of books available from Penguin in Holland, please write to *Penguin Books Nederland B.V., Postbus 195, NL–1380AD Weesp, Netherlands*

In Germany: For a complete list of books available from Penguin, please write to *Penguin Books Ltd, Friedrichstrasse 10 – 12, D–6000 Frankfurt Main 1, Federal Republic of Germany*

In Spain: For a complete list of books available from Penguin in Spain, please write to *Longman Penguin España, Calle San Nicolas 15, E–28013 Madrid, Spain*

FOR THE BEST IN PAPERBACKS, LOOK FOR THE 🐧

PENGUIN DICTIONARIES

Archaeology

Architecture

Art and Artists

Biology

Botany

Building

Chemistry

Civil Engineering

Commerce

Computers

Decorative Arts

Design and Designers

Economics

English and European
  History

English Idioms

Geography

Geology

Historical Slang

Literary Terms

Mathematics

Microprocessors

Modern History 1789–1945

Modern Quotations

Physical Geography

Physics

Political Quotations

Politics

Proverbs

Psychology

Quotations

Religions

Saints

Science

Sociology

Surnames

Telecommunications

The Theatre

Troublesome Words

Twentieth Century History

Dictionaries of all these – and more – in Penguin